D1202566

Creating a
Learning Commons

PRACTICAL GUIDES FOR LIBRARIANS

◎ About the Series

This innovative series written and edited for librarians by librarians provides authoritative, practical information and guidance on a wide spectrum of library processes and operations.

Books in the series are focused, describing practical and innovative solutions to a problem facing today's librarian and delivering step-by-step guidance for planning, creating, implementing, managing, and evaluating a wide range of services and programs.

The books are aimed at beginning and intermediate librarians needing basic instruction/guidance in a specific subject and at experienced librarians who need to gain knowledge in a new area or guidance in implementing a new program/service.

◎ About the Series Editors

The **Practical Guides for Librarians** series was conceived and edited by M. Sandra Wood, MLS, MBA, AHIP, FMLA, Librarian Emerita, Penn State University Libraries from 2014–2017.

M. Sandra Wood was a librarian at the George T. Harrell Library, the Milton S. Hershey Medical Center, College of Medicine, Pennsylvania State University, Hershey, PA, for over thirty-five years, specializing in reference, educational, and database services. Ms. Wood received an MLS from Indiana University and an MBA from the University of Maryland. She is a fellow of the Medical Library Association and served as a member of MLA's Board of Directors from 1991 to 1995.

Ellyssa Kroski assumed editorial responsibilities for the series beginning in 2017. She is the director of Information Technology at the New York Law Institute as well as an award-winning editor and author of thirty-six books including *Law Librarianship in the Digital Age* for which she won the AALL's 2014 Joseph L. Andrews Legal Literature Award. Her ten-book technology series, *The Tech Set*, won the ALA's Best Book in Library Literature Award in 2011. Ms. Kroski is a librarian, an adjunct faculty member at Drexel and San Jose State University, and an international conference speaker. She has just been named the winner of the 2017 Library Hi Tech Award from the ALA/LITA for her long-term contributions in the area of Library and Information Science technology and its application.

Titles in the Series edited by M. Sandra Wood

1. *How to Teach: A Practical Guide for Librarians* by Beverley E. Crane
2. *Implementing an Inclusive Staffing Model for Today's Reference Services* by Julia K. Nims, Paula Storm, and Robert Stevens

Titles in the Series edited by Ellyssa Kroski

Titles in the Series edited by M. Sandra Wood

Titles in the Series edited by Ellyssa Kroski

Titles in the Series edited by M. Sandra Wood

Creating a Learning Commons
A Practical Guide for Librarians

Lynn D. Lampert
Coleen Meyers-Martin

PRACTICAL GUIDES FOR LIBRARIANS, NO. 55

ROWMAN & LITTLEFIELD
Lanham • Boulder • New York • London

Published by Rowman & Littlefield
An imprint of The Rowman & Littlefield Publishing Group, Inc.
4501 Forbes Boulevard, Suite 200, Lanham, Maryland 20706
www.rowman.com

6 Tinworth Street, London SE11 5AL

Copyright © 2019 by The Rowman & Littlefield Publishing Group, Inc.

All rights reserved. No part of this book may be reproduced in any form or by any electronic or mechanical means, including information storage and retrieval systems, without written permission from the publisher, except by a reviewer who may quote passages in a review.

British Library Cataloguing in Publication Information Available

Library of Congress Cataloging-in-Publication Data
Names: Lampert, Lynn D., author. | Meyers-Martin, Coleen, 1964– author.
Title: Creating a learning commons : a practical guide for librarians / Lynn D. Lampert, Coleen Meyers-Martin.
Description: Lanham : Rowman & Littlefield, [2019] | Series: Practical guides for librarians ; no. 55 | Includes bibliographical references and index.
Identifiers: LCCN 2018038219 (print) | LCCN 2018043461 (ebook) | ISBN 9781442272644 (electronic) | ISBN 9781442272637 (pbk. : alk. paper)
Subjects: LCSH: Information commons. | Libraries—Space utilization. | Academic libraries—Planning. | Academic libraries—Information technology.
Classification: LCC ZA3270 (ebook) | LCC ZA3270 .L36 2019 (print) | DDC 025.5/2—dc23
LC record available at https://lccn.loc.gov/2018038219

♾™ The paper used in this publication meets the minimum requirements of American National Standard for Information Sciences—Permanence of Paper for Printed Library Materials, ANSI/NISO Z39.48-1992.

Printed in the United States of America

To my daughters Rebecca and Samantha.
As you grow from little girls into amazing women,
always remember that I love you both with all my heart.
Love, Mom.—L. D. L.

To my father, Francis C. Meyers,
who lives his life in service to his family.
Thanks, Dad.—C. M. M.

Contents

Figures and Tables

⑥ Figures

Tables

Foreword

When the World Wide Web exploded in the mid-1990s, many of us managing libraries realized we were at one of the great turning points of history, equal to Gutenberg's printing press: the initial fault line between the age of print and the digital age. Academic libraries first tried to cope with the explosion of web-based resources by wedging generic computer labs into traditional reference departments. That effort failed, for all too many reasons. A handful of university libraries then tried a new experimental model, first called the information commons (IC). I was hired by University of North Carolina–Charlotte in 1997 to start an information commons (then, perhaps the sixth or seventh in the United States) and had an article published two years later that drew much attention, "Conceptualizing an Information Commons." In 2006, my first book, *The Information Commons Handbook*, with contributions by Russ Bailey and Barbara Tierney was published. That book came out just as the transition from reference department to IC was gathering strong momentum, marking this period as the first phase of an ongoing transformation that continues to this day. Even then, the variety of IC examples prompted me to describe the model broadly: "The IC is not about technology per se, but more about how an organization reshapes itself around people using technology in pursuit of learning."

By 2005, the information commons had already begun to morph into something new, typically called a learning commons (LC), marking a second key transformational phase. Now there are many hundreds of these innovative library learning spaces—probably between 450 and 500 across the United States and Canada, with hundreds more across Europe, Central Asia, and the Pacific Rim. Lest anyone doubt the global impact of the IC/LC model, the evidence is ample and still vibrantly expanding. An exploration of representative variants on the model would literally require a world tour, with a few examples including the Brody Learning Commons at Johns Hopkins University; the Rolex Learning Center at École Polytechnique in Lausanne, Switzerland; and the recently completed Noor & Ann Lakhdhir Information Commons at the American University of Central Asia.

Concurrently, between 2006 and 2016, several more books and many more articles have greatly expanded the literature. Given the breadth of these writings, do we need another book now about learning commons creation and development? That was the question I asked myself as I began to read this newest entry to the field, *Creating a Learning Commons: A Practical Guide for Librarians*, by Lynn D. Lampert and Coleen

Meyers-Martin. Now, having completed this thoughtful, well-written, and carefully organized study, I submit that the answer is an emphatic yes. Yes, this is an important contribution for multiple reasons, external and internal, practical and conceptual. First, the authors examined the full extent of that literature and then extracted from it cogent and pragmatic lessons, which they insert at pertinent points throughout their chapters. Second, they went the extra mile to conduct their own updated survey on LC development across a range of library listservs, emerging to share important and original insights, grounded in their own estimable experiences in library management. And perhaps most significantly, they scan the current landscape in the context of technologies that continue to surge relentlessly ahead.

Only three months after *The Information Commons Handbook* was published, Steve Jobs announced Apple's first iPhone (January 9, 2007). Since then we have seen this wave of innovation produce new generations of smartphones, e-readers, interactive display walls, 3D printers, and immersive virtual reality environments. As these proliferate, new pedagogies emerge to harness and leverage their potential for learning and student engagement. As the authors perceptively state in chapter 11, "unlike past library service points, where students would come to access previously stored created information, almost all of these possible learning commons elements allow for students to create or get assistance in creating/authoring something. They share a commonality that supports a maker mind-set."

In 2018, I do not hesitate to repeat what I wrote two decades ago: we are still far closer to the beginning of the information technology revolution than we are to its end. Thus, as we appear to be entering yet another phase of our libraries' ongoing collective transformation, I strongly encourage librarians, faculty, and higher education administrators to let Lynn D. Lampert and Coleen Meyers-Martin be your guides to this rapidly evolving ecosystem of learning commons creation and design.

Donald Beagle

Preface

If you are picking up this book, you likely have been tasked with considering the creation of a learning commons within your academic library. Perhaps you are a librarian, library administrator, or a member of a task force recently assembled to create this new learning space within a library renovation project or the construction of a new library building. The work ahead of you may often seem overwhelming due to the high stakes, both fiscal and political, that come with any large-scale academic library construction project. A quick review of *Library Journal*'s annually published architectural issue articles and summative published data, gathered from academic libraries nationwide that reported new construction and renovation/addition projects, will reveal that learning commons projects remain one of the most prevalent type of library building project happening on college campuses across the United States (Fox, 2017). Indeed, in the past six years, almost all the highlighted *Library Journal* architectural issue projects exceed a six-figure budget, with the most successful and praised renovations typically totaling over $1 million. Given those fiscal pressures alone, most individuals charged with creating a new learning space within an academic library would likely feel some stress.

Any library remodeling project, big or small, is also always laden with pressures that go deeper than mere budgetary concerns. Academic libraries are shared spaces that are often seen as the heart of a college campus and in some instances sacred places where proposed physical changes can generate resistance and anxiety. In addition to the natural concerns that library personnel would have about any redesign project, individuals charged with leading a learning commons renovation will also have to contend with voiced concerns, ideas, and sometimes even demands from faculty, staff, students, campus administrators, donors, project partners, and engaged community stakeholders. Couple all of these above pressures with the fact that a learning commons task force will also have to deal with the external pressures of effectively evaluating the proposed plans of architects, contractors, designers, and other experts and it is common to start feeling like you wish you had an external resource to help you and your team filter through all the opinions and requests being lobbied your way. If you perhaps already find yourself facing any of the above-mentioned pressures, then this book will help you in your work.

What This Book Does

Creating a Learning Commons: A Practical Guide for Librarians is intended for academic librarians and library administrators charged with developing learning commons spaces within their libraries. For the past decade, physical changes in libraries have paralleled the reorientation of classroom learning in education. "Emphasis on student-led inquiry and collaborative learning has resulted in a trend toward flexible designs and interactive spaces" (Sullivan 2010, 130). It is no longer uncommon for libraries to house computer labs, tutoring services, writing centers, and even makerspaces. The development of learning commons spaces within libraries establishes more group and collaborative study areas. Students anticipate increased space to collaborate for academic purposes, and many libraries offer coffeehouses within them, creating a culture of an academic and social nature. More and more collaboration takes place within libraries as they transform their physical spaces. Effective learning commons design projects that are remodels typically transform an underused library space into an environment where peer-to-peer learning and social interactions between students and the campus community thrive. Ideally, a well-designed learning commons area provides students with comfortable and flexible furnishings, convenient access to mobile and fixed technologies, and inviting group and individual study spaces and creates an energy that promotes peer learning and community building.

Recurring Themes

Through a thoughtful exploration of best practices needed to design a multifunctional learning space, *Creating a Learning Commons* will assist academic librarians and organizations looking to innovatively integrate and further engrain their library's services into the fabric of their students' lives through resourceful collaborations with other campus departments and services. This book will help a professional

- examine critical research about the leading trends emerging within learning commons spaces and study the results of the Learning Commons Survey designed for this book;
- study how to implement engaging student spaces that offer a variety of zones for learning and separate nosier group learning activities from quieter individual study through the selection of flexible and functional furnishings;
- review important literature and gain expert advice through featured interviews with experienced learning commons professionals, including an architect, project manager, designer, and technologist;
- optimize communications with designers, architects, technologists, and other stakeholders;
- develop pre- and post-occupancy assessment strategies needed for multifunctional programming and services within learning commons settings; and
- identify best practices for implementing learning commons spaces in different library settings.

Creating a Learning Commons also provides readers with the results from the Learning Commons Survey, which was conducted to inform the writing of this book. Feedback from eighty respondents who shared their institutional experiences will likely help readers identify effective strategies toward the development of learning commons spaces in their own academic libraries. Survey results provide insight into the implementation processes, programming methods used by institutions across the country and beyond, and pervasive learning commons services and features.

⑥ Organization of the Book

Creating a Learning Commons is arranged to provide readers with a clear path through the necessary steps and processes needed to approach, develop, implement, assess, and sustain a learning commons design project.

Chapter 1 provides a history of the learning commons model by tracking its development from the information commons model and examining why learning commons designs are viewed as enhancing students' collaborative and social experiences within libraries. It lays the groundwork for how the reader can initially prepare for the development of a learning commons project.

Chapter 2 explores the impact that learning spaces in libraries have on student satisfaction and learning; identifies key campus stakeholders that should be consulted at the outset of the project; provides advice on how to best establish your learning commons creation task force for the programming; discusses the high potential for political pitfalls during the development stages of a learning space design vision; and describes how to effectively carry out a needs assessment to reveal critical institutional-specific data.

Chapter 3 examines ideal learning commons programming and dynamic partnership strategies. An overview of leading trends and characteristics within learning commons designs is also provided. A discussion of how to best consider potential learning commons floor plans and services, including active learning classrooms, is also presented. This chapter also introduces the results of this work's Learning Commons Survey.

Chapter 4 uniquely explores learning commons space design through in-depth interviews with an experienced architect, a designer, and a project manager who have extensive experience in contracted learning commons building projects. The chapter also examines how to discern where your project's funding streams will come from through a detailed overview of the *color of money* principle. Project implementation strategies and how to best plan for contingencies before, during, and after construction are included.

Chapter 5 studies the benefits of implementing a technology plan; discusses the differences between a strategic organizational plan and a technology plan; and describes the technology design process for new learning commons spaces. Related results from this work's Learning Commons Survey are also presented.

Chapter 6 discusses the preparation required to select and implement learning commons technologies. Readers will explore the value of technology needs assessments and identify best practices to implement effective learning commons technologies. This chapter also includes an in-depth interview with an experienced learning commons technologist, who discusses what role technologists should play in the development of a library's technology planning. Related results from this work's Learning Commons Survey are also presented.

Chapter 7 discusses best practices for identifying primary objectives for your marketing and promotion; how to prepare the foundation for designing effective communications; ideas for launching your campaign through a variety of formats; and how to select strategies and vehicles for communicating all needed learning commons marketing messages.

Chapter 8 describes the role of reference and instructional services within the learning commons setting; discusses how to conceptualize formal and informal instruction spaces in the learning commons; and posits how to successfully identify and coordinate learning commons outreach programming opportunities.

Chapter 9 examines how academic library assessment methods, tools, and best practices should inform post-occupancy learning commons assessment strategies. The chapter also reviews critical considerations that must occur when assessing space and student learning within academic libraries, with a discussion about lessons that have been learned when developing learning commons spaces from the Learning Commons Survey respondents. Finally, chapter 9 includes an interview with an assessment expert familiar with assessment challenges commonly found within academic library settings.

Chapter 10 focuses on how library-campus partnerships have evolved within learning commons settings and presents best practices for developing successful learning commons collaborations. In addition to discussing how library and student services partnerships can strengthen a learning commons space, this chapter also includes a reporting of results about existing learning commons partnerships and services from this work's Learning Commons Survey.

Chapter 11 examines current trends found in recent learning commons designs and reviews published predictions about the future features of library learning spaces. In addition to providing information on how to best weigh future learning commons expansion trends and options, this chapter also provides readers with an in-depth discussion of learning commons makerspaces.

Finally, the survey instrument, used to gather feedback from eighty respondents who work in academic libraries that offer learning commons spaces, can be found in appendix A. Appendix B offers a marketing action plan, which outlines step-by-step guidelines for carrying out a comprehensive promotional campaign.

◎ Making Best Use of the Book

Can a newly or redesigned learning commons found within academic libraries help better prepare students for learning and inquiry during their collegiate experience? The evidence found within published case studies and other discussions seems to suggest that the answer is yes. Therefore, when you are reading this book, it is imperative that you always keep your own campus student population and its unique needs in mind. When developing a learning commons design plan, simply duplicating what every other neighboring library is doing with its own learning commons is far too easy a trap to fall into and in most cases is not a viable option. Your learning commons design team will need to look at your institution's student profile data and review what typical students face when they arrive on your campus. Keep in mind that many of today's college students typically only connect outside of a classroom through technology (learning management systems) and social media. The exception to this pattern occurs when students have access to shared co-curricular learning spaces. Without dynamic shared common learning spaces being made available within academic libraries, many students will not be able to find available spaces to gather to study and exchange ideas, which is critical to their curricular and noncurricular needs. Making digital connections to peers is likely not enough to help acclimate many undergraduates who often study on large campuses, both residential and commuter. Today's students need dynamic study spaces, for both individual and peer learning, so that they can best engage in their work and develop connections to campus services, faculty, the community, and their peers. When dynamic learning spaces are thoughtfully placed within academic libraries, the possibilities for impactful programming opportunities that promote student success, reflect students' diverse needs, and house meaningful services are so exciting. As the renowned activist Gloria Steinem wrote in her book *My Life on the Road*,

> If there is one thing that these campus visits have affirmed for me it's that the miraculous but impersonal Internet is not enough. . . . [N]othing can replace being in the same space. That's exactly why we need to keep creating temporary worlds of meetings, small and large, on campuses and everywhere else. In them we discover we are not alone, we learn from one another, and so we keep going towards shared goals." (Steinem 2015, 123)

Learning commons spaces, when thoughtfully designed to include meaningful shared spaces and student-centered services within academic libraries, can help students achieve all of that and so much more.

References

Fox, Bette-Lee. 2017. "Welcome Home: The Comforts and Collegiality of Home Are Manifest in 82 Projects." *Library Journal* 142, no. 19 (November 15): 16+. *Expanded Academic ASAP.* http://link.galegroup.com.libproxy.csun.edu/apps/doc/A514657959/EAIM?u=csunorthridge&sid=EAIM&xid=ba3b0c71.

Steinem, Gloria. 2015. *My Life on the Road*. New York: Random House.

Sullivan, R. M. 2010. "Common Knowledge: Learning Spaces in Academic Libraries." *College & Undergraduate Libraries* 17, nos. 2/3: 130–48.

Acknowledgments

We undertook to write *Creating a Learning Commons: A Practical Guide for Librarians* as the result of our collaborative work and experiences during the development of our own academic library's learning commons. To say that the process of working to create a learning commons space within an academic library can be daunting is an understatement. Working to propose, design, market, implement, and assess a learning commons is a huge undertaking that involves a lot of effort and teamwork. The process also often demands breakneck-speed consultation, due to multiple pending deadlines, and fast-paced research to quickly respond to proposals with the best courses of action. While working to launch our campus learning commons at California State University's Delmar T. Oviatt Library between 2012 and 2013, we learned that there was a lack of published information offering research and proven best practices to librarians and library staff charged with learning commons planning duties. We often found ourselves working from scratch to develop floor plans, marketing approaches, and strategies to convey the process to both internal and external campus stakeholders. Along the way, we developed many survival tactics that helped guide us toward the research agenda that resulted in this book. We fervently hope that this book will assist others who find themselves similarly charged with developing a new learning space in their library. We have tried our best to think of everything we wish we knew before we started our journey.

First, we would like to acknowledge the following individuals who have helped us during the process of writing this book. Many thanks to Don Beagle, the director of library services at Belmont Abbey College in Belmont, North Carolina. Don truly is a learning commons innovator, and he was always so generous with his time and proven expertise. The following individuals also agreed to be interviewed for this book: Marianne Afifi (former associate library dean, California State University, Northridge), April Cunningham (Palomar College), Amber Jones (Tangram Interiors), Nate McKee (University of Washington), Brent Miller (Harvey Ellis Devereaux), and Ray Uzwyshyn (Texas State University Libraries). All of their thoughtful and detailed responses offer unique and professional advice about key aspects of learning commons planning. We also would like to thank all the individuals who completed our Learning Commons Survey. Many of these individuals also went the extra mile in their willingness to share photographs of their institution's learning commons features.

Second, we also owe many thanks to our wonderful editor, Sandy Wood, and publisher, Charles Harmon, who provided expert feedback throughout the writing process.

Third, we also owe a tremendous amount of thanks to our families for their patience and support. For Lynn: her husband, Andrew Diekmann; mother, Frances Lampert; and aunt, Sylvia Tapper for their love and support. Her daughters, Rebecca and Samantha, for "almost" always understanding why mommy could not immediately separate herself from her laptop while writing at night or on weekends. Her beloved dogs for hopefully understanding why consistent walk schedules were often deficient due to writing. And finally, her steadfast coauthor, colleague, and friend Coleen for always being supportive, organized, and agreeable to regularly discussing book project tasks over our "almost" identical Chinese lunch special orders.

For Coleen: her husband, Stuart Martin; son, Miles; and daughter, Madeleine for their consistent love and support. For their patience, in particular, during evenings and weekends when she spent many hours writing and rewriting. For their willingness to eat takeout way too many times, alter their weekend schedules on the fly, and serve as caretakers, bringing her cups of green tea when they saw that was what was needed. And finally, her friend and coauthor Lynn for her staunch support and whose passion for and dedication to the profession helped make the writing process rewarding.

And finally, we offer our sincere thanks to our colleagues in Interlibrary Loan Services at California State University, Northridge. We were so fortunate to have their prompt assistance whenever we needed to obtain resources beyond our own collection.

Learning Commons Library Spaces

A rose by any other **name** would smell as sweet.

—WILLIAM SHAKESPEARE, *ROMEO AND JULIET*

DETERMINING THE NEED for developing a new learning commons space will require thoughtful consideration and strategic planning. This chapter will address the historical emphasis of commons spaces and the current need for academic libraries to provide collaborative working areas in support of the twenty-first-century student. Initial considerations for developing an academic library learning commons space will be highlighted.

The History of the Learning Commons Model

Whether your library is planning on building a learning commons, research commons, information commons, or makerspace, it is imperative that your stakeholders realize that in essence the names or terms used for these spaces largely do not matter in the long run. What matters is that the services and functionalities offered within these spaces provide students, faculty, staff, and visitors with meaningful takeaways that solidify the feeling and reality that the library is proactively serving its clientele by fostering an environment conducive to student learning, collaboration, and growth. All that being said, anyone who has embarked on developing a new learning space in his or her library will likely tell you that what you are planning on naming a new space matters to a library and its stakeholders for many reasons, such as marketing, signage, fundraising, and services demarcation. Branding, marketing, and even something as basic as location codes in the library catalog are significant concerns to consider in terms of name selections.

Learning space designations used in libraries, whether they employ the use of *commons* or not, have many theoretical underpinnings, and therefore it is important to know about the terms that have been used to describe some of these spaces. For the purposes of this text, it is also important to understand why the term *learning commons* has more recently emerged as such a prevalent term. Within academic libraries, the use of the term *learning commons* began to saturate higher education settings within the last decade. Prior to that time, many libraries used the term *information commons*. As Elizabeth J. Milewicz notes, "Though the technology and services in the information commons have expanded over time, its character and emphasis have remained consistent: to provide a collaborative, conversational space that brings together technology, services tools and resources to support teaching and learning and encourage innovative ideas" (2009, 3). Joan Lippincott noted in 2009 that "the concept of an information commons is slippery—it means different things in different institutions—and there is no commonly accepted definition among those who manage information commons or those who study in them" (2009, 18). However, as Donald Beagle, Donald Bailey, and Barbara Tierney defined it, "a good Information Common brings together researchers, instructors, students, teachers and users, equipping them with the technology (computers, projectors, Internet access) and furnishings (workstations, conference rooms and classrooms, print stations) to meet the goals they set for themselves" (2006, xvii). They also theorized that there were three levels of information commons: physical, virtual, and cultural.

In terms of the shared characteristics found in many theoretical models and actual library settings, most information commons typically offer integrated services, access to technology via networked connections, technology, human support systems, and traditional library services on a physical level or platform. The first information commons settings began to emerge in the early 1990s after considerable theoretical discussions about new library models took place in the late 1980s out of a reaction to the computer revolution. Again, some of these dedicated library spaces shared different characteristics in both theory and practice, but by and large, an information commons typically debuted as a new section of a library designed to deliver and integrate access to technology and computing through the formation of large clusters of seating and access to networked terminals with nearby information technology (IT) help services.

An early example of this kind of physical information commons transformation and deployment can be found at the University of Southern California's Leavey Library Information Commons, which opened in 1994 and touted twenty-four-hour access (see figure 1.1).

According to one article describing the opening of this new facility, the Leavey Library was well received by students because of its successful merging of professional library and IT service assistance within once edifice.

Many students [who were] attracted to the Leavey first by the computers [additionally found] the content-expert reference librarians right there to help increase their under-

Figure 1.1. USC Leavey Library Information Commons. *Courtesy of the University of Southern California, on behalf of the USC Libraries Special Collections*

standing of the value of research consultation that librarians can provide. . . . The computer consultants, reference librarians and navigation assistants all work side by side in the Information Commons. (Helfer 1997, 38–39)

The Leavey Library also strove in its mission to incorporate technology into its teaching curriculum and launched a Center for Excellence in Teaching as well as a Center for Scholarly Technology dedicated to working with faculty members on curricular redesign and webpage development. A third Center for Excellence in Education was also established as an office dedicated to faculty pedagogical training.

Unlike the information commons example above, other libraries launched what Beagle and other experts studying these spaces branded as another information commons model—the virtual commons. A virtual commons can be described as a largely electronic library where online tools are marketed to support an institution's students, faculty, and staff as they increasingly require networked access to computer productivity software, online databases, and Internet resources. While a physical information commons relies a great deal on well-designed spaces, with a virtual commons a user sees the library as a resource connection from beyond the walls of the building through branding and marketing.

The cultural commons really best describes the social interactions that an information commons causes. Going beyond place and space, Beagle, Bailey, and Tierney described the cultural commons as "the social, political, legal, regulatory and economic envelop surrounding creative expression, public speech, popular and academic publishing and scholarly inquiry" (2006, 5). For all of its uses, the popularity of the term *information commons* really reflects the world that academic libraries were working within due to the launch of the information age. As Milewicz (2009) noted, the appeal of the term *information commons* did not mean that every library adopted the use of the phrase in naming the space.

For instance, the University of Iowa opened its information arcade in 1992. By and large, the major components of all of these new spaces included

- technology-rich environments (hardware, software, and digital content)
- Internet access
- user and information services
- group spaces

⊚ From Information Commons to Learning Commons: Why the Need for a Learning Commons?

So how and why did the learning commons emerge and more recently surpass the information commons model? One argument might be that in many instances, the learning commons is the combined embodiment of all three levels of the information commons Beagle outlined (physical, virtual, and cultural). But a true learning commons offers so much more than those areas of definition. A true learning commons also reflects that the transformed space is not only dedicated to providing access to networked information but also more importantly that it is dedicated to providing spaces that foster and support student learning by both individuals and groups. Scott Bennett notes that theorists like Beagle feel that a learning commons emerges when the physical resources of an information commons are "organized in collaboration with learning initiatives sponsored by other academic units, or aligned with learning outcomes defined through a cooperative process" (Bennett 2008, 183). By and large, this situation typifies the development of many learning commons in today's academic library settings.

Many of today's academic libraries, regardless of whether or not they have a learning commons, are increasingly being asked to share spaces with nonlibrary-related institutional units. Whether a library director is asked to consider providing space for a campus career center and its collection or campus student advisement services, a common question is how to best situate services so that they are visible and easily accessed. The collaborative process of absorbing nonlibrary campus units and services into existing library spaces can be very beneficial for the formation of a learning commons culture. The nonlibrary units that may exist in a learning commons through collaborative partnerships can be critical factors in helping libraries attract and sustain student interest. As a recent case study discusses, the placement of allied services and centers, such as student writing or tutoring centers, can be a key factor in engaging students and faculty to see the library as a place of student engagement and learning rather than merely a place to come to access materials or to study. It is also clear that another "possible benefit of [having] non-library units located in the academic library is that the increased building traffic could result in increased use of library services and collections" (Lux, Snyder, and Boff 2016, 114).

Sasaki Associates, an interdisciplinary planning and design firm, also published related information on shared library spaces in its 2016 report, *The State of Academic Library Spaces*. Receiving responses from 402 librarians representing 118 different institutions, the report breaks down how libraries with learning commons and other redesigned spaces have begun to incorporate academic enrichment programs into shared library space. Respondents for this survey commented that writing centers and other academic enrichment programs were the most likely to share library space after renovation or redesign projects, with 128 respondents commenting that they had an embedded writing center in their facility. Other commonly reported academic enrichment programs included language labs, math centers, and to a smaller extent, makerspaces (Sasaki Associates Staff 2016). It is also important to note that while collaboration between libraries and other academic divisions and academic enrichment units helps foster student learning by placing tutoring or writing centers in closer proximity to students, in order for a learning commons to thrive in an academic library, that library and its mission must foster student learning by being a teaching library above all else.

As information commons settings were emerging in academic libraries in the past two decades, another parallel trend was emerging—the teaching library. With the rise of the Internet, wireless access, and mobile devices, many spaces on college campuses can and could foster student access to resources and materials. However, the rise of academic libraries providing information literacy instruction and developing teaching models that support faculty and university curriculum in the past two decades also set the stage for the success of the learning commons spaces. Librarians can successfully argue that if an academic library does not have a strong instructional program, students will be less likely to see the library as a place where learning is supported. In fact, in the late 1990s theorists worried that without the emergence of teaching programs and the marketing of student-centered services, academic libraries would become the "deserted commons" or "the Deserted Library" as users logged in from home to access information resources that Internet search engines couldn't provide. Scott Carlson's 2001 article "The Deserted Library," published in the *Chronicle of Higher Education*, argued that increasing remote electronic usage and decreasing circulation statistics predicted the imminent decline and end of libraries, which would be supplanted by coffeehouses, bookstores, computer labs, and other more welcoming settings. Carlson's article hit more than a few nerves within the academic library community and generated important discussions about how and why students and faculty did or did not use the libraries.

From these trends and discussions and the decisions resulting from the assessment of library services, many academic libraries and institutions that either had or were developing information commons began to integrate teaching and learning characteristics into their designs and plans. The 2015 study *Learning Commons Benchmarks* reported that

> for more than 84% of the colleges in the sample, the information or learning commons was located exclusively in the library. For colleges in the highest tuition category, those charging more than $25,000 per year, only 72.73% located their information or learning commons exclusively in the library . . . 96.15% of public colleges had their entire learning commons located in the library while this was true of only 66.67% of private colleges in the sample. (Primary Research Group Staff 2015, 18)

This study, one of the only published studies of its kind, surveyed forty-four public and private institutions for their sampling of learning commons benchmarks and characteristics. Future research needs to provide greater assessment data that sheds light on how the growing number of learning spaces, such as learning commons designs, are impacting institutions and students.

Library Learning Commons Spaces on the Rise

Learning commons spaces have continued to multiply in academic libraries since they first appeared in the 1990s. Conclusive data on their rate of growth and ongoing development is lacking in a formal manner. However, Beagle has estimated the total number of library learning commons spaces within the United States to be well over three hundred (Donald Beagle, email communication, May 18, 2016). This number is likely a conservative estimate as it represents known or reported learning commons spaces. There may be other academic library learning commons spaces in existence that are not included within this estimate since there is no central research team or location that tracks this type of data and growth.

Pedagogy, Curriculum, and the Commons

Vast changes and developments have occurred within academic libraries during the last several decades in an effort to support student success. Libraries are answering the call to support pedagogical and curricular change (Lippincott, Vedantham, and Duckett 2014) within their buildings, and more specifically, within their physical layouts, virtual presence, and among the variety of resources and services they offer. With the continuing advances in technology, writers and scholars in higher education commonly assert the need for students to develop the ability to effectively communicate and collaborate through many forms of media (Jenkins 2009). These advances in technology will continue, as will the need and demand to develop skills that allow students to create and share information in a variety of mediums and formats. Countless course syllabi on college campuses exemplify this shift in pedagogy. Professors design assignments that require students to undertake research and to use technologies such as Google Sites, WordPress, Tumblr, iMovie, iPhoto, Skype, Wimba, VoiceThread, Blackboard, and more. Students also are asked to use other technologies such as webcams and digital drop boxes within their coursework (Lippincott, Vedantham, and Duckett 2014).

Using such technologies within their curriculum also provides professors with tools that support student interest and participation in their courses, as technology-based learning experiences can be more engaging and relevant to students (U.S. Department of Education, Office of Educational Technology 2015). This focus on developing student interest, in addition to building collaborative and technological skills within course curricula, will continue to grow and "provide students with opportunities to explore new media technologies and innovate in their academic work; increase individualization of assignments, which can also reduce plagiarism; and facilitate student expression in media that are not purely textual" (Lippincott, Vedantham, and Duckett 2014).

Libraries that offer learning commons spaces that include an array of technologies, and those that provide support for students in learning and using those technologies, play an important role for students to succeed in their coursework and within the development of twenty-first-century workplace skills. Faculty members' innovative pedagogical and curricular choices are altering the ways students create information and learn. Educators will continue to experience more "flexibility within their curriculum because the learning commons spaces encourage collaboration and innovative aspects of learning" (Kinkaid 2016). The growth of the library learning commons in academic libraries supports and underscores the pedagogical and curricular changes taking place within higher education today.

Learning Commons Spaces and Engagement

The phenomenon of growth in library learning commons spaces is also a response to student demographics, interests, and expectations. More and more libraries are taking steps to support their students' learning and working styles and to provide a rewarding and meaningful library experience. Studies reinforce the knowledge that students use the library for many purposes and in a myriad of ways (Duck and Koeske 2005; Lippincott 2012; Suarez 2007). In addition to using collaborative working spaces and numerous technologies, students of the millennial generation expect academic libraries to support the social aspects of learning within their college experience. They anticipate a comfortable library space that offers refreshments and provides wireless networking off campus, among many other state-of-the-art resources and services (Duck and Koeske 2005). These students often do their work alongside their friends and peers and have a tendency to multitask and to relate to one another through digital technologies. Using technologies to create new knowledge and art forms (Palfrey and Gasser 2008) within the library makes the needs of this generation on the cutting edge and unique from those students who have come before them. This generation is "having a great impact on the way higher education institutions are thinking about the technology infrastructure that they offer for students (and faculty) and on the types of learning environments, both physical and virtual, that they provide" (Lippincott 2012, 539).

Today's academic libraries are responding to how students digest and create information and how they collapse social and academic behaviors and activities. Doug Suarez (2007) led a study about student behaviors in an academic library to determine whether library spaces nurture academic engagement. He observed and determined several different types of behaviors by today's students and categorized them as either engaging, social, or leisure behaviors. He found that engaging behaviors generally contributed to desired academic and educational outcomes and include reading, writing, consulting notes or other works, using technology, and collaborating with other students while studying and working on assignments. Social behaviors include talking with friends, flirting, resting or napping, eating and drinking, and using cell phones within a personal nature. Leisure behaviors include playing games, talking on cell phones, and listening to music (Suarez 2007). The resources and services of the library commons, in addition to its physical space and virtual offerings, support this wide range of student interests and needs associated with their academic and social lives.

Initial Considerations for Developing Learning Commons Spaces

Undertaking the successful development of an academic library learning commons involves a planned and coordinated effort among various stakeholders and established library and campus partnerships. Creating a list of essential objectives and steps can support a streamlined process and serve as a road map that will guide stakeholders, project coordinators, and library administration through the multifaceted process. The following provides a strategic approach to establishing a learning commons space. Action steps to take include

- building a foundation for the project
- setting strategies for successful programming
- collaborating with architects, designers, and contractors and creating a budget
- developing a strategic plan for technology and identifying technology needs
- marketing and promoting the new space
- examining reference, instruction, and outreach practices
- launching and assessing services
- exploring the future of library spaces, including makerspaces

Building a Foundation for the Project

Library administrators must secure buy-in with campus administration, faculty, and those who work in the library for the successful development of the learning commons. Communicating the role and function of a learning commons and how it will affect students and align with the campus mission and vision is necessary in laying the essential groundwork from the beginning of the project. Open discussions in which library administrators share current literature and data about the benefits of a learning commons with campus and library stakeholders can help to shore up support (Weiner, Doan, and Kirkwood 2010). Campus and library personnel will be recruited during this time to build a team that will oversee the accountabilities and processes associated with the project. A needs assessment for library programming and services also must be carried out and communicated during the initial stages of the project. This assessment can be achieved through the use of surveys, focus groups, student and faculty advisory groups, comments, and tours. The needs assessment will identify the services, resources, and space required for planning and establishing a commons best suited for your specific library and campus (Whitchurch 2010). Chapter 2, "Building Your Foundation," provides further input and suggestions for developing buy-in and a needs assessment.

Setting Strategies for Successful Programming

It will be important to consider the ideal types of services your learning commons programming will offer. Dynamic service centers within learning commons spaces will vary according to individual campuses, library cultures, and needs but often will include media production resources, information technology support, equipment checkout, and research assistance. In more recent years, technology-enabled classrooms and/or active learning classrooms are being made available for students as well. These classrooms can be equipped with technologies that include computers and projectors, smartboards, videoconferencing capabilities, and video-editing equipment (Oblinger 2006).

Space allocation will also be an important factor to determine for your commons. Input on what is needed and desired may come from student surveys, ethnographic studies, designers, and other means. Usually a mix of collaborative spaces for learning and socialization as well as individual study areas are adopted. Determining the ideal research, study, and work environment will be a unique process for each institution. More information about services, active learning classrooms, and use of space can be found in chapter 3, "Partnerships and Strategies for Successful Programming."

Working with Architects, Designers, Contractors, and Budgets

Collaborating with architects, designers, and contractors will be a collective effort by the stakeholders within your learning commons project. Initially, those interested in participating in the development of the learning commons space within your library will serve on one general committee consisting of many team members. Smaller subcommittees will develop and coordinate with the different architects, designers, and contractors. Meetings will need to be held on a regular basis to keep everyone informed about the status of the project as well as to communicate any changes that need to be determined along the way.

Budgeting for the project will be handled by those within campus and library administration. Costs for consideration within the budget will include overall construction, consultation with architects and designers, building materials, labor, new technologies, marketing, and monies to support new learning commons staff. Pursuing university funding, in addition to external sources such as private monies and federal or corporate grants, will help to identify and secure financial support for the project (Cunningham 2016). Chapter 4, "Architects, Designers, Contractors, and Budgets, Oh My!," will discuss, in detail, many logistical considerations that you and your team may encounter during this collaborative process.

Developing a Strategic Plan for Technology and Choosing Technology

A technology needs assessment should be carried out during the initial planning stages of the project to identify the technologies essential to the new space. It will be important to consider and develop an infrastructure that will be able to support current technologies as well as technologies of the future (Chatas 2016; Uzwyshyn 2016). Gathering this information may take place through the use of student and campus surveys, focus groups, interviews, observations, and consultations with campus information technology. The technologies, resources, and services to consider for your commons will include

- desktop computing in the library
- technical support for computing
- power outlets and charging stations
- tablets and laptop needs and usage
- software and support for software
- reference services
- campus information technology support
- technology workshops and training
- printing, including 3D printing
- scanning services
- media production and makerspace resources

The project's overall budget will also play a role in determining which technologies and services can be offered within your commons. Chapter 5, "Strategic Planning for Learning Commons Technology," and chapter 6, "Choosing What Technology Goes into a Learning Commons," provide further details and discuss technology strategic plans, assessing technology needs, and working with campus information technology in order to develop state-of-the-art programming.

Marketing and Promoting the New Space

Developing and coordinating a multilayered marketing and promotional campaign that introduces the campus community to the benefits and opportunities of a new library learning commons will play a key role in the success of your commons. Tell your learning commons story to the campus community by identifying effective promotional objectives and selecting communication strategies and vehicles through the use of a variety of mediums and formats your campus audiences frequent most. There may be opportunities to partner with campus faculty and other departments to develop and streamline your messaging. Issues such as funding, staffing, and the timing of your marketing and promotions will need to be considered and tied into the overall vision and mission of the learning commons project. Chapter 7, "Marketing and Promotion," will provide more details, including best practices for library marketing campaigns and promotions.

Exploring Reference, Instruction, and Outreach

With the increase in library commons spaces, many academic libraries continue to consider the variety of ways the new space can provide reference, instruction, and outreach programming. It will be important to assess reference and instructional services pre– and post–learning commons occupancy and to properly evaluate their functionality and impact. Examining existing means of providing reference services will be essential. Establishing best practices for carrying out learning commons outreach within your library will also support programming that is impactful. Chapter 8, "Teaching and Learning in a Learning Commons Space: Reference Services, Instruction, and Outreach," provides more information on how to develop formal and informal instruction and outreach programming that is effective and meaningful.

Launching and Assessing Services and Lessons Learned

Ensuring that your new commons space effectively meets the needs of your students will require a coordinated assessment effort on behalf of your learning commons stakeholders. A needs assessment carried out during the initial stages of the project can measure how existing and proposed services can be offered in the new space. This information will help to determine the specific services that will be made available in your commons. Once the plan to provide services to meet the needs of your student body and campus is developed, it will be essential for you and your stakeholders to continue to assess your programming on a regular basis. This will support you in identifying the success and effectiveness of the services offered as well as the areas of service that require fine-tuning. Chapter 9, "Assessing Learning Commons Spaces and Reviewing Lessons Learned," will provide information about assessments as well as examples of lessons learned that can be used when developing learning commons spaces and offerings.

Partnering to Develop Student Services

The development of learning commons campus partnerships can strengthen student services and will continue to play an important role in offering services in specialized areas. Partnering with colleagues and identifying the ways in which a variety of services and centers can best provide their support and resources within your library's learning commons will be essential to success. The physical location of each service point within the commons will have an impact on supporting student success as well as the integration of these services. Successful integration will require a concerted effort by all service-point stakeholders involved. Identifying logistical considerations such as how library, information technology, tutoring, writing, and advisement staff will collaborate and communicate among themselves will be necessary. How will these service points work as partners to ensure they provide the best possible support to students? Research demonstrates that when collaborative learning commons spaces include tutoring, writing advisement, and other academic support structures, commons areas can successfully support the intertwined process of research and writing (Palomino and Gouveia 2011). Chapter 10, "Successful Learning Commons Partnerships," provides information on how to develop collaborative student services in learning commons spaces. This chapter also reports on the findings of the Learning Commons Survey and illustrates how services are being offered in academic commons spaces.

The Future of Library Spaces and Makerspaces

With the continued influx of technologies and collaborative working areas taking root in libraries, makerspaces, and other nontraditional library areas will continue to increase and broaden the opportunities available within academic libraries. Newly reinvigorated libraries that feature creative spaces that allow for both socialization and learning and that offer cutting-edge and technology-driven services will continue to develop. Each institution will determine its specific organizational needs; however, some trends in new offerings involve the inclusion of digital media centers, tutoring and advisement centers, exhibition spaces, flexible classrooms and/or makerspaces, and more. Displaying artwork in learning commons spaces, as discussed in chapter 10, "Successful Learning Commons Partnerships," continues to evolve, as does providing makerspace areas that allow for student experimentation, innovation, creativity, and do-it-yourself activities (Fourie and Meyer 2015). Makerspaces can be designed to be highly individualized to meet curricular and programming needs. They are frequently referred to as media studios, digital or idea labs, fablabs, hackerspaces, beta spaces, or tech shops (Fisher 2012). With a range of offerings found in these specialized labs, it will be important to determine the specific resources your library and learning commons will offer with input from students, faculty, and technology experts. Popular offerings include providing your users with the ability to use technologies such as 3D printers, laser cutters, digital media, computer software, fabrication software, tools for welding and woodworking, and recording studios. Chapter 11, "The Future of Library Learning Commons Spaces," will address the overall future of library spaces in addition to the learning and creating opportunities available in academic libraries.

ⓖ Key Points

Establishing a foundation of support and a strategic plan for developing a learning commons space are critical and important steps within the process. Such preparation creates the basis for a collaborative and efficient undertaking and for developing successful library programming.

- The majority of learning commons spaces found in academic institutions are primarily located in the campus library and often offer allied services dedicated to fostering and empowering student success through embedded writing and tutoring centers, makerspaces, and student advisement services.
- Today's learning commons spaces in academic libraries have evolved from earlier information commons models to promote collaborate learning spaces that promote peer learning and flexible space environments.
- The rise of academic libraries providing information literacy instruction and developing teaching models that support faculty and university curriculum in the past two decades set the stage for the growth and success of learning commons spaces.

- Developments in technology will continue to play a key role in enhancing the student experience and in designing learning commons spaces. Throughout the process, it will be important to consider student expectations that include access to collaborative working spaces and comfortable settings that can support the social aspects of learning and multitasking.
- Developing a successful learning commons space will involve strategic planning and support from many campus and library stakeholders. Collaboration, through the use of committees and subcommittees, will be necessary to coordinate the many aspects of developing the commons space and include assessing need, choosing technology, developing user-centered instruction, providing essential services, marketing and promoting, and developing support services such as writing and advisement centers.

The next chapter will discuss the process for carrying out an environmental scan and for conducting a needs assessment. Developing buy-in with campus and library stakeholders will also be addressed in chapter 2, "Building Your Foundation."

References

Beagle, Donald Robert, Donald Russell Bailey, and Barbara Tierney. 2006. *The Information Commons Handbook*. New York: Neal-Schuman.

Bennett, Scott. 2008. "The Information or the Learning Commons: Which Will We Have?" *Journal of Academic Librarianship* 34, no. 3: 183–85. https://doi.org/10.1016/j.acalib.2008.03.001.

Carlson, Scott. 2001. "The Deserted Library." *Chronicle of Higher Education* 48, no. 12 (November 16): A35–38. EBSCOhost.

Chatas, Jim. 2016. "Transforming School Libraries into Learning Commons: Five Keys to Success." *Stantec* (blog), February 2, 2016. https://ideas.stantec.com/blog/transforming-school-libraries-into-learning-commons-five-keys-to-success.

Cunningham, Carolyn. 2016. "St. Edward's University Learning Commons: Literature Review and Management Toolkit." Capstone project, University of Texas at Austin. https://repositories.lib.utexas.edu/bitstream/handle/2152/32016/cunningham%20capstone%20final%20report.pdf?sequence=3.

Duck, Patricia M., and Randi Koeske. 2005. "Marketing the Millennials: What They Expect from Their Library Experience." Paper presented at the Association of College and Research Libraries Twelfth National Conference, Minneapolis, MN, April 7–10, 2005.

Fisher, Erin. 2012. "Makerspaces Move into Academic Libraries." *ACRL TechConnect* (blog), November 28, 2012. http://acrl.ala.org/techconnect/post/makerspaces-move-into-academic-libraries.

Fourie, Ina, and Anika Meyer. 2015. "What to Make of Makerspaces: Tools and DIY Only or Is There an Interconnected Information Resources Space?" *Library Hi Tech* 33, no. 4: 519–25. https://doi.org/10.1108/LHT-09-2015-0092.

Helfer, Doris Small. 1997. "The Leavey Library: A Library in Your Future?" *Searcher Magazine* 5, no. 1: 38–41. EBSCOhost.

Jenkins, Henry. 2009. *Confronting the Challenges of Participatory Culture*. Cambridge, MA: MIT Press.

Kinkaid, Kami. 2016. "Learning Commons as an Extension of the Classroom." *Pfau Long Architecture* (blog), January 13, 2016. www.pfaulong.com/learning-commons-as-an-extension-of-the-classroom.

Lippincott, Joan K. 2009. "Information Commons: Surveying the Landscape." In *A Field Guide to the Information Commons*, edited by Charles Forrest and Martin Halbert, 18–31. Lanham, MD: Scarecrow Press.

Lippincott, Joan K. 2012. "Information Commons: Meeting Millennials' Needs." *Journal of Library Administration* 52, nos. 6–7: 538–48. EBSCOhost.

Lippincott, Joan K., Anu Vedantham, and Kim Duckett. 2014. "Libraries as Enablers of Pedagogical and Curricular Change." *Educause Review*, October 27, 2014. http://er.educause.edu/articles/2014/10/libraries-as-enablers-of-pedagogical-and-curricular-change.

Lux, Vera, Robert Snyder, and Colleen Boff. 2016. "Why Users Come to the Library: A Case Study of Library and Non-library Units." *Journal of Academic Librarianship* 42, no. 2: 109–17. https://doi.org/10.1016/j.acalib.2016.01.004.

Milewicz, Elizabeth J. 2009. "Origin and Development of the Information Commons in Academic Libraries." In *A Field Guide to the Information Commons*, edited by Charles Forrest and Martin Plymouth, 3–17. Lanham, MD: Scarecrow Press.

Oblinger, Diana G., ed. 2006. *Learning Spaces*. Washington, DC: Educause. PDF e-book. https://net.educause.edu/ir/library/pdf/PUB7102g.pdf.

Palfrey, John, and Urs Gasser. 2008. *Born Digital: Understanding the First Generation of Digital Natives*. New York: Basic Books.

Palomino, Norma E., and Paula F. Gouveia. 2011. "Righting the Academic Paper: A Collaboration between Library Services and the Writing Centre in a Canadian Academic Setting." *New World Library* 112, nos. 3–4: 131–40. https://doi.org/10.1108/03074801111117032.

Primary Research Group Staff. 2015. *Learning Commons Benchmarks*. New York: Primary Research Group.

Sasaki Associates Staff. 2016. *The State of Academic Librarian Spaces*. Boston: Sasaki Associates. http://librarysurvey.sasaki.com/.

Suarez, Doug. 2007. "What Students Do When They Study in the Library: Using Ethnographic Methods to Observe Student Behavior." *Electronic Journal of Academic and Special Librarianship* 8, no. 3 (Winter). http://southernlibrarianship.icaap.org/content/v08n03/suarez_d01.html.

U.S. Department of Education, Office of Educational Technology. 2015. "Learning." In *National Education Technology Plan*. Washington, DC: U.S. Department of Education. http://tech.ed.gov/netp/learning/.

Uzwyshyn, Ray. 2016. "Transforming Academic Libraries for the New Millennia." Paper presented at the Transformational Technology in Higher Education, Sixth Annual Conference and Expo, Denver, CO, March 24–25, 2016.

Weiner, Sharon A., Tomalee Doan, and Hal Kirkwood. 2010. "The Learning Commons as a Locus for Information Literacy." *College & Undergraduate Libraries* 17, no. 2: 192–212. http://docs.lib.purdue.edu/lib_research/131.

Whitchurch, Michael J. 2010. "Planning an Information Commons." *Journal of Library Administration* 50, no. 1: 39–50. EBSCOhost.

CHAPTER 2

Building Your Foundation

IN THIS CHAPTER

▷ Exploring the impact that learning spaces in libraries have on student satisfaction and learning

 ▷ Recognizing the high potential for political pitfalls during a learning space redesign

 ▷ Identifying the key campus stakeholders that need to be consulted

▷ Establishing buy-in and building your team for the programming

 ▷ Carrying out a needs assessment that will provide institutional-specific data

---

BUILDING A SOLID FOUNDATION for your learning commons undertaking will require you and your team to address a multitude of considerations and to carry out a series of action steps that will involve numerous project stakeholders. Included in this chapter are suggestions and guidelines for communicating the positive impacts of efficiently designed learning spaces, identifying key campus stakeholders, establishing buy-in with those stakeholders, and recognizing potential political risks within varied campus communities. Carrying out needs assessment strategies will also be discussed.

Scanning the Political Climate

Institutions may embark on developing a learning commons for many different reasons. Like any other campus building or remodeling project, the motivation for the construction of any new or renovated learning space can come from the highest echelons of a university's administration, via either a campus president or provost, or internally from the library director. Some learning commons projects may be initiated due to the need for physical upgrades to deteriorating and uncomfortable furnishings, advances in technology, and/or changes in the way students work in today's academic libraries. Still other learning space redesign projects may be triggered by a large donation with dedicated funds allocated to a facilities face-lift. Whatever the motivation, embarking on a learning commons development project requires careful consideration and planning. It also truly involves setting your institution up for success by making sure that all stakeholders and partners are always aware of project goals and the ultimate vision for the final learning commons design.

In the past decade or more, both practitioners and researchers have begun to focus more on the crucial thought process that goes into the development of successful new learning spaces within higher education settings. Many studies reveal that it is critical to design or redesign a library so that it reflects students' study needs and learning habits, both individual and group based. Studies, typically conducted outside of the United States, have also begun to examine whether there is a positive correlation between post–learning space/building user experience satisfaction with a preconstruction student needs assessment to measure what some refer to as a social return on investment or SROI (Watson et al. 2016). Studies such as *A Learning Space Odyssey* (Beckers 2016) have chosen to examine the alignment of all higher education buildings specifically from the perspective of students as an important user group. Libraries and their learning commons are ideal spaces for such studies as they offer a continuous laboratory for examining facility usage as well as user satisfaction with services and technology.

Since 2000, many researchers have begun to more deeply realize that just as "facilities could for example be essential to attract key research personnel . . . [their] impact on student perceptions of their pedagogic experience" was not as thoroughly scrutinized (Price et al. 2003, 212). It is also important to note that in the past decade, libraries and other dedicated quiet student study spaces have also begun to be considered in studies that examine the way that campus facility factors influence the decisions undergraduates and their parents make when picking the institution they will attend. Several studies have focused on how quality campus facilities, such as residence halls, fitness centers, and university grounds, impact a student's choice of university. For instance, the 2003 study "The Impact of Facilities on Student Choice of University" reported that "the availability of 'quiet' areas (e.g. library, study rooms)" was one of the higher-ranking factors out of two surveys intended to measure the most important factors related to student university selection (Price et al. 2003, 216).

Ideally, university presidents and provosts will recognize the significant importance that their institution's physical library setting plays in attracting, supporting, and retaining undergraduate and graduate students. However, for those institutions with older library facilities, campus leaders still often fail to realize that without attractive and technology-rich facilities that offer comfortable seating and dynamic learning spaces, students will be less likely to frequent the library for studying and peer-learning opportunities. Therefore, when scanning one's campus political climate, it is imperative to work to determine how those serving at the highest levels of the campus administration view and value the library's physical facilities.

It is also critical, for both library directors and other library personnel vested with the responsibility of working to develop a learning commons space, to both examine and nurture any collaborative alliances and mutually beneficial relationships across campuses before, during, and after any learning commons renovation project. Why, you may ask? For starters, unless the learning commons will be housed in a completely new facility, most learning commons redesign projects will be highly disruptive to existing library operations and facilities. In addition, the library is often seen as a commonly shared campus space about which many stakeholders, such as students and faculty, may have developed sentimental attachments and hardened expectations. It is critical not to lose sight of the fact that a library remodel can be fraught with political implications that may trigger multiple campus and community dustups.

As Colin Story notes in his article "Commons Consent: Librarians, Architects and Community Culture in Co-creating Academic Library Learning Spaces," "Constructing new or refurbished radical library learning spaces for a specific community inevitably involves the coming together of ad hoc groups of agents with fuzzy inter relationships to produce designs and realize projects" (2015, 572). When embarking on working with these various agents and stakeholders, it is imperative to always be aware of the political climate of your campus and work to develop a detailed knowledge of the current issues that may impact your project's budget and ultimate success. As Story admonishes, it is critical for your learning commons project managers to quickly determine what your project's most controversial and potentially politically sensitive plans may be and to develop strategies for including discussions of these "hot spots" in public forums such as town hall meetings or other campus presentations. These trigger areas will vary with each learning commons project—regardless of whether the planned learning space is a renovation or new construction.

Examples of typical project hot spots may include issues such as the addition of a café or dining facilities in the library, the removal or weeding of physical collections to make way for new study space furnishings, or the addition, fusion, or removal of library service points within a dynamic learning commons space. It is also essential not to neglect internal library personnel concerns and consternation over library remodeling plans. Some of the most commonly planned learning commons design features can evoke heated debates both within and outside of the library itself. Library leadership must remember to thoughtfully and promptly respond to publicly voiced concerns about learning commons planning. It is typical to find campus faculty and staff concerned about a learning commons project budget or the consolidation of service points to gain space for new blended services. The regular updating and dissemination of library renovation news can often help prevent unfounded rumors from gaining traction and creating political problems for the project. Providing all available details about the timeline, contingency planning during construction disturbances and/or closures, and budget will likely help assuage many who feel apprehensive about the changes a learning commons project can bring to a campus library.

Students are the single most important population that must be both considered and involved during any learning commons planning and development. A formal assessment of student satisfaction with existing library facilities and services is critical to formulating plans that will improve the library and enhance a future learning commons. Hopefully, any library entertaining the launch of a learning commons will already have ample longitudinal data about student satisfaction with library facilities and services. However, if this is not the case, the project should conduct this kind of assessment before embarking on design and planning. A failure to gather student input on desired services and space amenities would be a critical misstep.

In addition to student satisfaction surveys, students can also take part in focus groups that ask them to design and draw out future learning commons layouts or try out and comment on sample furniture that is slated for possible purchase. Taking the time to organize and market a furniture fair is an example of a planning investment that pays off huge dividends in the long run. When students, faculty, and staff get to test possible furniture pieces under consideration for the learning commons renovation, they are more likely to give critical feedback on comfort and usability. A successful marketing of "furniture fairs," via social media or library blogs, like those conducted at the Wentworth Institute of Technology, can also help document and narrate the inclusive story of how your library worked to gather input from student users and other campus stakeholders about learning commons purchasing and renovation decisions (Witlibrary 2015).

Figure 2.1. Furniture Fair. *Reproduced with permission from Wentworth Institute of Technology (2015)*

Unfortunately, per the 2016 Project Information Literacy (PIL) study *Planning and Designing Academic Library Learning Spaces*, this step is often not taken. "Less than a third of the sample (31%)" professionals interviewed in the PIL report "said they used formal methods to systematically collect user data as part of the planning process. Some stakeholders had surveyed students (27%) at the beginning of projects while others held focus groups (23%) for collecting data about library uses" (Head 2016, 2). In addition to conducting formal survey-based assessments, it is also critical to design student focus groups where project staff ask students what features or services might be desirable in a future learning commons and to consistently involve students in regular communications about the progress of plans, construction, and timeline for completion. Effective avenues for achieving outreach to students about the future learning commons include

- marketing in the student newspaper,
- working alongside student government leaders,
- addressing student groups and organizations,
- holding informational meetings where students can ask questions.

Collaborations with student government are essential for gaining support and marketing channels. In addition, it is also critical to reach out to university personnel charged with working with student services. Examples of other campus student services and/or units to consider collaborating with about learning commons planning include campus tutoring services, student athletics, writing centers, international student services, peer mentor groups, the career center, campus orientation services, and information technology services.

KEY STAKEHOLDERS TO BE INVOLVED IN ANY LEARNING SPACE REDESIGN

- Campus president and cabinet (vice presidents for finance, development, etc.)
- Provost
- Director of information technology or chief information officer (CIO)
- Facilities personnel and internal campus designers and architects
- Finance officers
- Deans of academic colleges/chairs of academic departments
- Faculty
- Library personnel
- Students (undergraduate and graduate)
- Community users

Library personnel charged with working on the development of a learning commons will quickly find that proposed changes to the physical space in their facility can potentially evoke passionate and sometimes critical responses from campus and community stakeholders. It is therefore imperative to work to create a culture of strategic planning that listens to and vets comments and concerns of students, professors, alumni, university managers, and library personnel not directly involved in project planning. A goal in this process is to make stakeholders and library users feel that they are a part of the process and essentially participants in the reimagining of the proposed new learning space. Clear and effective communication of project goals and processes is essential to the success of any learning commons endeavor. As reported in the PIL study *Planning and Designing Academic Learning Spaces* the most-cited requirement mentioned by the study's librarians and architects in effective learning commons planning was good communication.

> Continuous staff updates, ranging from individual meetings with library units to hosting campus-wide forums were critically important for establishing a sense of ownership for a new space, according to librarians. Taking time to build grassroots support with all constituents helped gain consensus about design choices at top levels later on, architects added. (Head 2016, 2)

Another essential planning step critical to this process involves reviewing the current physical state, both layout and condition, of your library facility. For example, question whether your building can physically handle the electrical upgrades needed to add several bring-your-own-device seating bars with multiple outlets within your learning commons. Or seek consultation with campus architects and/or other facilities personnel about whether existing walls can possibly be removed to expand an area and develop a more open floor plan. Knowledge of library floor plans and facility details like this matter greatly when planning a new learning space or learning commons. It is also critical to consider the future upkeep needs that a learning commons area will require post-occupancy. For instance, will the library need to develop a budget line for additional custodial services, annual painting, furniture refreshment and cleaning cycles, and technology upgrades given the likely increase in student facility usage?

⊚ Environmental Scan of Facilities and Working with Facilities Managers

Any remodel or new construction project being undertaken within a library can quickly reveal what library administration does not know about their facilities. As library director Sarah Houghton noted in her blog posting titled "Must-Have Skills for Today's Library Director" (2014), "It is amazing how many of us have absolutely no experience, background, or skill in managing a building. . . . It's just not something you think about." Hopefully, as personnel move forward on any learning commons project, someone within the library will have a solid grasp of physical floor plans, access to spreadsheets of the current problems in the building, and a solid relationship with the campus facilities planning and management team. Most likely this individual will be the library facilities manager or a member of your library's facilities team. A well-organized library, regardless of size, should have either an individual or a number of key personnel dedicated to managing building furnishings and planning for renovations, planning for disaster and evacuation, enforcing safety and emergency guidelines, and maintaining building and patron security. In addition to the library having staff with these responsibilities, a university campus will also have facilities managers on staff dedicated to the library building and any university construction projects.

⊚ Developing a Foundation for Support

Each library learning commons will be unique to its institution and university culture. The size of the campus, academic department focus and programs, in addition to campus demographics will have an impact on the nature of the learning commons programming. "A key component of the planning process is to understand the campus perspective, student learning styles and preferences, and the role of the campus library. The combination of those factors will result in a learning commons that supports its own institutional priorities" (Weiner, Doan, and Kirkwood 2010, 194). From a practical perspective, the academic library learning commons provides its users with physical and virtual spaces and state-of-the-art technologies. Access to resources and services, in addition to opportunities for student and campus collaborations and partnerships, all take place in a comfortable, adaptable, and educational setting. Academic libraries continue to develop these spaces to support student success in the face of current academic demands and twenty-first-century skill-set expectations. Any plan to develop a learning commons space within an academic library should be unique to specific campus user needs and conform to the mission and values of that particular university (Whitchurch 2010).

Library Leadership

Library administrators will need to play a leading role in gaining stakeholder support for the development of the new learning commons space. Building relationships with campus donors, deans, department heads, and other administrators will be one of the most important responsibilities of library administrators (Weiner, Doan, and Kirkwood 2010). Library leaders must communicate the vision of the learning commons and convey how the day-to-day workings and offerings of the commons will support the mission, vision, and values of the university as a whole. Keeping abreast of current literature and best practices in relation to learning commons spaces will be essential for the library director or dean, associate dean, and other library leadership. Library administrators will need to serve as experts about learning commons spaces and the development process (Weiner, Doan, and Kirkwood 2010).

Making the case for a new learning commons space should be supported by sound reasoning and grounded in accurate facts (Watson and Hubsher 2016). This can be done through the use of gathered data that will demonstrate the need for the new commons resources and services. Some of this information may be library specific and drawn from the assessment data carried out during the initial planning stages of the project. Conducting a needs assessment will provide library leadership with data that can illustrate and inform others about the need and benefits of the new space and offerings. Details about carrying out a needs assessment will be addressed later in this chapter. Results of the assessment, which can include student interviews and individual campus or institutional surveys within research studies, can be shared. Using existing campus data concerning student services usage can also be a valuable source of information for making a case to create a learning commons housed in the library. University stakeholders may find value in the model as it brings student support services together in one location (Weiner, Doan, and Kirkwood 2010).

In addition to garnering support from campus donors, deans, department heads, and other campus leadership, library administrators will need to gain support from stakeholders within the library. This will include speaking and listening to all library employees, students, and library volunteer groups. Building support for the new space and programming will take time and involve a series of meetings and presentations that provide the opportunity for library stakeholders to ask questions and to voice any possible concerns. During this initial period, library leadership will need to address any concerns and communicate the benefits of developing a learning commons within the library. Field trips to visit other learning commons and guest speaker presentations with reference to the project can help to build support and consensus for the programming. Allocating additional staff and financial resources toward the development of a new learning commons will need to be addressed with library stakeholders (Weiner, Doan, and Kirkwood 2010). Finally, those library employees who will be impacted due to the addition of the commons will need to be provided with specific information as to how their positions will be affected. During this initial phase of the project, library stakeholders will be invited to participate in the planning process and to serve on the management teams and committees that will carry out and oversee the project.

Buy-In for Programming

According to Gary Fitsimmons in "Resource Management: People Gaining Buy-In" (2009), effective leadership identifies and uses employee connections to an organization to gain buy-in when possible. These employee connections to a library can provide a context and bring meaning to each individual's work. For some employees with a strong connection, they view what they do at the library as their life's work. However, others may be motivated predominately by a paycheck. Regardless, library leadership can frame its messaging to appeal to those specific connections. It will be important for library administrators to be involved with all phases of the project and to shore up continuous support throughout the process. General strategies for building support and buy-in for your project can include Susan Ashford and James Detert's (2015) research on "issue selling." They suggest the use of seven tactics to gain buy-in. The following strategies may be useful:

- Tailor your pitch—know your audience's goals and values.
- Frame the issue—demonstrate importance through the big picture.
- Manage emotions on both sides—listen and speak carefully and respectfully.
- Get the timing right—identify the best time to raise your ideas.
- Involve others—build a coalition for support.
- Adhere to norms—identify preferred organizational approaches and data.
- Suggest solutions—implies thought and respect for the process.

It will be essential to establish trust, interest, and involvement with all campus and library stakeholders in order to carry out successful learning commons programming. Using effective communication strategies can support library leaders in managing the relationships within this process. Involvement from all stakeholders will be important from the beginning and into the management of an up-and-running commons space. "Buy-in is not just acceptance, but active support. Having stakeholder buy-in is not just, 'Okay, go do that' from your manager. It is, 'Okay, I want to help you achieve that' from every stakeholder" (Bier 2015, 56). Securing this level of agreement will help to ensure a collaborative process.

Building the Team

Developing your project management team will begin during the initial phases of your learning commons project when library administration is reaching out to campus and library stakeholders in order to build support. Invitations for participation can be made at meetings and presentations. If there is a library administrator other than the library director or dean managing the day-to-day processes of the project, he or she may want to make a list of committees or teams that need to be created in order to manage specific areas of the project, including but not limited to construction, design, facilities, technologies, marketing and campus communications, and collaborations with campus information technology, tutoring, and advisement. It may be useful to have a chair or lead for each committee or team. These chairs or team leaders should meet with library leadership on a regular basis to keep everyone informed on progress and to receive feedback about changes to the planning and programming, which will need to be addressed throughout the process. Committee or team members can be composed of campus and library stakeholders, including

- library administrators and employees;
- campus administrators;
- students;
- faculty members;

- student services personnel;
- information technology staff;
- tutoring and advisement personnel;
- facilities staff;
- donors.

Developing project committees and teams that include a broad range of stakeholders will help to create transparency in the process and add a range of perspectives to the programming (Weiner, Doan, and Kirkwood 2010).

Planning Documents

Creating planning documents in reference to specific areas of your learning commons programming and in reference to managing the logistical aspects of the project will be helpful in order to monitor progress. A document that includes all project goals and a timeline for goal completion throughout the process will also help to keep team members aligned and on track. Creating these documents and checklists can support a smooth and collaborative process. An overall learning commons strategic planning document can outline the vision, mission, and scope of the new space, resources, and services offered. Operational planning documents can address goals and strategies concerning the project's design, facilities, budget, teams, services, technologies, marketing, and collaborations. Resources and examples of learning commons project planning documents can be found at www.lib.ncsu.edu/sites/default/files/huntlibrary/documents/102508_ppd.pdf.

Needs Assessment

Performing a local needs assessment will guide the creation of a learning commons that will meet your specific institutional needs and help to identify new initiatives and programs to be offered. This research also will provide valuable input in determining how your library's physical space should be repurposed or redesigned. Overall, the needs assessment process and its results will help to determine and prioritize needs and provide a structure for your planning documents (Lynn 2011). Your needs assessment can be carried out using many of the methods that will be employed to assess your learning commons programming once your commons is established. Through evaluation of the gathered results, the services and ideal space allocations for your learning commons should become evident based on the goals and mission of your library and university (Whitchurch 2010).

Several methodologies will need to be used in order to gain reliable information concerning the addition or renovation of your learning commons. Various tools and approaches, formal and informal, quantitative and qualitative, should be carried out in an effort to gather a broad range of data that represents the needs of your particular institution. Gathering and using relevant quantitative data includes considering service desk statistics, group study room usage, and gate count. These data are generally more meaningful when they are analyzed over a period of time (Bailey and Tierney 2008). Qualitative evaluation is considered more subjective overall than quantitative data but is still useful when considered as part of a whole. Surveys, focus groups, and usability studies are several methods of gathering qualitative data. The following provides a guideline by which the needs assessment programming can be carried out. Those conducting the assessment will need to determine

- a well-defined purpose for the study;
- the individuals best suited to conduct the assessment;
- the methods and instruments to be used;
- the manner in which the assessment will be administered;
- the data that should be gathered; and
- how the information will be used (Bailey and Tierney 2008).

Impartial individuals who have some background knowledge about the topics being discussed and assessed should be assigned as moderators. Those responsible for the resources and services being evaluated should not be involved in this part of the process. It is also important that the stakeholders who serve on the committees or teams that design and serve as moderators of the needs assessments instruments share similar characteristics with the library's user population (Marczak and Sewell 2018). Well-designed assessment strategies, instruments, and planning activities will ultimately provide information that will assist in allocating resources for programming. The collection and analysis of the data will support and guide informed decision-making and help to prioritize goals for the development of a mobile, functional, and flexible library space that supports the needs of twenty-first-century students (Lynn 2011). Among the needs assessment instruments, tools, and data-gathering activities that are used for such programming are

- site visits to similar libraries with learning commons;
- review of current literature on the subject of learning commons;
- student and faculty focus groups;
- ethnographic studies;
- ideal space design exercises (drawings of collaborative spaces);
- interviews and surveys;
- environmental scan;
- analyzing service desk, group study room and specialty lab statistics, and gate count;
- photo diaries (images of favorite and least favorite spaces);
- online campus-wide survey of library resources and physical space;
- survey of incoming freshmen;
- evaluation of other learning commons websites;
- assessment of library employee work areas, including circulation, reference, and office space (Andrews and Wright 2015; Bailey and Tierney 2008; Lynn 2011).

Focus Groups and Usability Studies

Focus groups, usability studies, and surveys are among many user-centered research tools that assist researchers in understanding user needs, behaviors, and attitudes. These methods provide researchers with opportunities to observe and gather direct user feedback. User-centered research tools assist researchers in understanding how users live their lives so that the organizations serving them can respond to user needs with informed solutions (Veal 2016). Focus groups and usability studies are two types of user-centered evaluative instruments that, if conducted, are sometimes carried out in conjunction with each other. Focus groups are structured interviews that gather users' expectations and preferences about

resources and services. Generally, data derived from focus groups will be somew[...]
tive, but the information gleaned can be extremely useful in determining user-speci[...]
and preferences (Bailey and Tierney 2008). Usability studies are often carried out [...]
focus groups are conducted and can help to determine how easily patrons can use libr[...]
services. The main goal of usability studies is to "identify usability problems, collec[...]
qualitative data, and determine participants' overall satisfaction" (Veal 2016). Together,
focus groups and usability studies results can provide data about user preferences and
expectations as well as identify specific aspects about the usability of library resources
and services.

Surveys for Needs Assessment

Surveys are another form of user-centered research gathering. Organizations generally
design their own survey instruments and sometimes share them with other libraries.
These surveys can be adapted, fairly easily, for other institutional needs (Bailey and
Tierney 2008). Generally, these assessment tools aim to consider and determine existing
space allocation and usage within the library and learning commons and to identify the
resources and services most desired by users. Such surveys will generally ask users to provide feedback about the following areas and more:

- Group study spaces
- Places for quiet individual study
- Computing and other technology resources
- Electrical outlets
- Group presentation practice rooms
- Active learning classrooms
- Furniture
- IT assistance
- Tutoring
- Media lab
- Reference assistance (Lynn 2011)

Needs assessment surveys can be advertised on the library website, distributed through
campus student government organizations, shared within social media, and sent by
email. Specific student cohorts can also be invited to participate in the needs assessment
programming and often will include input from freshmen during first-year freshmen
programming (Lynn 2011). Needs assessment resources can be found at https://learning
spacetoolkit.org/.

Ethnographic Studies and Ideal Space Design Exercise

Additional methods of gathering user-centered data include employing ethnographic strategies. Through the use of ethnographic tools, researchers attempt to understand user's behavior from the user's point of view. Unlike other forms of traditional assessment-gathering
strategies that ask specific and highly practical questions, ethnographic-based inquiry places
the researcher in the users' environment for nondirected observation. This form of research
is generally not as efficient as other forms of data gathering, but it can provide researchers
with the context held by patrons who use the library (Anderson 2009).

An ideal space design exercise is an informal, user-centered method of determining student preferences and expectations. The Bissett Collaborative Center at the Albert R. Mann Library at Cornell University used this method to gather specific information about how their students were working collaboratively in the library. They arranged for thirty-eight students to participate in the exercise and asked them to draw their ideal collaborative library spaces. They also conducted ten-minute interviews with the students about their drawings and preferences. The information from the brief interview was recorded on the back of the drawings. Pizza and soda were provided to enhance the experience. The top results from the drawings and interviews found that students wanted group study rooms, windows with views of nature, plants, comfy chairs and couches, whiteboards, and mobile furniture, among other offerings (Andrews and Wright 2014). The information gathered from this type of research can provide direct and practical feedback about user preferences and behaviors.

Carrying out a wide range of needs assessment strategies that include both quantitative and qualitative methodologies will support a comprehensive data-gathering effort and help to identify new initiatives and programming to be offered within your learning commons. Such institutional-based assessment will help to ensure the services, resources, and space identified within your findings will establish a learning commons best suited for your specific library and institution.

⑥ Key Points

When establishing a foundation for your learning commons development and programming, keep in mind the following considerations and recommendations:

- A careful review of your current library facility or new building blueprints can help ensure your project vision is achievable.
- Examination of the political strengths and weaknesses of your library's image, budget forecast, and ranking on campus will support a thoughtful and effective planning process.
- Library spaces or services that are "nonnegotiable" for remodeling or restructuring within the campus community will need to be identified at the beginning of the planning process. Prematurely announcing plans to augment these "sacred cows" could wreck acceptance of design plans.
- Successful learning commons space plans will be unique to your specific campus and user needs and will conform to the mission and values of your institution.
- The vision of your learning commons must be communicated to campus and community members. Library leaders will be involved with these communications during all phases of the project to secure stakeholder buy-in throughout the entire process.
- Successful project committees or teams will include a broad range of stakeholders. This will help to create transparency and add a range of perspectives.
- The use of planning documents to manage the logistical aspects of the project will be helpful in monitoring progress and help to keep all on track.
- The implementation of qualitative and quantitative assessment tools to carry out your local needs assessment will support the creation of a learning commons space that meets your specific institutional needs.

In the next chapter, designing professional floor plans for learning as socialization will be discussed. Developing active learning classrooms and creating dynamic services centers will also be addressed. Finally, chapter 3, "Partnerships and Strategies for Successful Programming," will begin reporting on the findings of a survey that explores the development and popular offerings of academic library learning commons spaces.

⑥ References

Anderson, Ken. 2009. "Ethnographic Research: A Key to Strategy." *Harvard Business Review*, March 2009. https://hbr.org/2009/03/ethnographic-research-a-key-to-strategy.

Andrews, Camille, and Sara E. Wright. 2014. "Crowdsourcing Design: Using the Ideal Space Design Exercise to Gather Student Feedback." Paper presented at Educause, NorthEast Regional Computing Program Annual Conference, Providence, RI, March 24–26, 2014. www.educause.edu/sites/default/files/library/presentations/NC14/PS05/Nercomp-crowdsourcing-final-Wright-Andrews.pdf.

———. 2015. "Library Learning Spaces: Investigating Libraries and Investing in Student Feedback." Paper presented at the Association of College and Research Libraries Creating Sustainable Community Conference, Portland, OR, March 25–28, 2015. www.ala.org/acrl/sites/ala.org.acrl/files/content/conferences/confsandpreconfs/2015/Andrews_Wright.pdf.

Ashford, Susan J., and James R. Detert. 2015. "Get the Boss to Buy In." *Harvard Business Review* 93, nos. 1–2. https://hbr.org/2015/01/get-the-boss-to-buy-in.

Bailey, Russell, and Barbara Tierney. 2008. *Transforming Library Service through Information Commons: Case Studies for the Digital Age*. Chicago: American Library Association.

Beckers, Ronald. 2016. *A Learning Space Odyssey*. Enschede, Netherlands: University of Twente. http://doc.utwente.nl/100427/1/thesis_R_Beckers_revision.pdf.

Bier, Laura. 2015. "Securing Team Buy In for EVM." *PM Network* 29, no. 2: 56–57. www.pmnetwork-digital.com/pmnetwork/february_2015?pg=58#pg58.

Fitsimmons, Gary. 2009. "Resource Management: People Gaining Buy-In." *Bottom Line: Managing Library Finances* 22, no. 1: 21–23. https://doi.org/10.1108/08880450910955404.

Head, Alison J. 2016. *Planning and Designing Academic Library Learning Spaces: Expert Perspectives of Architects, Librarians and Library Consultants*. Project Information Literacy Research Report. Practitioner Series. Seattle: University of Washington. www.projectinfolit.org/uploads/2/7/5/4/27541717/pil_libspace_report_12_6_16.pdf.

Houghton, Sarah. 2014. "Today's Library Director, Part 2: Partner Relationships, Facilities Management, and Reading a Budget." *Must-Have Skills for Today's Library Director* (blog), December 10, 2014. www.sirsidynix.com/blog/2014/12/10/today-s-library-director-part-2-partner-relationships-facilities.

Lynn, Valerie A. 2011. "A Knowledge Commons Needs Assessment." *College & Research Libraries News* 72, no. 8 (September): 464–67.

Marczak, Mary, and Meg Sewell. 2018. "Using Focus Groups for Evaluation." Alternative Methods for Collecting Evaluation Data. University of Arizona. Accessed May 7, 2018. https://cals.arizona.edu/sfcs/cyfernet/cyfar/focus.htm.

Price, I., Fides Matzdorf, Louise Smith, and Helen Agahi. 2003. "The Impact of Facilities on Student Choice of University." *Facilities* 21, no. 10: 212–22. https://doi.org/10.1108/02632770310493580.

Storey, Colin. 2015. "Commons Consent: Librarians, Architects and Community Culture in Co-creating Academic Library Learning Spaces." *Library Management* 36, nos. 8/9: 570–83. https://doi.org/10.1108/LM-05-2014-0057.

Veal, Raven. 2016. "How to Conduct User Experience Research like a Professional." *Careerfoundry* (blog), September 5, 2016. http://blog.careerfoundry.com/ux-design/how-to-conduct-user-experience-research-like-a-professional.

Watson, Karen, and Robert Hubsher. 2016. "Facility Planning: The Strategic Plan and Its Essential Place in Your Library Project's Success." *eBulletin.* www.nyla.org/max/4DCGI/cms/review.html?Action=CMS_Document&DocID=723&MenuKey=eBulletin.

Watson, Kelly J., James Evans, Andrew Karvonen, and Tim Whitley. 2016. "Capturing the Social Value of Buildings: The Promise of Social Return on Investment (SROI)." *Building and Environment* 103: 289–301. doi:10.1016/j.buildenv.2016.04.007.

Weiner, Sharon A., Tomalee Doan, and Hal Kirkwood. 2010. "The Learning Commons as a Locus for Information Literacy." *College & Undergraduate Libraries* 17, no. 2: 192–212. http://docs.lib.purdue.edu/lib_research/131.

Whitchurch, Michael J. 2010. "Planning an Information Commons." *Journal of Library Administration* 50, no. 1: 39–50. doi:10.1080/01930820903422370.

Witlibrary. 2015. "Furniture Fair Fun." *WIT Library Renovation Blog: Renovation Updates for the Douglas D. Schumann Library & Learning Commons,* December 7, 2015. http://blogs.wit.edu/library-renovation/2015/12/07/furniture-fair-fun/.

CHAPTER 3

Partnerships and Strategies for Successful Programming

THE SUCCESSFUL PLANNING AND PROGRAMMING of your learning commons will require project leaders and stakeholders to become very familiar with existing and/or planned building floor plans to ensure your new learning spaces can be designed for exploration and socialization. Using the strategies and preexisting tools of other successful institutional projects can support your team in implementing a workable plan. Preassessments of existing library facilities and programming can be carried out during this period of the process. Addressing and instituting many of the current trends taking place in today's learning commons spaces can support a desired outcome.

Envisioning Professional Floor Plans for Learning as Socialization

When thinking about designing a learning commons in academic libraries, it is critical to remember that every learning space serves its own unique purposes for its clientele and campus. Just like a library's print or electronic book collection, what is available at a neighboring library's learning commons may not suit your campus or its needs.

The layout and structure of every library building varies. The various ways in which a learning commons is used and valued also differ. Moreover, while most of today's academic libraries offer similar service points (circulation, reference, course reserves, and interlibrary loan), it is important to remember that these traditional library services and operational functions should not dictate the layout or design of your learning commons. As academic libraries have moved toward becoming teaching libraries with dedicated library instruction classroom spaces in the past two decades, new learning spaces should also possibly reflect the move away from being solely repositories of physical collections arranged around access service points. Today's academic libraries need to strive to provide spaces that support both unmediated learning through individual or peer group study spaces that offer cutting-edge technologies and active learning spaces where librarian-led information literacy instruction can foster inquiry and knowledge creation. Well-placed customer service points are also critical features in any library space, but their locations should not dictate design considerations without thinking about how and when students will need to use them during their learning endeavors.

⌾ Floor Plans for Socialization

Before embarking on developing the layout and design of your library's learning commons, it is critical to take stock of how your primary clientele will likely use the space for learning and socialization. It is imperative to think about your entire facility layout floor by floor. Will students come to your learning commons for study space, access to technology (Wi-Fi or networked desktop computing), access to collection materials, and/ or to seek assistance from staff (reference desk, writing center, information technology help desk, etc.)? Will the learning commons become a space where students meet over coffee in a café to study for a class or to socialize? When planning a learning space, it is important to think of all of the possible features and services that may make your learning commons both attractive and beneficial to all users. Moreover, how will different learning areas and services within your learning commons model flow from area to area or floor to floor within your building?

A preassessment of building usage patterns can help your learning commons design team plan future layout possibilities by examining how students currently use existing furniture, group study spaces, computer labs, and other study areas. Hopefully, your library has conducted user satisfaction assessments that included queries about the comfort and utility of existing study spaces and their layout. If your library does not have this kind of data, you may want to consider developing a homegrown assessment instrument to measure user satisfaction and/or preferences for future facility upgrades. If you do not have time to develop a homegrown instrument to measure satisfaction with your facility, you may want to consider implementing an instrument like LibQual+. LibQual+, an assessment instrument developed by the Association of Research Libraries (ARL) and Texas A&M University in 2000, asks respondents to rate selected aspects of library service, including elements related to "library as place" on a Likert scale of 1–9 (1 being the lowest and 9 being the highest). There is a great deal of helpful literature about how libraries have benefited from LibQual+ assessment projects. Much of the research reporting results from within the LibQual+ category of "library as place" shows how libraries have been able to successfully assess how users view their library environment prior to or after renovations.

For instance, within the LibQual+ category "library as place," the following aspects can be surveyed:

- Library space that inspires study and learning
- Quiet space for individual activities
- A comfortable and inviting location
- A getaway for study, learning, or research
- Community space for group learning and group study (Cribb, Hanken, and Gottipati 2015)

Through a preassessment like LibQual+ and/or other similar instruments that offer opportunities for open-ended responses about existing facilities and services, libraries may be able to learn which furnishings are not comfortable for long hours of studying or that the second floor has poor lighting or that there are too few power outlets to charge laptops on every floor. Undoubtedly, many existing library buildings that were constructed before the growth of computing in libraries will be in need of common upgrades related to power and ergonomic seating and computing offerings.

Sharing Learning Commons Trends and Commonalities with Stakeholders

As Matthew Simon notes in discussing the trends in recently renovated library spaces within the United States, most newer space renovation projects share some of the following common characteristics and space renovation goals:

- Highly flexible spaces to support a wide variety of activities
- Storage areas for extra chairs, smart boards, computers, and replacement parts
- Modular furniture that can be readily reconfigured into conference rooms, traditional classrooms, or computer laboratories, in addition to relaxed study and learning environments
- Redundant telecommunications [persistent Wi-Fi] to provide access to local servers and the internet
- Additional electrical support to provide power, for use or recharging of student-owned devices
- Acoustical conditioning to reduce the intrusion of conversations, lecturers, phone use, or sudden intrusive sound which distracts learning
- Lighting that provides a range of light intensity
- Access to restroom facilities for the off-hours occupants of learning spaces
- Access to service kitchens [or cafés] to provide refreshments for meetings, conferences, team projects, or receptions
- Hard-wired overlapping security with video surveillance, hard-wired to campus or town security (Simon 2013, 33–34)

In addition to these characteristics, it is also important to think of the shared changes that have been consistently noted with recent renovations of older library spaces—for example, moving away from book collections–based spaces, jam-packed with high shelving or large microfiche cabinets. Many libraries have opted to move lesser-used materials to off-site storage facilities when hosting on-site automated storage and retrieval systems is not possible.

Ideally, deliberate and multistep space allocation studies need to be undertaken before presenting any final design to stakeholders. There are many proven strategies and tools that can help a learning commons implementation team and campus partners become familiarized with the complex process of thinking about space allocation or reallocations. As Camille Andrews notes, "Toolkits [like the Learning Space Toolkit] have been developed to help librarians work through these challenges and engage users of the library in the process of renovating spaces and rethinking services" (Andrews, Wright, and Raskin 2016, 648). A resource like the Learning Space Toolkit is a great instrument for a learning commons planning team to consult before they even interview potential architects or designers. Thoroughly understanding how to talk about learning spaces with stakeholders, designers, and architects is not as obvious as it might seem. For example, the Learning Space Toolkit offers users a Learning Space Taxonomy that provides detailed help in developing and organizing learning space profiles of existing or future spaces so that all learning styles and needs are addressed in space planning. Before planning learning commons space designs and/or components, it is critical to consider how space can be broken down by these essential categorizations, arrangements, and possible foci. The Learning Space Toolkit's Learning Space Taxonomy provides five major taxonomy categories broken down into intricate subcategories for maximum space-planning consideration (see the textbox).

Resources like North Carolina State University's (NCSU) Learning Space Toolkit offer learning commons planning teams a road map and versatile tools and techniques to guide the project through the planning process. However, every planning team also needs to be willing to delve deeply into their own organizational psyche and mission to ask pertinent planning questions. According to Scott Bennett, there are six key critical questions that must be asked of every facility before embarking on designing a new learning space. Bennett's posed questions can be summarized as follows:

1. What is it about the learning that will happen in this space that compels you to build (or redesign) a brick-and-mortar learning space, rather than rely on a virtual one?
2. How will this space be designed to encourage students to stay in the library to study?
3. Should this learning space design cater to individual study and/or collaborative study?
4. Will the space foster open collaboration and shared spaces among various groups within the campus community (undergraduates, graduates, faculty, staff, and community users)?
5. Should this space be designed to provide additional opportunities for faculty-student exchanges beyond the classroom?
6. How will this space enhance educational experiences? (Bennett 2007)

While cocurricular learning is taking place in the settings of many academic libraries, some institutions have not updated their facilities to meet the more social learning needs of students. This is unfortunate, as "the function of an academic library as an information retrieval space . . . has become weaker [and] use of physical space remains important as student learning space: many students spend long periods in the library to conduct their own studies and research" (Cha and Kim 2015, 274). For decades, an academic library's food restrictions, single-occupancy cubicles, and strict adherence to complete

LEARNING SPACE TAXONOMY

1. Activities [how the space may be used]

    1.1. Focus: listening, meditating, reading, studying, viewing, etc.

    1.2. Create: building, designing, editing, filming, producing, sketching, writing, etc.

    1.3. Collaborate: brainstorming, demonstrating, discussing, meeting, presenting, performing, video conferencing, visualizing, etc.

    1.4. Share: assisting, teaching, tutoring, advising, etc.

    1.5. Socialize: eating and drinking, gaming, networking, etc.

2. Components [what can go in the space]

    2.1. Display

    2.2. Seating: mobile ergonomic chair, fixed ergonomic chair, tablet-arm chair, lounge seating, café seating (lighter weight), bar stools, booth, etc.

    2.3. Work surface: table, workstation, tablet-arm chair, booth table (fixed)

    2.4. Writing surface: mobile whiteboards, fixed whiteboards, blackboards, smartboards

    2.5. Production: printer, copier, plotter, 3D printer

3. Technology

    3.1. Basic: access to power, wireless connectivity and general computing: self-service

    3.2. Enhanced: large screen or multiple displays, specialized software, production tools, access to general staff assistance

    3.3. Advanced: immersive displays; specialized hardware and facilities; access to expert staff assistance

    3.4. Experimental: prototyping emerging technologies or spaces; dedicated specialized staff

4. Attributes

    4.1. Ownership: individual institution; shared between organizational units

    4.2. Access: open; bookable; dedicated; mediated

    4.3. Flexibility: none (fixed); low (slight layout changes); moderate (moveable furniture); high (low switching cost)

    4.4. Enclosure: enclosed; partially enclosed; open [example: study rooms]

    4.5. Group size: individual; two-people; small (3–6 people); medium (7–10 people); large (11+ people)

    4.6. Support services: high touch; medium; low; none

    4.7. Atmosphere: formal (conventional setting configured for research or work); informal (accommodate for casual settings for research, work and social activities); versatile (setting can be used for both formal and informal); cyclical (ambiance can change with time of day, activity protocols, lighting, etc.)

5. Audience: undergraduate; graduate; faculty; external/public; mixed

(NCSU et al. 2018)

This information, "Learning Space Taxonomy," is a derivative of Learning Space Toolkit's Learning Space Taxonomy by North Carolina State University et al., used under CC BY by Lynn D. Lampert and Coleen Meyers-Martin.

silence greatly limited the likelihood of finding environments conducive to peer learning or student socialization. The awareness that students crave comfortable spaces that can serve as cocurricular extensions of their classrooms continues to grow. Studies show that students want multifunctional spaces within libraries where they can enjoy a café setting, use computers and Wi-Fi, take advantage of single- and group-occupancy study areas, and write papers or work on presentations. While online course forums within learning management systems may allow for group chat, only a physical library space, such as a learning commons, can simultaneously provide refreshments, computers, and access to spaces designed to allow students to gather and learn from one another. For any library facing opposition to the utility and return on investment potential of physical upgrades or renovations in the Google age, it is imperative for the learning commons implementation to provide ample examples via photos and presentations of successful learning commons projects through town halls and other campus communication vehicles. These open forums should not only emphasize future design elements. They should also provide the campus community clear ideas of how the newly designed spaces will enable student learning and improve services.

Active Learning Classrooms

Universities and colleges across the United States are developing active learning spaces and classrooms on their campuses in response to pedagogical changes, student demographics, and developments in technology that allow for a more hands-on active learning approach. Pressure from employers to develop students who possess twenty-first-century proficiencies that include problem solving, effective communication skills, and teamsmanship are also considerations for those in higher education (Beichner 2014; Valenti 2015). These active learning spaces allow for student interaction within the learning process and can support students to acquire the competencies employers are seeking. There are a wide range of active learning spaces across the country and beyond that offer a variety of technologies and resources that are often referred to as *technology-enabled active learning spaces*, *active learning classrooms*, *smart classrooms*, and *experiential learning spaces*, to name a few. For the purposes of this discussion, *active learning classrooms* will be used to represent all of these spaces that often are different in their focus but similar in their goals to provide technology-rich, interactive educational settings. The nature of these classrooms and the resources available in each space will depend on the institutional mission and academic programming of individual campuses and libraries. In this way, these learning spaces ultimately represent an institution's philosophy about teaching and learning (Oblinger 2005). "An active, collaborative teaching and learning philosophy is often manifested in a different design. Space can either enable—or inhibit—different styles of teaching as well as learning" (Oblinger 2005, 14).

In general terms, active learning classrooms are characterized by technology-rich settings that foster small-group collaboration, a rich media work environment, and furnishings that enable students to reconfigure the space easily (Valenti 2015). Many of these classrooms offer a space with round tables that intentionally lacks an obvious orientation. Technologies offered will vary as some classrooms will possess an abundance of resources while other classrooms will provide the technological basics, depending on individual institutional philosophies and resources available. Common offerings of many active learning classrooms include Wi-Fi, power outlets for connecting devices, whiteboards, tables for writing, and technologies that allow for presentations. A more in-depth look at active learning classroom offerings as represented in case studies will be discussed later in this chapter.

How Active Learning Classrooms Support Student Learning

Learning research indicates that student competencies can be successfully developed through interactive, exploratory, and social settings. According to Diana Oblinger (2005), learning is enriched when students are asked to think critically and conceptually with both peers and professors. Active learning classrooms support learning as both social and active activities that allow students to engage in dialogue, collaborate, debate, role-play, solve problems, and present their work publicly. Research shows that the learning that takes place in active learning spaces enhances student success (Garrett 2014). An analysis of 225 published studies on the effects of active learning in science, technology, engineering, and math courses revealed that students in active learning settings, on average, achieved 6 percent higher on their examination scores compared to those in traditional classrooms. In addition, students attending classes in traditional lecture classrooms were 1.5 times more likely to fail than students attending class in active learning classrooms (Freeman et al. 2014).

Learning space assessment data from the University of Minnesota revealed faculty attitudes concerning the use of active learning classrooms and how they change the learning experience. According to interviews and surveys, faculty members believed the use of active learning classrooms

- changed or deepened student-instructor relationships,
- provided an environment where learning could easily take place,
- shifted roles to a "learning coach" or facilitator, and
- minimized class preparation time and allowed more focus on course content since the space was already designed for collaboration (Whiteside et al. 2009).

Student feedback on using active learning classrooms at the University of Minnesota was favorable in that students believed active learning classrooms:

- provided an effective space for teamwork and collaborative projects,
- helped students feel more connected to their professor and classmates, and
- encouraged discussion (Whiteside et al. 2009).

SCALE-UP Classrooms at North Carolina State University

SCALE-UP (student-centered active learning environment with upside-down pedagogies) classrooms are active learning spaces designed to facilitate student interaction, collaboration, and participatory learning (Soderdahl 2011). According to Robert Beichner (2014), these classrooms were first developed at North Carolina State University (NCSU) in the mid-1990s and have often been used as a model for replication. Hundreds of institutions have adopted the instructional spaces and pedagogies used within these active learning settings. The SCALE-UP classrooms have the look of a restaurant, with seven-foot-diameter round tables that seat three teams of three students each for a total of nine students at each table. A laptop is available to each team, and laboratory equipment is located in nearby closets. Plenty of large whiteboards cover the walls, and computer projection screens are located at each end of the room. An instructor station that includes a document camera, and in many instances a tablet PC as well, is usually located in the center of the configuration. The classroom layout allows students to easily interact and provides the instructor with the opportunity to make contact and engage with all students during the sessions (Beichner 2006).

Short videos and pictures depicting SCALE-UP classrooms at NCSU and other institutions across the country can be seen at http://scaleup.ncsu.edu/.

Technology-Enabled Active Learning at MIT

Technology-enabled active learning (TEAL) is a teaching format that incorporates lectures, simulations, and hands-on experiments that take place in a learning environment based on the "studio physics" model (MIT 2016a). Developed in the late 1990s to address the "mismatch between traditional teaching methods and how students actually learn," these active learning techniques and spaces provide students with the opportunity to experience interactive engagement during the learning process (MIT 2016b). Classroom innovations from other institutions, including NCSU's SCALE-UP program, were adopted and customized to meet the educational demands of the Massachusetts Institute of Technology (MIT) physics courses. A three-thousand-square-foot TEAL classroom offers thirteen round tables that seat nine students each. Computers are provided to each group in order for them to collect experiment data and view lecture slides (MIT 2016b). More than a dozen whiteboards are located in the classroom, and an instructor workstation is located in the center. Eight video projectors with screens are placed at the classroom periphery. Students in these classes use animated simulations to support them to visualize concepts and to carry out experiments in groups. Instructors no longer lecture from a set location and are better able to facilitate interaction (MIT 2016b).

TILE at the University of Iowa Library

Active learning classrooms are developing in academic libraries in response to changing pedagogies, student demographics, and continued technological advances that allow for their incorporation into the classroom. In 2010, the University of Iowa began developing active learning spaces on its campus and converted a traditional library classroom into the university's prototype for active learning spaces called the TILE classroom—transform, interact, learn, engage (Soderdahl 2011). The campus leaders for this initiative were guided by the SCALE-UP classroom at NCSU, the TEAL room at MIT, and the University of Minnesota's active learning classrooms. One of the defining characteristics of the TILE initiative was its focus on applying active learning concepts to include the social sciences, arts, and humanities disciplines. Active learning spaces and classrooms at other institutions generally emerged from the science disciplines (Soderdahl 2011).

The TILE classroom's orientation mirrors those active learning spaces at NCSU and MIT in that they offer seven-foot-diameter round tables that seat nine students each. NCSU research on design indicated that seven-foot-diameter tables permit conversations, yet they are still large enough to avoid crowding and small enough for efficient use of space (Beichner 2006). Each table is equipped with three laptops, one for each group of students. This decision also was based on NCSU's research, which demonstrated a shared computer per each team worked better than a computer per each student. The smaller footprint and lower screen height of laptops offer advantages over desktop computers (Beichner 2006). Each table is wired with cables for video and data in addition to power adapters. The tables are equipped with an Extron video switcher and push-button controller connected to a wall-mounted fifty-five-inch LED TV. Wi-Fi is widely available throughout the classroom. An instructor station located in the center of the room creates a setting without an obvious orientation, is wheelchair-accessible, and contains a desktop computer, Blu-ray player, document camera, and laptop connection. There are two ceiling-mounted projector displays and six TVs at the perimeter of the room (Soderdahl 2011). An additional discussion of active learning classrooms can be found in chapter 8, "Teaching and Learning in a Learning Commons Space: Reference Services, Instruction, and Outreach," of this book.

The Learning Commons Survey

In an effort to identify effective strategies toward the development of learning commons spaces in academic libraries, a survey was developed to explore the implementation processes and programming methods of other institutions across the country and beyond. Using SurveyMonkey, a questionnaire of fifty-one questions that included both multiple choice and short answer was developed and disseminated. The following listservs were included in the distribution of the survey and were selected due to their learning or information commons, learning spaces, makerspaces, library services, access services, technology, and administrative components to their membership interests. These listservs are

- infocommons-l@listserv.binghamton.edu (Information Commons Interest Group)
- lita-l@lists.ala.org (Library and Information Technology Association)
- uls-l@lists.ala.org (University Libraries)
- large-psd@lists.ala.org (Public Service Directors of Large Research Libraries)
- acr-dghps@lists.ala.org (ACRL Heads of Public Services Discussion Group)
- stars-l@lists.ala.org (News and Information about RUSA-STARS programs)
- learningspace@listserv.educause.edu (Educause Learning Spaces Group)
- rss-l@lists.ala.org (Reference Services Section)
- transforming-libraries-web-group@lists.ala.org (Transforming Libraries Web Group)
- acr-ilialumni@lists.ala.org (ACRL Immersion Alumni) and
- acrlframe@lists.ala.org (ACRL Framework Group).

Those taking the survey were invited to forward the questionnaire to others who work in academic libraries that offer learning commons spaces. The specific goals of the survey were to gather information for identifying strategies for developing and implementing learning commons spaces within academic libraries and to support others to find the answers to common questions such as, What state-of-the-art technologies and student-centered services are available in today's learning commons spaces? What is the impact of including makerspaces as well as writing and advisement centers within the academic commons? How are these pioneering spaces being assessed? For a full list of survey questions, please see appendix A.

The questionnaire was distributed beginning October 2016 through December 2016. Eighty respondents completed the survey on a self-selected basis. Only responses from completed surveys are discussed. Respondents of the survey were provided with the option of remaining anonymous or providing their contact information for further follow-up. Some respondents filled out the survey on the basis of a team and/or individually based on their responsibilities within their institutions. As this is not a random sample, the survey results are not representative of all academic libraries that offer learning common spaces.

The majority of the eighty survey respondents and their academic library learning commons spaces are located throughout the United States. Four respondents originate from Canadian libraries with learning commons offerings, and there is one respondent each from libraries in Ireland and Pakistan. Thirteen respondents did not disclose their location. Figure 3.1 identifies the percentage of respondents from the different types of libraries participating in the survey. Figure 3.2 identifies the jobs or roles of the respondents who completed the survey.

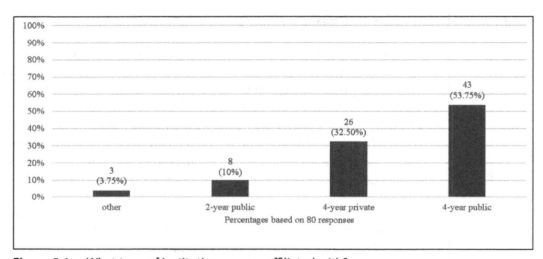

Figure 3.1. What type of institution are you affiliated with?

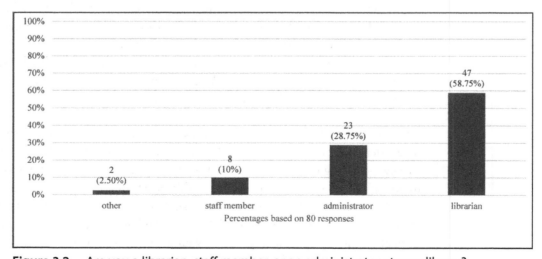

Figure 3.2. Are you a librarian, staff member, or an administrator at your library?

Respondents reported the development, establishment, and opening of their learning commons spaces to have taken place throughout various years within the date range of 1998 through 2017. Further survey results will be discussed in this chapter and in the remaining chapters, which address specific academic library learning commons implementation processes and programming explored in the survey.

Active Learning Classrooms and the Learning Commons Survey

The Learning Commons Survey addressed the prevalence of active learning classrooms within academic libraries and how those classroom offerings engage students in an effort to promote interactive and educational experiences. Of the eighty respondents to the survey, forty-seven (58.75 percent) respondents reported offering some form of active learning classroom within their learning commons and/or library. The following are the offerings reported to be made available in the active learning classrooms of the survey respondents:

- Internet access and a wireless system
- Computers, laptops, and iPads (PC and Mac)
- HDMI laptop inputs and cables (for student devices)
- LCD and LED monitors, including wall-mounted flat panels
- Smartboards, whiteboards, glass tops, and walls for writing
- Tables, including mediascape, and moveable furniture
- Projectors, LCD, and LED displays and data visualization walls
- Videoconferencing, video recording, and webcam streaming
- One Button Studio (open-source software by Penn State that offers simplified video recording setup), http://onebutton.psu.edu/
- Presentation practice space
- Digital document cameras
- Microphones and speakers, including surround sound
- Lecterns or smart podiums
- Large TVs and Blu-ray players
- Green screens
- Conference-style seating
- Dedicated workstations for those with disabilities per ADA recommendations
- Audio and video digital technologies by Crestron Equipment, www.crestron.com
- ClassSpot (http://tidebreak.com/products/classspot) and TeamSpot (http://tidebreak.com/products/teamspot), software that allows for productive group work

Several survey respondents were currently developing or updating their active learning classrooms during the time of the survey distribution. A handful of respondents reported that their libraries offered active learning classrooms in a space other than their library's learning commons. Overall, academic library active learning classroom offerings vary based on university and library vision and goals, student demographics, and the resources available for developing these educational and interactive classroom spaces.

Developing Active Learning Classrooms

Active learning classrooms provide students and faculty with an environment that supports collaboration, exploration, and discovery. Chris Kobza (2015) of the University of Oklahoma recommends the following general considerations for developing an active learning space. When creating an active learning classroom, it will be important to do the following:

- Identify a vision for the space. Will the focus be on **technology or flexibility**? Sometimes technology and flexibility do not go hand in hand. Identify what is more important.
- Let your budget work for you, not against you. Start with identifying what you want to provide in the classroom and then consider how you can achieve it. An active learning space can be created at all different budget levels.
- Nonnegotiables will need to be determined. What resources are absolutely necessary for your vision of an active learning classroom? This usually involves providing writing spaces such as whiteboards, technology for basic presentations, dedicated displays, Wi-Fi, power outlets, and flexible furniture.
- Real estate matters. Ensure there is enough space for students to spread out and move around.
- Plan for the long term. Consider the long-term operational and sustainability issues of the space. Be mindful that technologies will continue to evolve and require support.

Adopting other institutions' successful strategies for developing active learning classrooms and reviewing the literature on the subject of learning space design can also be useful during this process. Other resources that can assist in the planning and management of active learning classrooms include FLEXspace, which is an online resource designed for those in higher education who are building or renovating classrooms. FLEXspace offers a planning tool and the opportunity to locate a best-practice model for a project. This tool makes available a searchable open-access repository that includes collections of high-resolution images, line drawings, floor plans, spec sheets, videos, case studies, and research papers that describe physical learning spaces. These materials have been contributed to the repository by people from around the world. Each item in the collection contains contact information for its contributor and allows for users to follow up concerning a specific learning space implementation (Stephens et al. 2016).

Another useful tool associated with learning space design is the Learning Space Rating System. This tool provides a way to assess and score a classroom's design to see how well it supports active learning. In this way, it can be a useful device during the planning stages and throughout the management of an active learning space (Cevetello et al. 2015).

More information about FLEXspace and its resources can be found at http://flexspace.org/, and information about the Learning Space Rating System can be found at www.educause.edu/eli/initiatives/learning-space-rating-system.

⊚ Laying the Groundwork for Dynamic Learning Commons Services

During the planning stages of your project, you and your team will want to identify the range of services that will be offered in your learning commons. Technologies and support for those technologies, space allocation, department and campus partnerships, and budgeting as well as staffing resources will need to be considered as they will impact your programming and offerings. Services associated with technology will continue to remain extremely important to students as they navigate academic demands. Additionally, since technology continues to change the way information is delivered, those services that support student access to that information will remain a vital component to leading cutting-edge offerings. "The challenge for libraries and librarians, then, is to think of technology not only as particular visible 'systems' that need to be designed and managed, but also to think of technology as an integral part of service" (Dempsey 2015, 24).

Technologies as Services

The need for students to access digital information will continue to grow. Successful learning commons spaces will continue to offer expanding electronic and digital collections through dynamic discovery systems. Access to free computing and Wi-Fi should be available in addition to printing services that include wireless and 3D printing. An area that offers equipment checkout that will loan students iPads, tablets, laptops, cameras, and other devices associated with multimedia projects will be anticipated. Students and other users will continue to access library resources through your library's mobile technologies. An area that provides IT support to use these technologies will also need to be considered and made available. Finally, widening your "library discovery services" to include the discovery of institutional resources will also be a service that will grow in demand (Harris 2016). Training and support in the form of workshops and one-on-one instruction will be useful to support new software systems and will help to round out your learning commons technology offerings.

Student Support Services

In addition to providing access to numerous technologies, offering a variety of student support services in your commons will enable your learning commons to foster a "library as a place" environment. Many academic libraries have considered sociologist Ray Oldenburg's concept of the "third place" "to inspire their thinking, seeing libraries as a place that is neither home nor workplace but a space for self-directed community engagement and a sense of belonging" (Fister 2015, 43). With the addition of many student support services such as research and reference, IT, tutoring, advisement, writing, and media centers located in one convenient location, many learning commons spaces create an environment that supports student academic success in addition to providing a sense of community.

According to Richard McKay (2014), planning these spaces in a successful manner will include designing for functionality. Some practical considerations when developing learning commons spaces will include

- identifying which service desks will be merged and which service desks will be kept independent depending on the nature of the resources and services as well as existing partnerships;
- separating noisy areas such as service desks and collaborative spaces from quiet study areas;
- placing copiers and scanners near the reserve desk and other service areas associated with copying;

- locating printing services near student and public computing terminals;
- providing plenty of signage that will assist in locating services and resources within the commons and the library as a whole.

When services and the space allocated for those services are designed in a thoughtful manner, providing a learning commons that is conducive to collaboration, discovery, and knowledge creation naturally aligns itself with successful learning commons programming. Research indicates that library learning commons spaces have become significant because "as a place where students can meet, talk, study, and use 'borrowed' equipment, the learning commons brings together the functions of libraries, labs, lounges, and seminar areas in a single community gathering place" (Lippincott and Greenwell 2011). In addition, many libraries and learning commons spaces now offer group study rooms and areas, longer library hours, a café or place to eat, and comfortable seating that is inviting and convenient.

Service Centers and the Learning Commons Survey

The respondents to the Learning Commons Survey introduced in this chapter identified the most common service desks offered in their commons areas and/or libraries. Figure 3.3 illustrates the services desks and centers that are most frequently made available in the learning commons spaces of the eighty survey respondents.

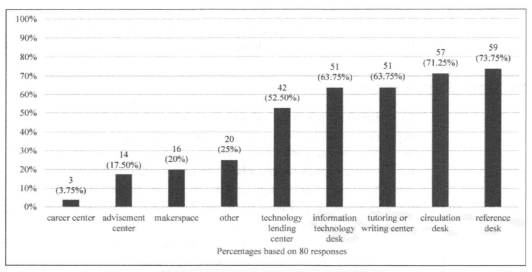

Figure 3.3. What are all of the service centers your learning commons offers to your student users? Select all that apply.

Many survey respondents reported to have shared service desks or centers that varied in offerings per each individual institution. Commonly reported merged service desks included circulation and information technology desk combinations in addition to reference and circulation desks coupled as single service points. Service desks other than those combined were reported to be nearby in the learning commons or in the library building. Each institution determined the most practical format for their service points depending on their existing physical service areas, staffing and resources, and student feedback. Some respondents reported a single service point for all services, while others reported eliminating some formal service desks all together. Several respondents said they did not offer a formal reference desk in their learning commons but instead provided equivalent services through an office setting or reference roving. Pedagogy also played a role that impacted choices for combining or not combining service desks. Some respondents preferred to keep particular service desks distinct and separate, such as writing and tutoring services. Those who responded with "other" reported offering services or desks that include an information desk, data and digital humanities consulting, a multimedia service desk, special collections, a Center for Retention and Advocacy, and a Center for Innovative Learning. Further discussion of learning commons services and service centers will be discussed later in chapter 10, "Successful Learning Commons Partnerships."

Key Points

When creating library learning spaces for the purposes of collaboration, socialization, and exploration, the following points may be considered to aid in the process:

- Each learning space should serve a unique set of user community needs.
- Preassessment of building usage patterns will assist your learning commons design team.
- Active learning classrooms will facilitate student participatory learning when designed with intent.
- Active learning classroom offerings will vary based on university and library vision, goals, and student demographics.
- Adopting other organizations' and other institutions' successful strategies for developing learning spaces and active learning classrooms will be useful and save your team time.

The next chapter discusses working with designers while highlighting innovative and award-winning learning commons designs. Budgeting for your learning commons project will also be addressed.

References

Andrews, Camille, Sara E. Wright, and Howard Raskin. 2016. "Library Learning Spaces: Investigating Libraries and Investing in Student Feedback." *Journal of Library Administration* 56, no. 6: 647–72. doi:10.1080/01930826.2015.1105556.

Beichner, Robert J. 2006. "SCALE-UP North Carolina State University." In *Learning Spaces*, edited by Diana G. Oblinger, 29.1–29.6. Washington, DC: Educause. PDF e-book. https://net .educause.edu/ir/library/pdf/P7102cs16.pdf.

———. 2014. "History and Evolution of Active Learning Spaces." *New Directions for Teaching and Learning* 2014, no. 137 (Spring): 9–16. https://onlinelibrary.wiley.com/doi/full/10.1002/ tl.20081.

Bennett, Scott. 2007. "First Questions for Designing Higher Education Learning Spaces." *Journal of Academic Librarianship* 33, no. 1 (January): 14–26. doi:10.1016/j.acalib.2006.08.015.

Cevetello, Joseph, Shirley Dugdale, Adam B. A. Finkelstein, Richard Holeton, Melaine Kenyon, Phillip Long, Carole Meyers, Jennifer Strickland, and Jim Twetten. 2015. "The Learning Space Rating System." *Educause Learning Initiative*, October 5, 2015. https://library.educause .edu/resources/2015/10/7-things-you-should-know-about-the-learning-space-rating-system.

Cha, Seung Hyun, and Tae Wan Kim. 2015. "What Matters for Students' Use of Physical Library Space?" *Journal of Academic Librarianship* 41, no. 3: 274–79. doi:10.1016/j.acalib.2015.03.014.

Cribb, Gulcin, Tamera Hanken, and Swapna Gottipati. 2015. "Evaluating Library Spaces while Developing a 'Culture of Assessment.'" Presentation at Northumbria International Conference on Performance Measurement in Libraries and Information Services, Edinburgh, Scotland, July 20–22, 2015. http://ink.library.smu.edu.sg/library_research/57.

Dempsey, Lorcan. 2015. "Technology Co-evolves with Organization and Behaviors." In *New Roles for the Road Ahead: Essays Commissioned for ACRL's 75th Anniversary*, edited by Nancy Allen. Chicago: Association of College and Research Libraries. http://acrl.ala.org/newroles/?page_id=243.

Fister, Barbara. 2015. "Repositioning Library Space." In *New Roles for the Road Ahead: Essays Commissioned for ACRL's 75th Anniversary*, edited by Nancy Allen. Chicago: Association of College and Research Libraries. http://acrl.ala.org/newroles/?page_id=251.

Freeman, Scott, Sarah L. Eddy, Miles McDonough, Michelle K. Smith, Nnadozie Okoroafor, Hannah Jordt, and Mary Pat Wenderoth. 2014. "Active Learning Increases Student Performance in Science, Engineering, and Mathematics." *Proceedings of the National Academy of Sciences* 111, no. 23: 8410–15. www.pnas.org/content/111/23/8410.full.

Garrett, P. B. 2014. "The Evolving Classroom: Creating Experiential Learning Spaces." *Educause Review*, October 13, 2014. http://er.educause.edu/articles/2014/10/the-evolving-classroom-creating-experiential-learning-spaces.

Harris, Sasekea. 2016. "Distinctive Services in Academic Librarianship." *New Library World* 117, nos. 9/10: 596–625. doi:10.1108/NLW-05-2016-0036.

Kobza, Chris. 2015. "5 Tips for Active Learning Space Design." *Educause Review*, June 22, 2015. Video, 2:54. http://er.educause.edu/multimedia/2015/6/5-tips-for-active-learning-space-design.

Lippincott, Joan, and Stacey Greenwell. 2011. "7 Things You Should Know about the Modern Learning Commons." *Educause Learning Initiative*, April 11, 2011. https://library.educause.edu/resources/2011/4/7-things-you-should-know-about-the-modern-learning-commons.

McKay, Richard. 2014. "Building a Learning Commons: Necessary Conditions for Success." *Community & Junior College Libraries* 20, no. 3: 107–12. doi:10.1080/02763915.2015.1056705.

MIT (Massachusetts Institute of Technology). 2016a. "TEAL—Technology Enabled Active Learning." MIT iCampus. https://icampus.mit.edu/projects/teal/.

———. 2016b. "TEAL Technology-Enhanced Active Learning." MIT iCampus. http://web.mit.edu/edtech/casestudies/teal.html.

NCSU (North Carolina State University), brightspot, AECOM, and Institute of Museum and Library Services. 2018. "Learning Space Taxonomy." Learning Space Toolkit. Accessed May 12, 2018. https://learningspacetoolkit.org/space-types/learning-space-mind-map/index.html.

Oblinger, Diana. 2005. "Leading the Transition from Classrooms to Learning Spaces." *Educause Quarterly* 28, no. 1. http://er.educause.edu/articles/2005/1/leading-the-transition-from-classrooms-to-learning-spaces.

Simon, Matthew. 2013. "US Projects and Trends." In *Better Library and Learning Space: Projects, Trends, Ideas*, edited by Les Watson. London: Facet.

Soderdahl, Paul A. 2011. "Library Classroom Renovated as an Active Learning Classroom." *Library Hi Tech* 29, no. 1: 83–90. doi:10.1108/07378831111116921.

Stephens, Lisa, Rebecca V. Frazee, Jim Twetten, and Joseph Moreau. 2016. "FLEXspace." *Educause Learning Initiative*, April 12, 2016. https://library.educause.edu/resources/2016/4/7-things-you-should-know-about-flexspace.

Valenti, Mark. 2015. "Beyond Active Learning: Transformation of the Learning Space." *Educause Review* 50, no. 4. https://er.educause.edu/articles/2015/6/beyond-active-learning-transformation-of-the-learning-space.

Whiteside, Aimee, Linda A. Jorn, Ann Hill Duin, and Steve Fitzgerald. 2009. "Using the PAIR-up Model to Evaluate Active Learning Spaces." *Educause Review* 32, no. 1. http://er.educause.edu/articles/2009/3/using-the-pairup-model-to-evaluate-active-learning-spaces.

CHAPTER 4

Architects, Designers, Contractors, and Budgets, Oh My!

IN THIS CHAPTER

▷ Exploring learning commons space design

▷ Discussing project implementation with an architect, designer, and project manager

▷ Planning for contingencies before, during, and after construction

▷ Identifying the color of your money

EMBARKING ON A LEARNING COMMONS development or renovation project can be exciting due to the promises of the completed space. However, it also can present itself to be a monumental undertaking as a result of the different stages and numerous elements involved. Architects, designers, contractors, and project managers all play essential, yet unique, roles in creating institutionally specific envisioned spaces. Understanding and establishing partnerships with these key players can support a manageable and streamlined process. Knowledge of budgeting and the various avenues for its sources will also serve as the foundation for a successful learning commons venture.

Getting Started with Learning Commons Space Design

Identifying your institutional values concerning teaching pedagogies and learning principles, opportunities, and outcomes will be the first step in designing a flexible and dynamic learning space. You can begin this process by asking a series of questions about the nature of the educational experiences to be offered to students using the learning commons. The answers to those questions will serve as a guidepost within the design and development periods of the project as well as throughout the later stages of construction. The need to make adjustments and modifications to different elements of your project plans will likely be a common occurrence due to the nature of construction and its sometimes unanticipated circumstances. Therefore, identifying the types of activities and learning opportunities that are to take place in the new space will be essential to ensure that these identified, valued goals remain at the forefront of the project (Johnson and Lomas 2005). Also, the different types of services to be offered and support for those services in the new learning space will need to be determined ahead of time. This knowledge will support the team in making project decisions that consistently align with the identified learning opportunities and outcomes for the new space.

During the process of designing a new library space that will shape and very often define student educational experiences, project team members will want to ask, "What do we want to happen in this building?" (Bennett 2003, 27). In his article "First Questions for Designing Higher Education Learning Spaces," Scott Bennett (2006) poses questions discussed previously in chapter 3, "Partnerships and Strategies for Successful Programming," of this book. These questions include addressing how physical spaces can enrich educational experiences and encourage students to spend more time studying productively. See chapter 3, "Partnerships and Strategies for Successful Programming," of this book for the complete list of questions. Identifying the answers to such questions will enable the architects and designers involved on the project to plan for flexible and dynamic learning experiences that support institutional values and student demographics.

The work of Chris Johnson and Cyprien Lomas (2005) suggests taking the following steps when initially designing a new learning space in an academic library.

1. Identify the institutional context—values, culture, strengths, and limitations—for the space that will be constructed.
2. Specify the learning principles that are meaningful to the context of the institution.
3. Define the learning activities that will take place in the space and that support the institutional values.
4. Develop clearly articulated design principles that support the identified learning principles and activities.
5. Create a set of requirements that will be communicated to those who will carry out the renovation.
6. Determine the methodology for ongoing evaluation and assessment of the new space.

Many resources and materials are available to support the designing process. In addition to the Learning Space Toolkit (https://learningspacetoolkit.org/) and the Learning Space Rating System (www.educause.edu/eli/initiatives/learning-space-rating-system), which were introduced in chapters 2, "Building Your Foundation," and 3, "Partnerships and Strategies for Successful Programming," of this book, other guides to support the planning process include the Learning Spaces Collaboratory's publication *A Guide: Planning for Assessing 21st Century Spaces for 21st Century Learners* (Narum 2013) and Educause's *Learning Spaces* (Oblinger 2006).

In addition to the suggestions mentioned above, according to the 2007 *Academic Library Building Design: Resources for Planning Document*, authored and currently maintained by the Association of College and Research Libraries (ACRL) and Library Leadership and Management Association (LLAMA) joint Designing Spaces for Higher Education Task Force, before your team consults with any architects, designers, or contractors about designing a new library space, there are several important documents and resources that you will need to review, consult, and provide to all members of your design team before the project progresses. These include

- institution and library vision, mission, and/or goals statements
- institution and library strategic plans
- campus master plans
- campus history, culture, and demographics
- library needs assessment and environmental scan
- documents from other library [building/design] projects
  - concept documents
  - building programs
  - architectural plans [including floor plans]
  - construction budget
- standards—national, regional, and state standards and guidelines for library facilities
  - ADA (Americans with Disabilities Act) requirements www.ada.gov/
  - LEED (Leadership in Energy and Environmental Design) certification www.usgbc.org/
- tours of other libraries in construction or recently completed
- library building consultants, www.libraryconsultants.org

Additional important works and resources that your team will want to consult before visiting other model learning commons or interviewing and hiring architects, designers, and contractors include LLAMA's 2011 *Building Blocks for Planning Functional Library Space*; Les Watson's 2013 book, *Better Library and Learning Space: Projects, Trends and Ideas*; and William Saanwald's 2016 *Checklist of Library Building Design Considerations*.

⦿ Award-Winning Library Designs

"No one now plans an academic library without a learning commons" (Bennett 2015, 215). This declaration cannot be any more evident than as witnessed through the renovations and construction taking place within academic libraries across the country. In an effort to highlight the best and most innovative and inspiring academic library reconfiguration projects, the *Library Journal*'s New Landmark Libraries Award acknowledges academic libraries for innovative new construction and renovations that create inspired learning spaces. Selected winners of the award demonstrate excellence in design and construction, sustainability, functionality, innovation, and beauty. Trends within the award-winning designs and facilities include projects that make extensive use of glass (windows, walls, and skylights) to bring daylight into interior spaces and technology to be integrated within the designs and planning through the use of raised flooring in many cases.

The James B. Hunt Jr. Library at North Carolina State University and the Mary Idema Pew Library Learning and Information Commons at Grand Valley State University are two recent winners that offer innovative service models, peer-to-peer interaction, and other programming (Rodgers 2016). Additional award-winning designs include the James Branch Cabell Library at Virginia Commonwealth University, the Charles E. Odegaard Undergraduate Library at the University of Washington, and the Charles E. Shain Library at Connecticut College (see figures 4.1 and 4.2).

Figure 4.1. Charles E. Odegaard Undergraduate Library, University of Washington, atrium and first floor. *Photo by John Pai*

Figure 4.2. Charles E. Odegaard Undergraduate Library, University of Washington, first floor. *Photo by John Pai*

According to Emily Puckett Rodgers (2016), there are seven trends that can be identified within the designs, planning, and implementation of these award-winning library spaces.

1. Data-driven design—Libraries increasingly are studying learning spaces and usage patterns of academic libraries before they design their own new spaces.
2. Smart collection management—The use of on-site automated storage and retrieval systems are decreasing the footprint of collections.
3. People-centered services—Innovative service models use peer mentors and cross-trained staff at centralized service points.
4. Pedagogical prowess—Award-winning libraries offer active learning classrooms that support informal and formal learning.
5. Life-cycle thinking—Innovative library spaces support collaboration and quiet study, addressing every stage of the academic process.
6. Visualize it—Interactive media and visualization walls engage students in both research and creative expression.
7. Enhance the campus—Sustainable efforts of these projects incorporate elements of regenerative design.

The most innovative academic library spaces demonstrate excellence in designs that have the capacity to bring student learning and teaching pedagogies to a new level.

Expert Discussions on Creating Dynamic Learning Commons Spaces

Each learning commons building or renovation project will be unique to its institution's vision, mission, goals, values, demographics, and the resources available to support the proposed programming and new learning space. Consultation with experts who handle such projects on a daily basis provides firsthand knowledge and experience that can be useful to those embarking on such a large-scale venture. The following are excerpts from interviews with three professionals who have worked extensively on library learning commons development and/or renovation projects.

Interview with a Learning Commons Architect

Brent Miller (see figure 4.3) has been instrumental in the planning and design of higher education facilities in Southern California. As the managing principal of Harley Ellis Devereaux's (HED) Los Angeles office, he has been responsible for over three hundred higher education projects and brings over twenty-six years of experience. Brent's focus on the development and implementation of integrated and sustainable "learning spaces" can been seen through his many campus-related projects. His passion for the development of new learning spaces has increased student collaboration and student success. He is an expert in developing consensus among multiple stakeholders and believes that campus design must be contextual within the campus environment while providing learning opportunities for students.

How are innovative learning commons designs creating contemporary places for collaboration and study?

In our approach to supporting student success, we have found learning occurs outside the classroom as much as it does inside the traditional classroom. Learning commons are one of the nontraditional learning environments being embraced on university campuses to create opportunities for students to engage and collaborate. The goal is to provide flexible environments that allow for different levels of engagement and learning styles to occur—from an independent learner to collaborative group study—giving an opportunity for the student to self-select the most appropriate learning style.

Figure 4.3. Brent Miller. *Courtesy of HED*

What are some of the academic libraries and other projects you have worked with in this manner?

USC [University of Southern California] Leavey Library; USC Doheny Library; California State University, Los Angeles, Kennedy Library Master Plan; California State University, Northridge, Oviatt Library Learning Commons; Pepperdine University residence hall; California Lutheran University student commons; University of California, Irvine; and University of California, Davis, student housing developments.

What steps do you take when developing an architectural plan for a library learning commons? What is your process?

It is critical to hold the vision/mission of the institution as sacrosanct and fully realize the university's goals and outcomes for the learning commons. We work with our clients to develop the path forward with the goals for the project in support of the university's mission. We advocate that the design process be inclusive and transparent so all staff/stakeholders have ownership of the project and believe that better ideas are developed in a group versus isolation. Utilizing this process provides clarity—everyone may not agree on the solution, but it is important that they understand why the solution was selected.

What are your overall goals as an architect when you create plans to develop a library learning commons?

Our goals are twofold. First, we aim to create spaces that are reflective of the mission/vision of the institution—which goes hand in hand with the second goal, to provide a pathway for student success.

What design principles are important to you as an architect when developing a learning commons?

Our design principles are focused around four main ideas:

1. Transparency—Spaces should allow students to see and be seen, creating opportunities for interaction and engagement.

2. Flexibility—Students should be able to easily rearrange the space to meet their functional needs.
3. Variety—Learning styles are unique to the student and the commons needs to offer the space type that best suits the learning style.
4. Technology—Wi-Fi is critical to support student needs.

Are there specific design elements you can comment on that can enhance service delivery and user experience?

In addition to furniture selections that support the design principles, we include whiteboards, group study rooms, and technology to enhance group interactions to support the student. Also, special consideration is paid to acoustics, lighting, and indoor air quality. Those components cannot be overlooked as they directly correlate to the usability of the space. The selections should make the space feel comfortable and inviting while being ergonomic and sustainable.

What do you think is important for those in the library to know about developing and designing a library learning commons from an architect's perspective?

Clearly articulating the vision and project goals is the most critical component to a successful design process. This will help guide the architect and stakeholder group in making decisions that will best support the institution.

What kind of preparation information do you need to receive from clients before embarking on a design?

If we are being asked to engage in the project after the feasibility phase of the project, we will need the schedule, budget, and vision. It would be helpful to have student surveys from the feasibility phase.

Interview with a Learning Commons Designer

Amber Jones (see figure 4.4) has been in the interiors business since 2007, working at two Southern California Steelcase dealers, and has found a home at Tangram Interiors for the last three years. Amber now runs the Education Team for Tangram, which was the largest education provider for Steelcase in the country in 2016.

In the last decade, Amber has worked on well over twenty different library spaces within K–12 schools and higher education campuses. She will be the first to tell you that each campus has its own difficulties and each challenge should be met with excitement and pride as designers, like Amber, effectively change the way students learn across their state.

Are you a designer that specifically works with higher education/education K–12 clients?

I am the director of the Education Team for Tangram Interiors. My focus is on

Figure 4.4. Amber Jones

K–12 and higher education learning environments, which includes twenty-first-century active learning classrooms, dynamic libraries, and learning spaces outside of the classroom, as well as bringing the staff and administration areas up to par so that everyone on campus can support the learning of each student in the best way possible.

What are the most common mistakes that libraries make when entering the design process on a learning space redesign or learning commons project?

One mistake we often see is that they assign one person to make the decisions on what *they* think is comfortable and what is not. The goal for a learning commons is choice and control—choice over where you learn for the day and control over your environment. So with that in mind, as you design the space, you must have options. Multiple different options should be available for sitting while you work on different styles of work. For example, do I need to share media content? Do I need visual privacy to avoid distractions? Can I get this work done at a lounge chair? Or do I need to be plugged in and working at a computer?

The biggest thing to remember when kicking off a project like this is that one size does not fit all. I like to remind people of how they studied when they were in college. Everyone had their favorite spot in the library or in the student union and everyone's spot was different. So create choices that allow for people to select *their* favorite place to learn. Lastly, plan learning zones within the learning commons to help isolate noisier activities away from quieter activities.

Would you say that you urge clients to consider function over form or form over function in designing library spaces?

Form and function are equally important. We must specify spaces that meet the needs of both the students and the staff. If the furniture only supports one of the two mentioned, then the space will fail. It's important to allow for moveable furniture that will grow and move based on the students' needs for that space that day, but you also need to create spaces for library administration to easily be able to support the students' needs. The flow of the space has to make sense with the way the staff moves throughout the day, but not in such a way that it puts the staff's needs ahead of the needs of the students and how they move through the space.

In working on learning space design projects are you ever presented with assessment data (needs assessments of what staff and students want)?

Yes, which makes programming a space much easier and more collaborative. One example we see often is the data provided on the amount of private schedulable rooms that the space has and the data that supports how often they are booked and how many students are using those rooms. From this information, we can decide how many rooms we must plan for and what size those should be. Or we will get a count for how many students are recorded in the space and at what times. This allows us to plan for a certain number of people in the space with the furniture plan and to specify appropriately. The more data and research that can be collected in advance of programming a new space, the better the space will support future needs.

How do you work with technology considerations in a learning commons design process? What typically comes into consideration?

Some of the key factors in technology in a learning commons would be:

1. Content sharing using technology. The ease of the sharing is crucial. If it's too cumbersome, it doesn't get used. Is the technology easy to swap out as new technology becomes available?
2. Whiteboards for brainstorming solo and in groups; mobile, full-wall whiteboards; and fixed boards in specific rooms.
3. Easy locations to drop in and access a computer for five to thirty minutes.
4. Easy locations for printing (throughout the space).
5. Access to power . . . *everywhere*!

One thing to remember is that new technology can't replace the need for low-tech whiteboards. Both have a place in a learning environment.

What questions do you ask before you begin any design project? What information is most important?

We always start with "why?" We need to understand what issues we are trying to solve before we begin creating possible solutions. It's helpful to know the problems with the space and the dreams for how the space should function before we start coming up with solutions.

What guidelines or structures need to exist to foster collaboration between a designer and client?

Open communication and feedback. Our designs are only as good as the feedback we get from the customer. Open, honest feedback and multiple in-person meetings will always create a trusting relationship, and those relationships almost always end in a successful space.

When working on furnishings, colors, and fabrics, what are some common pitfalls that higher education clients often make?

Fabrics and finishes need to be as hardworking as the furniture that is going into the space. Materiality plays a powerful role in the process of creating emotional connections and can alter the feel of a space instantly. For areas that aren't going to be supervised all the time, the material must be wipeable so that if something does get spilled and doesn't get cleaned up right away, the furniture isn't ruined. Wipeable doesn't mean vinyl on everything either; there are some great fabrics and finishes that perform very well in a high-use space that are more visually exciting than a solid vinyl and certainly more comfortable. I would also advise the group to think about a once- or twice-a-year cleaning to keep their investment cared for and maintained well.

If you were interviewing a designer for a learning commons project—what would be three key questions you would ask them to answer before hiring them?

I would ask to see images or do a job walk of three of their favorite spaces. I would ask why these projects were their favorite and have them explain how they became engaged in the project and have them walk me through how the process went. I would ask for references from projects they worked on and speak to those customers directly and have them tell me how they felt throughout the process and how they felt once the project was complete.

Interview with a Learning Commons Project Manager

Marianne Afifi (see figure 4.5) was associate dean of the Oviatt Library at California State University, Northridge, during the Oviatt Library's $2.5 million library learning commons renovation project. Prior to coming to California State University, Northridge, she served in various roles at the University of Southern California (USC) Libraries. She holds an MLS from the University of California, Los Angeles, and an MBA from USC and is a member of the American Library Association (ALA) and the Association for Information Science and Technology (ASIS&T). Her specific roles on the project were library project manager and project liaison for the two concurrent projects that tied into the overall renovation of the library. These projects were the library café and the university's learning resource center, each of which was funded separately and the work was performed by different contractors. As a liaison on the projects, Afifi needed to stay abreast of the schedules and progress on those projects in order to coordinate with the library's learning commons project.

What were the greatest challenges involved in managing this project?

Managing this project on top of my regular duties was the greatest challenge. On the project level, a tight budget and timeline were the other two major challenges. Although I was not personally administering the budget, I needed to communicate to the library dean any major decisions that impacted the budget. The project had a very tight timeline consisting of four summer months when the student population was greatly diminished. The library was kept open during the whole time, and construction took place chiefly in the evenings,

Figure 4.5. Marianne Afifi. *Photo by Lee Choo, Courtesy CSU Northridge*

further increasing some costs. The budget was very tight, and additional funds had to be allotted due to construction issues and partly to take advantage of opportunities that arose to refurbish areas while the project was ongoing. Communication among all stakeholders was also a challenge due to the tight timeline. Other, smaller challenges involved getting various campus services to realize the urgency of our project and to hold them to the tight timeline.

How did you stay organized while managing such a large project?

I relied on a great team of colleagues, who took on various tasks. For example, one of my colleagues was a de facto co–project manager, while others took on smaller tasks. The whole project was a great team effort. I prioritized activities related to the projects and obtained permission from the dean in terms of being able to postpone some of my own work. In terms of day-to-day management, since the project took place in the summer, many meetings and regular semester activities were not taking place, thus freeing up some time. I kept meetings with my staff to a minimum, although meetings with the designers, construction groups, vendors, trades, and library staff involved in the construction took up that extra time for me. I created to-do lists for each project, the learning commons, the café, and the learning resource center. I used my calendar extensively to ensure that I was aware of the deadlines, and I worked many extra hours to make sure that we were on track. I also tried to communicate as much as possible with internal and external stakeholders, and even though that was time consuming, it helped me stay organized. For example, I sent out weekly messages reporting on the construction; these messages were also sent to a blog. When excessive noise was anticipated, I advised library personnel to adjust their schedules if possible and recommended messages to be given to library users concerning the construction noise.

What do those who are planning to develop a learning commons need to be aware of and pay special attention to in order to be successful?

The most important factor is to do upfront research in terms of what you and your constituents expect from the project. The users' interests and needs should be considered by way of focus groups and surveys. The planners need to read current literature on learning commons, attend conferences where the learning commons is a theme, or join groups discussing learning spaces in general. Anecdotal data can round out the ideas that can be constructed from research and surveys but should not be relied on solely. Vendors should be invited to show their latest products that relate to these spaces, or at minimum, library staff need to visit exhibits relating to library space at conferences. Some furniture vendors whose clients include educational institutions often do their own research and can contribute to the overall planning effort. A view to the future with as much flexibility built into the plans should guide the planning, as rapid change in the overall environment can affect the final physical and technological environment of the learning commons.

Another important consideration in planning is that the architects and space planners may have a different view of how the space should be configured even if you as the "owner" have done your homework and have shared your vision of the plan. Therefore, being upfront and as precise as possible with your ideas will go a long way toward making the architects and designers understand your point of view. One needs an awareness of the fact that administrators of a campus may have other ideas and may be able to redirect the project into unanticipated directions, thus potentially invalidating the preparatory work that you have done. An awareness that there is potential conflict around every corner is essential, as is listening carefully. Outside forces and unforeseen events can impose changes to the plan. Building and renovation are not exact sciences, and there are many factors that can influence change while a project is developing. Therefore, flexibility within reason is essential, as is standing your ground when unreasonable change is proposed.

The library's administration and the library staff should be communicated with at all critical points before, during, and after the project. Town hall meetings and frequent updates on the project's progress, even if there is very little of it at times, is essential. Communication should also be with stakeholders in the form of social media and signage, and a marketing plan should be developed to create anticipation and excitement about the new space.

What "tips" would you give to those within an academic library who are beginning to plan for the development of a learning commons within their library?

My tips would be to gather a small team, including staff with different interests and strengths. For example, it is difficult for some people to deal with constant up-to-the-minute change (which is the norm in any project where construction and or refurbishment is involved). The team members must be aware of that fact and must be selected to be creative, flexible, adaptable, self-motivated, and to be good communicators. The team should clearly articulate what is wanted in the learning commons and be able to work with architects, designers, and technologists on the final design. At a minimum, one team member should have the skills to oversee the programmatic aspects of the learning commons, another should be responsible for the day-to-day oversight and be the liaison to library staff, another should be responsible for the technology aspects of the project, another for marketing, and another to serve as liaison to the library administration. Team members must be patient, articulate, and be prepared to spend the time it takes to plan and implement. When asked to participate, they should be able to get a reduction in their other work in order to have the ability to spend enough time on the project. While much of the physical work will be carried out by others, the team members need to be involved to ensure that the result is what they had originally planned. Also, the team members must interact with their colleagues in the different library departments and understand how they are affected.

What was your experience working with contractors, and is there anything you would like to share about that experience that may benefit others embarking on such a project?

Each of the projects going on in the library—the learning commons, the café, and the learning resource center—had a contractor representative, a campus project manager, and a "local" project manager (which I was for the learning commons). While the contractors and project managers for the café and learning resource center were not working directly with the library project, I attended all their weekly meetings to learn about their processes and how they affected the work on the main project, the library leaning commons. Thus, I was able to coordinate with our own project and avoid a variety of conflicts.

I attended weekly construction meetings that included the library's own contractor, campus project manager, and architect. The construction meetings consisted of the contractor reporting on the project's progress and issues that needed to be addressed. The architect was called on to clarify plans and design issues. My role was to ask questions, get a handle on the timeline, find out about major potential disruptions which could impact services in the library, and ensure that the work was moving forward according to plan.

I made it a point to understand the language and vocabulary of building so as to ensure that I knew exactly what was being done. I felt that the contractors and campus project managers appreciated my interest and knowledge and therefore the atmosphere in the meetings was collegial and productive. As is the case with most building projects, there were mostly men sitting around the table, which was different from a typical library meeting, where the majority tends to be women. I was often the only woman in the room, but I never felt that I was at a disadvantage because of it and was treated respectfully and as an equal member of the team, although the general language in the meetings was quite different from that of library meetings. I also learned to talk to tradespeople and campus service staff such as electricians and information technology staff and to ask the right questions. The lesson learned when dealing with contractors is to respect the complex work contractors need to manage, use the "trust but verify" attitude, take a stand when necessary but also be flexible when the situation calls for it. I learned to respect the construction project managers, as they are working in a very fluid environment, have many different "bosses," and must deliver on time, on budget, and with no mistakes.

Is there anything else you would like to add about developing a learning commons in the academic library?

Developing a learning commons is a major undertaking. The library must make a commitment in terms of time and human as well as financial resources to be able to make the learning commons a success. The library must communicate the process outline, completion date, and available subsequent services to a wide variety of stakeholders on the campus, especially the students and other relevant departments, such as information technology and learning resource centers. The library needs to consider the learning commons as an organic element of the organization that must change with changing learning technologies and student preferences. It is essential to have the support of campus administrators who are responsible for campus facilities design and construction. They can smooth the way for the project to proceed according to plan. The library must do due diligence in terms of checking and rechecking with campus or external experts during the planning and construction in order to avoid costly mistakes.

Other Experts to Consult When Working on a Learning Commons Project

The addition of a learning commons and/or any open-space learning environment with large seating areas with workstations or conversational furniture tends to produce a nosier atmosphere in an academic library. Therefore, it is also a wise idea to refer to an acoustic consultant when planning your library's learning commons. If you can't locate or budget for an acoustic consultant, you should review the literature and consult with other experienced learning commons project managers and library directors about how they addressed noise adjacency issues from social seating areas, classrooms, and cafés. Noted expert on both information and learning commons programming Donald Beagle shared information about his experiences with acoustic noise assessments in libraries (Donald Beagle, email communication, May 10, 2017). Beagle relayed that it is important to consider how seating arrangements can impact sound travel and noise in different-sized areas. He also shared his experiences in working on a floor plan with a furniture vendor and acoustic consultant to assess how to best mitigate potential noise that might disturb students in a large study area that contained both seating and workstations.

Figure 4.6 depicts a floor plan with lines and circles. These lines and circles were added by a consultant who, according to Beagle, was "estimating the vectors of louder directional sound (lines) and the resulting nebulous 'sound-cloud' around various furniture clusters (circles)." Beagle shared how the circles "usually extend wider at openings in the furniture module. But notice that we don't seem to have circles overlapping all over the place. This all assumes normal conversation volume, not shouting, of course" (Donald Beagle, email communication, May 10, 2017).

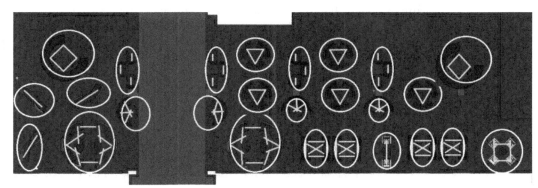

Figure 4.6. Acoustic visualization. Straight, triangle, and square or diamond-shaped lines: directed vectors of primary sound from conversations or from workstations and other digital devices. Circles and ovals: probable extensions of secondary carryover sound marking range of "noise." *Space, planning, and design by Kelli Jo Dixon, Agati Furniture. Soundfield and vector renderings by Donald Beagle.*

**FURTHER RECOMMENDED READING ABOUT
LIBRARY ACOUSTICS AND ACOUSTIC CONSULTANTS**

Markham, Benjamin. 2003. "A Survey of the Acoustical Quality of Seventeen Libraries at Princeton University." *Acoustical Society of America Journal* 114: 2316.

——. 2004. "Acoustic Comfort in Libraries." In *Inter-Noise and Noise-Con Congress and Conference Proceedings*, no. 8: 619–23.

——. 2006. "Wireless Technology and Library Acoustics." *Journal of the Acoustical Society of America* 119, no. 5: 3402.

Swallow, John, Michael Wesolowsky, and Todd Busch. 2015. "This Ain't Your Daddy's Library—the Challenges of Modern Library Acoustics." *Canadian Acoustics* 43, no. 3: 32–33.

⑥ Planning for Contingencies

Unless you are embarking on a completely new building-site project, you will need to consider how a remodel and/or significant construction project will impact existing library services. Contingency planning is something that all libraries need to think about in terms of loss of services from natural disasters, power outages, and other emergencies. In terms of planning for contingencies during construction, your team will need to work with the project contractor and architect to determine how to best stage the timing of certain construction phases.

According to the 2016 *Handbook of Research on Disaster Management and Contingency Planning in Modern Libraries*, "accidents happen more frequently during periods of renovation and construction. Additionally, at these times, crews often disable building protection systems" (Decker and Townes 2016, 147). This means that in addition to having to potentially worry about moving services desks, collections, staff, and furnishings, your planning team also needs to consider how planned and unforeseen power and water outages may impact library services and building safety. It is also not uncommon for construction equipment to emit smoke or fumes that can set off fire alarms and potentially cause damage from building fire sprinkler systems. Keeping all of this in mind, it is imperative to try to determine answers to the following questions:

1. Will the library be able to stay open during the entire remodel?
2. Will certain collections or library services points need to be closed or relocated during construction?
3. Will emergency exits and full egress be useable during each phase of construction?
4. Will any phase of the construction impact adjacent service areas?
5. Will library building shutdowns be required during any phase(s) of construction? Also, will there be planned temporary disruptions to HVAC, electrical, water, fire alarm, or sprinkler system functionality for construction safety, needed upgrades, or repairs?
6. Will elevators, escalators, and/or stairs be accessible throughout all phases of construction?
7. Will additional signage be needed to communicate closed areas or the need for caution in construction zones?

8. Will construction noise make library personnel and/or patrons unable to occupy the building in comfort?
9. Have the fire marshal and building code inspector been consulted about any potential need for revamping or relocating fire alarms and sprinklers?
10. Will the library's security system need to be disarmed to allow for the comings and goings of construction crews and workers?

According to Ayub Khan, author of *Better by Design: An Introduction to Planning and Designing a New Library Building*, in addition to contingency planning, all library remodeling and construction projects should practice sound risk-management practices. Khan implores project managers to

- Identify the [project's] risks;
- Assess the chances of each [risk] occurring;
- Analyse the impact of the project on organization if the risks do occur;
- Identify measures that can be taken to prevent [risks] from occurring; and
- Identify contingency needs and arrangements which can soften the effects of known problems (Khan 2009, 31).

Khan also recommends that project managers compile a risk register, which should be updated regularly throughout the entire project. In addition to all of these risk-management planning efforts, it is also imperative that all library personnel be continuously updated about known safety concerns or building contingency planning. This can be achieved through regular detailed emails, a construction project blog, or a regularly maintained project website.

⟲ Working within Your Budget: What Is the Color of Your Money?

At some point during your library team's numerous meetings with campus administrators, building and safety planners, budgeting administrators, architects, designers, and contractors, you may hear someone use the term the *color of money* while discussing your learning commons project budget. Rest assured that these "experts" are not referring to Monopoly board game money; rather, they are describing how university funds often work and are typically allocated for building projects. The term *color of money* refers to the source and/or purpose of funding and/or allocation source and its spending limitations or restrictions. Most university units and divisions have many different "colors of money" to work with as they typically have funding streams that come from different lines within a university budget.

Depending on whether or not your library is a state- or publicly funded institution, those charged with working on a learning commons implementation budget may need to consider whether or not funding streams will come from public funding or private sources such as donations. Indeed, navigating the funding sources for the creation of any learning commons, as well as continued maintenance and future upgrades, can be a true challenge. As Susan E. Parker, deputy university librarian at the University of California, Los Angeles, reminds readers in her "Game of Funds: Strategies for Strong and Healthy Library Budgets," "academic libraries typically have a lot of one 'color' of money in the form of general and unrestricted funds" (2016, 50).

After surveying forty-four libraries about the financing of their learning commons projects, the Primary Research Group staff reported in their 2015 *Learning Commons Benchmarks* study that

- 25% of those sampled had financing that came from the library capital budget.
- 34.09% reported that the library operating budget was a source of start-up funding.
- 27.27% of colleges sampled obtained grants, of which close to 39% in the sample used grants at least in part to finance their commons.
- For 27.27% of colleges sampled, money came from academic or administrative departments of the college other than the library.
- The overall reported total cost of developing a learning commons ranged from $60,000 to $6,000,000. (Primary Research Group Staff 2015, 23)

It is imperative for those charged with your learning commons budget oversight to project from the outset of the entire project just how much funding you will need and whether or not the university will need to help the library find ways to swap any "color of money" when and if existing lines of funding will not allow for needed purchases and/or expenditures. Multiple sources of funding streams should be considered when possible. For instance, grants may need to be obtained in order to fund technology initiatives. Moreover, it is also important to plan for unforeseen construction costs. Just as each learning commons project should plan for physical contingencies for safety, it is advisable to have a contingency budget and to assume that costs will likely go over by a minimum of 10 percent. Therefore, you will need to know what "colors of money" will be available for construction costs, furnishings, technology, staffing, marketing, signage, future post-occupancy maintenance of furniture and equipment, and other related learning commons expenditures.

◎ Key Points

As you prepare to work with architects, designers, contractors, and budgeting officers on planning your learning commons and its physical offerings, consider the following recommendations and guidelines in order to establish and maintain effective communication between these critical professionals and your library's learning commons implementation team:

- A thorough review of your institution's mission and familiarization with campus values concerning teaching pedagogies, learning principles, curricular programming, and desired student learning outcomes by your learning commons planning team members will help to ensure a flexible and dynamic learning commons design.
- Trusted experts in library architecture and design, like those interviewed in this chapter, who have successfully worked on similar projects at peer institutions can provide firsthand knowledge and identify best practices that will inform your team's decision-making processes.
- Campus building-management personnel, library facilities coordinators, project contractors, and architects can best determine how to stage certain known problematic construction phases (e.g., the noisiest and/or those with planned power outages) in order to develop contingency planning for services and egress as needed.

- The total project budget for your learning commons will require careful planning. Library administration will need to determine whether or not your university can help the library find ways to swap any "color of money" or obtain needed capital through additional external sources of project funding such as grants or donations.

In the next chapter, the need for a strategic technology plan for your learning commons will be discussed. The importance of developing a comprehensive strategic plan that considers both existing campus and library information technology infrastructures and their roles in supporting technologies within your learning commons space will also be explored.

References

ACRL (Association of College and Research Libraries) and LLAMA (Library Leadership and Management Association) Designing Spaces for Higher Education Task Force. 2007. *Academic Library Building Design: Resources for Planning Document.* http://acrl.libguides.com/c.php?g=459032&p=3138007.

Bennett, Scott. 2003. *Libraries Designed for Learning.* Washington, DC: Council on Library Resources. www.clir.org/wp-content/uploads/sites/6/pub122web.pdf.

———. 2006. "First Questions for Designing Higher Education Learning Spaces." *Journal of Academic Librarianship* 33, no. 1: 14–26. http://libraryspaceplanning.com/wp-content/uploads/2015/09/First-Questions-for-Designing-Higher-Education-Learning-Spaces.pdf.

———. 2015. "Putting Learning into Library Planning." *portal: Libraries and the Academy* 15, no. 2: 215–31. doi:10.1353/pla.2015.0014.

Decker, Emy Nelson, and Jennifer A. Townes. 2016. *Handbook of Research on Disaster Management and Contingency Planning in Modern Libraries.* http://proquest.safaribooksonline.com/?fpi=9781466686243.

Johnson, Chris, and Cyprien Lomas. 2005. "Design of the Learning Space: Learning & Design Principles." *EDUCAUSE Review* 40, no. 4 (July/August). www.educause.edu/ir/library/pdf/erm0540.pdf.

Khan, Ayub. 2009. *Better by Design: An Introduction to Planning and Designing a New Library Building.* London: Facet.

LLAMA (Library Leadership and Management Association). 2011. *Building Blocks for Planning Functional Library Space.* Lanham, MD: Scarecrow Press.

Narum, Jeanne L., ed. 2013. *A Guide: Planning for Assessing 21st Century Spaces for 21st Century Learners.* Washington, DC: Learning Spaces Collaboratory. www.pkallsc.org/wp-content/uploads/2018/04/LSCGuide_PlanningforAssessing.pdf.

Oblinger, Diana G., ed. 2006. *Learning Spaces.* Washington, DC: Educause. PDF e-book. www.educause.edu/research-and-publications/books/learning-spaces.

Parker, Susan E. 2016. "Game of Funds: Strategies for Strong and Healthy Budgets." In *Practical Strategies for Academic Library Managers: Leading with Vision through All Levels*, edited by Frances C. Wilkinson, 45–59. Santa Barbara, CA: Libraries Unlimited.

Primary Research Group Staff. 2015. *Learning Commons Benchmarks.* New York: Primary Research Group.

Rodgers, Emily Puckett. 2016. "Learning Life Cycle: New Landmark Libraries 2016." *Library Journal*, September 2016. http://lj.libraryjournal.com/2016/09/buildings/lbd/learning-life-cycle-new-landmark-libraries-2016/#.

Saanwald, William. 2016. *Checklist of Library Building Design Considerations.* Chicago: ALA Editions.

Watson, Les. 2013. *Better Library and Learning Space: Projects, Trends and Ideas.* London: Facet.

CHAPTER 5

Strategic Planning for Learning Commons Technology

TODAY'S ACADEMIC LIBRARIES typically offer an array of technologies and technology services within their physical and virtual walls. It is not uncommon to see computer labs, robust networks, software, and other information technology equipment available for use through library services or partnerships with campus information technology divisions. Therefore, it is imperative during the initial planning and post-occupancy phases of any learning commons space not to neglect technology planning and simultaneously to balance strategies with the overall technology structures and policies of the library and/or existing campus information technology. Whether your team is planning on adding classrooms, a makerspace, technology-rich study rooms, or any other type of additional new learning space for your learning commons, strategic technology planning strategies should be implemented. This chapter will discuss the importance that strategic technology plans bring to learning commons spaces in libraries, the benefits of working with technologists, the technology design process for new learning spaces, and best practices for developing and sustaining a technology plan.

⊚ What Is a Technology Plan?

Most academic libraries currently implement strategic-planning strategies within their organizations. It is typical to see library management deploy planning mechanisms to develop and/or revise existing strategic plans on a cycle of three to five years. Strategic planning is typically defined as "a systematic process of envisioning a desired future, and translating this vision into broadly defined goals or objectives and a sequence of steps to achieve them" (Roberts and Wood 2012, 10). It is imperative to remember that a strategic organizational plan, replete with an organizational mission and vision statement, a set of core values, developed goals, and strategies, as well as a plan for implementing and assessing the plan and later revising the plan as needed, does not mean that all your library's planning needs are fulfilled. Indeed, the majority of strategic-planning cycles tend to work more broadly, envisioning service themes, organizational goals tied to the university's larger mission, and long-range planning cycles balanced around the current and future needs of a library's collections and services. In comparison to a strategic technology plan, a library's overall strategic plan could best be described as the overall "long-range plan" for the organization.

A technology plan is a different planning tool in comparison to a library's overall strategic plan. Not much has changed in terms of the typical absence of formalized technology-plan cycles within academic libraries, which John Cohn, Ann Kelsey, and Keith Fiels noted in their *Writing and Updating Technology Plans* (2000). In fact, it is still the case that

> academic librarians must initiate their own planning processes . . . and remain cognizant of their institution's articulated mission and knowledgeable about the emerging technologies that will support the changing environment of higher education . . . while taking an integral part of whatever technology planning activity occurs on their respective campuses. (Cohn, Kelsey, and Fiels 2000, 15)

Less than a quarter of the Learning Commons Survey respondents reported that their library had a technology plan in place. Figure 5.1 identifies the number of respondents who reported that their library and or learning commons has a technology plan.

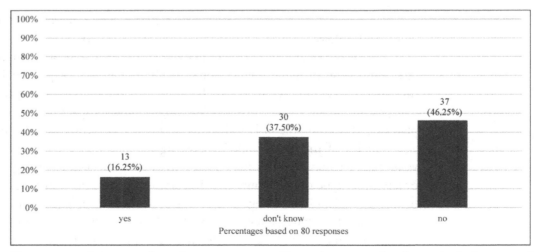

Figure 5.1. Does your learning commons or library have a technology plan? *Courtesy of the author*

Ideally, a technology plan is a detailed guide that describes how a given organization will employ technology to help accomplish its goals. The plan is created by envisioning a shorter timeline of no more than three years and typically must be updated frequently to respond to the rapid changes in technologies. It is far too easy a pitfall for many organizations to neglect to include a wide spectrum of stakeholders in their technology planning. This is problematic because consultation with the technology-planning process ideally should be broad and tied to larger institutional information technology needs. Without wide consultations, a library's overall technology plan may be fraught with implementation and sustainability problems down the road.

Regardless of whether you are working at an academic, public, or special library, technology plays a huge role in the deployment of services and collections in any organization. According to the New Mexico State Library's "Checklist for a Library Technology Plan," there are many critical steps that cannot be overlooked in creating a technology plan checklist. This document states the following as components of a good technology plan:

- Is based on broad participation and ownership by the library, its board, patrons, and others in the community consuming the library's technology services.
- Is consistent with the perspective of the long-range plan already established by the library.
- Has long-term goals (up to three years) and realistic short-term goals (six months to one year).
- Includes assessment of the current status of library staff knowledge, skills, and abilities.
- Includes assessment of current facilities, hardware, and software.
- Includes not only assessment of hardware and software, but also assesses items such as connectivity, materials, policies, and procedures.
- Has the support of the board, the administration, and any funding bodies.
- Recognizes the full spectrum of user needs and expectations and allows for differences.
- Has a staff development/training plan to build levels of expertise.
- Recognizes changes in staffing patterns and budget allocations necessary to implement new technologies.
- Considers what it will take to maintain the equipment and other technology products.
- Recognizes a life cycle for hardware and software and anticipates updates and replacement.
- Has an explicit and well-defined evaluation component.
- Provides for periodic review of needs and plans, while allowing for revisions.

(New Mexico State Library 2012)

⑥ Achieving Balance between Strategic Plans and Technology Plans

As you are developing any new learning space, it is no surprise that you need to keep your organization's overall mission and goals in mind. The same is true when developing innovative technology services and programming for these new spaces. In fact, the process of developing a technology plan truly requires that your learning commons planning team familiarize themselves with the current and past strategic plans and initiatives to gain perspective and institutional groundings on future goals and needs. According to TechSoup for Libraries, a nonprofit devoted to making technology and technology education available and affordable to nonprofits and libraries all over the world, there are many perils innate in deciding to develop a strategic technology plan without consulting the overall strategic plan. In their *Cookbook for Success*, TechSoup for Libraries reminds library leaders that without a strategic plan in place, technology-planning conversations will not be focused, and it is typically more common to fall into the trap of selecting recent technologies that have appeal due to popularity rather than need. In addition, the *Cookbook for Success* also reminds planners that a technology plan will help your team "prioritize your technology objectives . . . and reminds you who you serve and [prioritizes] technology projects that you've worked on in the past and projects that are still underway" (TechSoup for Libraries 2017).

ⓖ Writing Your Technology Plan

There are many books on technology planning in libraries. Helpful works include *The Complete Library Technology Planner* (Cohn and Kelsey 2010); *Technology for Results: Developing Service-Based Plans* (Mayo 2005); *Writing and Updating Technology Plans* (Cohn, Kelsey, and Fiels 2000), and *Technology Planning: Preparing and Updating a Library Technology Plan* (Matthews 2004). Common themes and best practices for writing a technology plan emerge in each of these works and others. Some of the commonly identified steps that are encouraged before embarking on writing a technology plan for a library and/or its learning commons include

- identifying key information technology (IT) leaders on your campus to consult about IT infrastructure, support, licensing, hardware, software, and budgeting;
- compiling a complete list of current technology resources/equipment, including both hardware and software (make certain to note the age of items and check on warranty status);
- examining your current IT support staff structure and training programs for personnel to develop and sustain skill sets;
- reviewing your existing strategic plan and any previous technology plans if they exist;
- assembling a task force of stakeholders (IT, library technologists, librarians, staff, budget personnel, networking specialists, etc.) to meet to develop your new technology plan;
- collecting examples of working technology plans that are in place at other academic libraries to help generate ideas and talking points.

Working technology-plan documents, for both libraries and/or learning commons, are typically composed of key sections outlining a library's technology vision, goals and outcomes for technology programming areas (web presence, networking, discovery systems/online catalogs, computer labs, technology-rich learning areas such as learning commons and/or makerspaces, digitization efforts, data management, and training/user support), evaluation plans, and budget. See the box on "Sample Technology Plans" for current online examples of well-done library and/or learning commons technology plans within academic libraries.

Many academic libraries will also publish statistics and reports about the use of technology within their libraries, and more specifically their learning commons, within their annual reports. See the "Sample Learning Commons Assessment Reports" box for helpful examples of this kind of evaluation and assessment reporting.

SAMPLE TECHNOLOGY PLANS

Brown University Libraries Technology Plan, http://library.brown.edu/dt/LORI TechnologyPlan2015.pdf

University of West Florida Libraries Strategic Technology Plan, http://libguides.uwf .edu/ld.php?content_id=8253725

Cypress College Technology Plan, http://library.cypresscollege.edu/uploads/72/tech plan.pdf

SAMPLE LEARNING COMMONS ASSESSMENT REPORTS

University of Iowa Libraries, www.lib.uiowa.edu/commons/files/2014/07/Learning -Commons-2013-14-Academic-Year-Report.pdf

University of Connecticut (UConn Libraries) Annual Assessment Report, http://learning commons.uconn.edu/about/UConn_Learning_Commons_Report.pdf

Simon Fraser University: Student Learning Commons Reports, www.lib.sfu.ca/system/ files/28741/slc_annual_report_2015_16.pdf

⊚ Checking In with Technology Experts: The Role of the Technologist

Just as it is typical to find that libraries often reach out to consultants when developing and launching new strategic plans, many organizations also choose to employ technologists to develop a technology plan for their learning commons or their entire library. Within higher education and academic library settings, a technologist may be employed to help libraries and librarians explore new technologies and test-drive innovation within media labs or burgeoning makerspaces. As Mackenzie Brooks and Margaret Heller note, while "any librarian can and should be paying attention to the tools that make their work better and their patrons' lives easier, whether or not emerging technologies is in his or her job description," there are many challenges that present themselves in striving to keep up with emerging and effective technologies (2013, 189). Many librarians and other personnel working within academic libraries may regard themselves as technologists. However, within the scope of developing a learning commons, in terms of its physical layout and programming, it is far more common to find that a library has initially consulted a technologist from within their campus information technology division and then later created a position dedicated to managing the technology and its training needs within the learning commons.

Learning commons project leaders and administrators should keep in mind that an effective technologist should ideally be "knowledgeable about broad trends, specific technologies that will be used, and [know] how to apply technologies to specific user and project owner goals. . . . The technologist keeps all stakeholders informed, invested and engaged around how technology advances the goals for the space" (NCSU et al. 2018). According to the Learning Space Toolkit's "Role of the Technologist Chart" (NCSU et al. 2018), some of the central roles, skills, and tasks that a technologist working within a learning space planning team should be expected to fulfill include those found in table 5.1.

Table 5.1. NCSU et al.'s Learning Space Toolkit's "Role of the Technologist"

ROLE	SKILLS	ACTION/DELIVERABLES
Communicator	Ability to translate technology concepts in non-technical language to project stakeholders	Bring key issues to the attention of stakeholders at each phase of the project (design, programming, implementation)
Technology advocate	Ability to present vision and inspire enthusiasm for the technology and what it can do in the space	Presentations to key audiences; provide specific documentation related to solutions (services, costs, and staffing)
Futurist	Ability to look at emerging technology trends and apply them to the specific domain	Presentations to key audiences
Strategist	Ability to identify potential solutions and select the best path forward for the overall project from the technology perspective	Build the technology vision asks: what is unique on campus and how can the library support? Engage partners to design high-level solutions; prepare technology plan for project
Researcher/tester	Ability to research new technologies and their applicability to project needs	Prototype and carry out desk research to support technology-related decisions throughout the project
Implementer	Project management; resource and personnel management	Engage with consultants and integrators to ensure that the functions as designed are implemented in the technology in the spaces

Source: Chart by North Carolina State University is licensed under CC BY.

The role of futurist is one of the most important for any learning commons technology consultant. Technology trends change so rapidly within higher education and society at large that it is imperative for libraries to keep up with user needs in terms of hardware, software, and important skill sets.

Ⓖ Interview with a Technologist

Nate McKee (see figure 5.2) serves as the director of Academic Technologies at the University of Washington (UW) Seattle campus. Academic Technologies is a unit within Academic and Student Affairs in the Office of the Provost and includes two departments, Learning Technologies and Classroom Technologies and Events. Nate's units provide support for many educational technologies and learning spaces that enable and facilitate teaching and learning for faculty, staff, and students in the UW community. His teams specialize in supporting instructional technologies, designing formal and informal learning spaces, instructional design, and the largest student computing facility on campus. Nate's primary goal is to help people achieve their teaching and learning objectives by leveraging technology in innovative and meaningful ways. Prior to his work at UW, Nate created, managed, and incrementally expanded the University of Houston (UH) Libraries Learning Commons from 2008 to 2014. He was integral in securing donor support for student training classrooms and a fully functioning professional recording studio to support innovative multimedia projects.

Please briefly describe your current (UW) and past (UH) roles as a technologist working on library learning commons technology planning.

I was hired as the first manager of the University of Houston (UH) Learning Commons in June of 2008, and upon starting that role, I worked directly with a task force of librarians who had researched potential space layouts and services that would best suit the predicted needs of the student population. Over the six years that I spent in that position, I quickly learned

Figure 5.2. Nate McKee. *Courtesy of University of Washington*

that what we had assumed was not always in alignment with what actually worked when attempting to build a space that was conducive to collaboration, innovation, and support of student success. The task force empowered me with a lot of latitude to experiment with different staffing and support models but expected me to be very mindful about how we would turn the Learning Commons into a sustainable and forward-thinking facility for our student population.

Prior to opening the Learning Commons, our staff developed a basic survey instrument to help us understand what our users expected, why they had decided to use the space, and some demographics about what they studied and how far along they were in their educational journeys. We included questions that asked specifically what they would like to see in the space, and after reading many of the responses, we were able to glean information beyond what other schools might need but specifically what *our* students needed. While some schools were rushing to explore edge technologies and exciting new inventions, our students were overwhelmingly asking for more infrastructure support (better Wi-Fi, Ethernet connections, BYOD [bring-your-own-device]–friendly furniture, etc.) instead of things like 3D printers and the like. As a result, I often advocated for meeting those needs first and reserved fringe and innovative investment opportunities for the bleeding-edge services.

We expanded the Learning Commons several times during my tenure at UH. Each time, we were careful to pay attention to feedback from the survey results to ensure that we were continually iterating on the best parts of the facility and its technology while making improvements to the elements that our students identified as being important to them and their success. In many cases, this included faster computers, expanded software offerings, and training and mentorship opportunities. I found the relationship between myself and the task force, and later the department that oversaw library public services and spaces, to be very collaborative and supportive, and looking back I see the use of student feedback as being the lynchpin in our success over time.

Since I took the role of director of Learning Technologies at the University of Washington I have overseen the direction and operations of another major learning commons facility in the Odegaard Library. We have a team who maintains the space and works directly with a subset of our student government that offers funding to individuals and departments who request funding for student-focused technological services. In that relationship, our team supports the technology and spaces while reporting usage statistics and patterns of need to the committee, and in return they provide us with funds to continually refresh the oldest technologies and keep the software titles up to date. We have recently been fortunate to gain a form of recurring funding from this committee that has helped us to create a predictable workstation and equipment refresh cycle. In return, we provide them with lots of information about how the resources are being used and what the students expect from our informal learning spaces.

Where you currently work (UW), does your academic library learning commons have a strategic technology plan? If no, how do you plan for technology life-cycle strategies, the assessment of existing hardware and software usage, and determine what technologies should be maintained or removed from the learning area?

At the University of Washington, our learning commons support team has devised a five-year plan for workstation refreshes of the approximately four hundred computers in our main facility in Odegaard Library. We based this timeline on the fact that most of our workstations come with a five-year warranty, and with our funding coming exclusively from student fees, we want to get the most usage out of their investment as possible. When computers exceed the five-year warranty, we often find new uses for them and occasionally offer them to other departments on campus who may have technology needs as well.

To address usage information about the computers and software, our team uses a Sassafras product called KeyServer, which allows us to install a client on each workstation that sends anonymized information about which software titles were used, the length of visit, and the frequency at which unique visitors return to the spaces. We often use data from these reports to help the funding committee understand the user base and what we predict to be common need when funding proposals are presented each quarter.

What primary technologies (hardware/software/other technology services) have you helped to deliver in the academic library learning commons environments at the University of Houston and/or the University of Washington?

At the University of Houston, we offered a mix of PCs and Apple workstations with a variety of STEM-focused software titles like MATLAB, AutoCAD, and some development consoles, as well as multimedia creation and design titles like Adobe Creative Suite, etc. We also offered workshops and technology training sessions, one-on-one support for software titles offered in the lab, and a two-chambered recording studio to help students record high-quality audio materials for their projects. Similarly, the learning commons at the University of Washington offers a blend of Apple and PC workstations with several of the same software titles above as well as a recording studio and a video-conferencing facility.

Is your library solely in charge of maintaining/reviewing the technology plan for your learning commons or does campus IT play a collaborative role?

At the University of Houston, the technology plan was created and maintained within the library organization exclusively, with input from campus partners and departments when available. At the University of Washington, the team that is responsible for the day-to-day maintenance, upgrades, and operations of the learning commons works directly with the administration of the Odegaard Library to ensure that the facility meets needs of the students in a holistic way.

Did you/do you have a technologist consulting on current or future learning commons technologies?

While at the University of Houston, I had the primary role of technologist and consultant when it came to keeping an eye on new technologies and service offerings. However, many librarians and members of the initial task force also participated in piloting new ideas and testing possibilities in the space as well. At the University of Washington, our systems support team is primarily responsible for researching new software titles, new technologies, and new ways of delivering services to our students. My current team within Learning Technologies includes nine full-time employees and roughly sixty student assistants, and anyone and everyone is welcome to help shape the future of our spaces, including the learning commons.

What methods/tips would you recommend in order to sustain, fund, and upgrade learning commons technologies given the rapid changes in technology that can typically make it difficult to identify future technological developments and needs?

During my time at UH, I was fortunate to meet many different donors who were very interested in supporting our student population, and over time we were able to foster ongoing relationships with them that helped to fund upgrades to both the equipment and the physical plant. While the majority of our operational budget was provided by administration, much of our innovative experiments were funded by outside sources. Per that model, I'd highly encourage any learning commons staff to think critically about ways in which their services and spaces might be attractive to outside entities. As technology often evolves at rapid paces, it is important to help administration *and* outside funding sources understand what a typical useful life cycle might look like. For example, a typical workstation could easily see five years of usage, on average, before it would need to be replaced. However, some software titles iterate and evolve annually and over time can add a great deal to the cost of ownership of the workstations themselves.

As I mentioned earlier, at the University of Washington we're fortunate to have the support of the student technology fee coordinated by our campus technology funding committee. That committee collects a fee from all students and then determines how to spend the funds based on proposals offered each quarter. As a result of our willingness to use data and evidence to support our requests for new technology and services, they've been very supportive of our efforts in return. At present, we're guaranteed an annual funding level that allows us to ensure that all workstations are replaced by the end of their warranty life cycle, all software titles supported in the space are paid for, and the studios are given similar refresh funding to replace damaged or out-of-date items when necessary.

Is there anything else you would like to add about the importance for developing and/or maintaining a strategic technology plan (formal or informal processes) in an academic library learning commons?

Anecdotally, the one thing that has been the most important to my success at both the University of Houston and the University of Washington has been our willingness to learn about how our students use the technology and services we provide. We don't often write multiyear strategic plans because frankly, technology evolves so quickly in some cases that it isn't fruitful to do so. However, by combining a strong team of technologists with an ear to the ground on new innovations and emerging technologies, it's easy to stay focused on what your team should do moving forward. That being said, it's also crucial to stay in lockstep with the strategic goals and initiatives of the library, information technology, and the university as a whole. I may have been lucky in all my endeavors, but I have embraced a certain degree of uncertainty when planning spaces. So far, all parties involved have been responsive to changing needs, heavily utilized and largely appreciated by our students. I could not ask for much more!

POPULAR RESOURCES FOR PLANNING ABOUT THE FUTURE OF LIBRARY TECHNOLOGY WITHIN LEARNING SPACES

Educause Learning Initiative (ELI) is a community of higher education leaders and professionals focused on teaching and learning, learning principles and practices, and learning technologies. ELI sponsors an annual meeting as well as publications and special initiatives, such as Seeking Evidence of Impact. (www.educause.edu/eli)

The New Media Consortium (NMC) Horizon Project charts the landscape of emerging technologies relevant to teaching, learning, research, creative inquiry, and information management. Each year it releases a Higher Education Report, which is a collaboration between the NMC and ELI. This report outlines the top trends in the one-year, two- to three-year, and four- to five-year horizons. (www.nmc.org/nmc-horizon/)

Pew Internet and American Life Project produces reports exploring the use and impact of the Internet on Americans. Many of the Pew reports give insight into how young people engage with technology in educational settings. (www.pew internet.org/)

Technology Design Process

In addition to developing a strategic technology plan that will help define how technology will be implemented within your library and any of its new learning spaces, it is also imperative to work out a technology design plan for your learning commons. The North Carolina State University Learning Space Toolkit describes the ideal learning space technology design process as requiring the following elements:

Vision: Create a narrative for the role of technology, how will it support service goals, and what the long-term direction will be

Program: Develop a technology design and near-term plan, from endpoints to infrastructure

Specify Requirements: Specify what people will be able to accomplish in each space, and the individual technologies to be purchased and installed

Life-Cycle Implications: Analyze the long-term hidden costs of each space to gain an overall picture of sustainability and resource commitment

Engagement with Partners: Learn what stakeholders may be involved at different phases and how best to engage them. (NCSU et al. 2018)

When it comes to developing a vision for how technology will be used within a new learning space, it is important to think of how a given new space should support student learning that may be assisted by technology. For instance, will a student or a group of students need access to power outlets, wireless connections to Internet access, computing, software, printing, scanners, data visualization, and digital audiovisual-recording creation tools to support their coursework? As Mary Augusta Thomas notes, "The library building program should carefully delineate the roles of each room in the building and the technology used in each. . . . If technology is a means of access, does it extend a student's ability to learn, and does it enhance the learning process?" (2000, 414). Diana Oblinger (2005) also suggests that learning commons planners question how the information technology and support staff programming will enhance students' understanding of how to use technology to support their learning and skill set within the envisioned space.

ⓖ Key Points

As you prepare to work on developing a technology plan for your learning commons, consider the following recommendations and guidelines in order to establish and maintain a viable technology plan that will allow your learning commons technologies to remain cutting edge and sustainable:

- Familiarization with your institution's mission and existing campus and library technology planning documents and policies by all members of your learning commons planning team will be essential.
- Consultation with successful and trusted experts in campus information technology and library technology will help to gather firsthand knowledge and to develop practical plans that will inform your team's decision-making processes. Also, budgeting for a technologist to assist with the development of your technology plan will be useful if your organization does not already have an individual who can fulfill that role.
- A review of existing technology plans found at other academic libraries and published learning commons annual reports that may be applicable to your library's setting can provide meaningful input.
- A survey of published reports of library and learning commons technology trends and an awareness of emerging student technology skill-set needs that may exist in relation to careers and majors will assist your team in developing a relevant technology plan.

The next chapter will explore popular technologies commonly found within learning commons spaces, how to plan a technology needs assessment, and discuss the current learning commons technology landscape with a technology expert working in an academic library setting. Ideas for how to carefully plan each proposed technology element will also be discussed.

References

Brooks, Mackenzie, and Margaret Heller. 2013. "Library Labs. (Accidental Technologist)." *Reference & User Services Quarterly* 52, no. 3: 186–90. www.jstor.org.libproxy.csun.edu/stable/refuseserq.52.3.186.

Brown University Libraries. 2015. *Brown University Libraries Technology Plan.* http://library.brown.edu/dt/LORITechnologyPlan2015.pdf.

Cohn, John, and Ann L. Kelsey. 2010. *The Complete Library Technology Planner: A Guidebook with Sample Technology Plans and RFPs on CD-ROM.* New York: Neal-Schuman.

Cohn, John M., Ann L. Kelsey, and Keith Michael Fiels. 2000. *Writing and Updating Technology Plans: A Guidebook with Sample Policies on CD-ROM.* New York: Neal-Schuman.

Cypress College. 2014. *Cypress College Technology Plan 2014–2017.* http://library.cypresscollege.edu/uploads/72/techplan.pdf.

Matthews, Joseph R. 2004. *Technology Planning: Preparing and Updating a Library Technology Plan.* Westport, CT: Libraries Unlimited.

Mayo, Diane. 2005. *Technology for Results: Developing Service-Based Plans.* PLA Results Series. Chicago: ALA Editions.

NCSU (North Carolina State University), brightspot, AECOM, and Institute of Museum and Library Services. 2018. "Role of the Technologist Chart." Learning Space Toolkit. Accessed May 12, 2018. https://learningspacetoolkit.org/technology/role-of-technologist/index.html.

New Mexico State Library. 2012. "Checklist for a Library Technology Plan." OCLC WebJunction. www.webjunction.org/documents/webjunction/Checklist_for_a_Library_Technology_Plan.html.

Oblinger, Diana. 2005. "Leading the Transition from Classrooms to Learning Spaces." *Educause Quarterly* 1, nos. 7–12: 15–18. https://er.educause.edu/articles/2005/1/educause-quarterly-magazine-volume-28-number-1-2005.

Roberts, K., and D. Wood. 2012. "Strategic Planning: A Valuable, Productive and Engaging Experience (Honest)." *Feliciter* 58: 10–11. EBSCOhost Academic Search Premier.

TechSoup for Libraries. 2017. *Cookbook for Planning and Decision Making.* www.techsoupforlibraries.org/Cookbooks/Planning%20for%20Success/Planning%20and%20Decision%20Making/strategic-and-technology-plans.

Thomas, Mary Augusta. 2000. "Redefining Library Space: Managing the Co-existence of Books, Computers, and Readers." *Journal of Academic Librarianship* 26, no. 6: 408–15. doi:10.1016/S0099-1333(00)00161-0.

University of West Florida. 2013. *University of West Florida Libraries Strategic Technology Plan.* http://libguides.uwf.edu/ld.php?content_id=8253725.

CHAPTER 6

Choosing What Technology Goes into a Learning Commons

OFFERING RELEVANT AND INNOVATIVE technologies lies at the heart of developing an effective and successful academic library learning commons space. This chapter will discuss the research and planning required when choosing and implementing learning commons technologies that address specific campus-community needs. The importance of carrying out a proper technology needs assessment will be addressed, and survey data illustrating the most popular learning commons technologies currently being offered is included. Finally, an interview with a technology expert will underscore the myriad of issues to consider when identifying, implementing, and managing technology in the academic library learning commons space.

Technologies in Learning Commons Spaces

State-of-the-art, carefully planned academic library learning commons spaces offer integrated technologies throughout a variety of learning spaces and service points. According to Lauren Pressley in "Charting a Clear Course: A State of the Learning Commons," "At this point, the literature indicates that most learning commons spaces utilize a mix of library provided computers and a Bring Your Own Device model" (Pressley 2017, 115). However, creating and adopting a library-specific technology plan or technology needs assessment instrument, as discussed in chapter 5, "Strategic Planning for Learning Commons Technology," of this book, will enable library administrators, librarians, and staff to align their services and resource offerings with campus-community needs. According to Susan McMullen (2008) in "US Academic Libraries: Today's Learning Commons Model," while thriving academic library learning commons spaces include social and academic-based components such as coffeehouses, tutoring, and reference services, these successful spaces also offer many of the following technologies:

- **Computer workstations clusters**—These computer configurations are often called *pods* or *clusters* and are designed for functionality. Other popular workstation designs include circular or octagonal pods or a variation on a square design that provides four separate work points (see figures 6.1 and 6.2).
- **Wired collaborative-learning or group study spaces**—These flexible working spaces can take the form of rooms or open areas. Many group study spaces offer technologies that include computing with large monitors, power to plug in devices, whiteboards, and more. These spaces often can be reserved online through reservation software such as Springshare's LibCalendar (see figures 6.3 and 6.4).
- **Service/help desks**—Service points are integrating research and technological assistance at a single desk or at separate colocated desks to provide support in identifying and locating information resources and receiving assistance with software and hardware issues.
- **Technology loaning centers**—These locations within learning commons spaces provide students with the opportunity to borrow laptops, tablets, headphones, cables, and many other computing peripherals associated with the technologies offered within the commons.

Figure 6.1. Computer workstations at the James B. Hunt Jr. Library, North Carolina State University. *Courtesy of NCSU Libraries*

Figure 6.2. Computer workstations at the Marriott Library, University of Utah. *Courtesy of Marriott Library, University of Utah*

Figure 6.3. Active learning booths at the Charles E. Odegaard Undergraduate Library, University of Washington. *Photo by @LaraSwimmerPhotography, www.swimmerphoto.com*

Figure 6.4. Group study space at the James B. Hunt Jr. Library, North Carolina State University. *Courtesy of NCSU Libraries*

- **Presentation support centers**—High-end PCs and Apple computers that include full suites of Adobe's Macromedia software are offered in these centers. Audio editing, large-format printing, and web content development with video, audio, and animation are also commonly available.
- **Instructional technology centers for faculty development**—Some institutions offer faculty centers that provide instructional-design support and strategies for teaching with technology.
- **Electronic or smart classrooms**—These classrooms are designed for laptop use, with only the projector and instructor workstation permanently fixed in the classroom. This allows for flexibility (McMullen 2008).
- **Makerspaces**—This flexible and dynamic work environment allows students to experiment and learn hands on with various technologies, including 3D printing, multimedia-editing and computer-programming software, recording-studio technologies, scanning, arts and crafts, and more.

Technology Needs Assessment

In order to determine the technologies that will best serve your campus community and support your existing technological resources and offerings, you and your team will want to carry out a technology needs assessment, via a survey or questionnaire, with a specialized technologist or another expert within the technology field when available. This undertaking will help to identify current and potential oncoming technologies that can emerge in the future. The results from this effort will enable you and your library stakeholders to understand the resources necessary to meet the expectations and needs of your students and campus-community members. The first step in beginning a technology needs assessment is to develop an inventory or to carry out an environmental scan of the technology assets that currently exist in your library (Morgan 2017). As discussed in chapter 5, "Strategic Planning for Learning Commons Technology," taking a complete inventory of technology assets is also a key step in developing a thoughtful technology plan. This can be done by creating a spreadsheet to track your technology inventory. According to Morgan, elements to consider for inclusion in your tracking can be

- computer networks;
- individual computers (installed software and hardware);
- printers, laptops, tablets, and other peripherals;
- classroom technologies, including overhead projectors and tablet-charging carts;
- Internet connectivity, including email, web services, and WAP (wireless access points);
- telecommunications assets;
- database subscriptions;
- human resources and the physical space to support the offered technologies.

The next phase in the technology needs assessment process will involve conducting a needs analysis through the use of several different tools in order to obtain relevant user input and gain a multitude of perspectives for developing a flexible and state-of-the-art learning commons technological plan and offerings. The data collection tools to be used for your needs analysis can include interviews, focus groups, surveys, and analysis of services desks and study room statistics (Morgan 2017).

Another additional approach to consider employing when assessing how students currently use library and/or learning commons technologies is an anthropological/ethnographic analysis like those conducted at the University of Rochester by Nancy Foster and Susan Gibbons in 2007 or the "How Are Students Actually Using IT" study conducted at the University of Wisconsin–Madison (Cooley, Malaby, and Stack 2011). While surveys can be effectively delivered alone, when combined with ethnographic studies that call for the observation of student interactions with learning commons technologies, a learning commons team can directly observe the usage of technology-rich areas and affiliated hardware/software within newly added learning areas. In order to document how your institution plans to assess how learning commons technologies are being used during the post-occupancy stage of operations, the learning commons planning team should ideally state which assessment efforts and instruments will be implemented within the technology plan.

Visit http://guides.acu.edu/learningcommons to see the Abilene Christian University Brown Library Technology Satisfaction Survey listed within their planning documents.

Following the interviews and surveys of students, faculty, and other campus-community members, look for themes in their responses in order to establish specific stakeholder expectations. The overall goal of this particular needs assessment process will be to identify the technologies in your learning commons offerings that may be lacking or insufficiently supported. Determining the exact technologies that will need to be acquired and/or installed, and how those technologies will be secured, will follow with further consideration, research, and discussion.

Dr. Ray Uzwyshyn (see figure 6.5) is currently director of collection and digital services for Texas State University Libraries. Previously, he served as director of online libraries for the American Public University System, head of digital and learning technologies for the University of West Florida and web services librarian for the University of Miami. Ray possesses a PhD (New York University, media studies), MBA (IT management), and MLIS (University of Western Ontario). He has chaired the American Society of Information Science and Technology's Special Interest Group in Visualization (SIGVIS) and served as a grant reviewer for the Bill & Melinda Gates Foundation and the Institute for Museum and Library Services. Ray's specialties include information systems, online education, information visualization, learning commons technologies, data repositories, multimedia possibilities for digital libraries, and new information technology (IT) infrastructure implementation.

How do you determine which technologies and IT services should or can be offered in an academic library learning commons?

For determining appropriate technologies for a learning commons, my philosophy is that a preliminary environmental scan should be conducted both at one's local university—interviewing academics, students, and administrators—as to needs and simultaneously forming a committee to survey best practices among North American learning commons at libraries and in universities and colleges in general. There are always three or four institutions that are constantly being mentioned at the leading edge of innovation. These should be looked at more closely for what they are doing and whether it is feasible to follow their lead or build on their information. It's ideal to be synthesizing what has been done previously so your institution's choices are not merely following the past leaders' infrastructures but rather are marrying the technology possibilities to one's particular environment and specific university or college.

Figure 6.5. Dr. Ray Uzwyshyn

For example, a liberal arts college will naturally have different needs from a research 1 university, and a STEM-based polytechnic will have different needs from a large state teaching university. This is where the stakeholders come in. It is very useful to compile and synthesize their comments and evaluate their needs, both present and perceived. A committee should review both the environmental scan and best practices with the principals and from there forward a set of recommendations to the architects/engineers and university planning to consider. This will generate a list of what services/centers should be offered. What can be offered will always also be dependent on budget exigencies. From there, determinations and choices will need to be made on higher levels. I am also of the opinion that the more visionary choices should be taken from the pragmatic or mundane and that donor and university-wide angles should always be considered. This is always a bigger win, more exciting, and in the long run of much more pragmatic value to the entire institution. Technology is always moving forward, and it is good to position your institution at least at the top of the middle.

What are the primary technologies to be offered in today's academic library learning commons, and once primary technology needs are met, what other technologies could be offered to enhance student experience?

Primary technologies that should be offered in today's academic library learning commons include makerspaces, 3D printer labs, visualization labs, themed moveable centers, instant theaters, viz walls, data visualization labs, artificial intelligence labs (i.e., Watson-type facilitation for academic/student disciplinary infrastructures), in-house library e-Presses, and Internet of Things labs. These are all also technological infrastructures that can be built iteratively. For example, one begins with a prototype lab, say for a 3D printer lab: a single printer/scanner and HR infrastructure and progressively builds out from there. Once the initial infrastructure is in place with a point person or two, these technological infrastructures can naturally expand with the trajectories being pursued in these areas. Also, the excitement here is with the intersection of ideas and synthesis of technologies. This is where the action really takes place among these newer areas. My idea on enhancing the student experience has to do with innovatively working with the human resource infrastructure so that there is a facilitator or facilitators that work among the technologies. Helping faculty and students implement these types of possibilities and also making them aware of what is possible is done through best practice examples, show and tells, and surveys of what is going on in the wider global landscape in which we currently exist. To note, the larger idea is not to have "technologists" enable "technologists" but rather to have technologists enable humanists, social scientists, and scientists. Those not working in technological areas need to marry their particular disciplinary content and possibilities with the technology. That is a worthy endeavor that requires staff and administrators to be thinking on these larger synthetic levels.

How important is a strong collaborative partnership between campus IT and the library in developing a learning commons?

A strong collaborative partnership between campus IT and the library is extremely important in developing a learning commons. There will be divergent viewpoints between camps and also methodologies in accomplishing projects. These occur naturally. Differences in perspective, while being respected, need to be synthesized. IT services are usually very product oriented. Libraries and librarians are usually service oriented and service organizations. The important human touch is also sometimes lost in IT organizations and their produced applications or services (i.e., the user interface, service infrastructures). We've learned especially in the last ten years that the "user" should not be ignored. The danger of not having a strong collaborative partnership, say for a 3D printing lab, puts the lab's resources at risk of devolving into a service that only can be utilized by very technically adept students. IT needs to be included every step of the way, but the larger goal is to humanize and democratize these technologies and services for wider university use. This is where the subject librarians and "nontechnical" library staff come in—they need to be included and also take leadership roles in outreach and perspectives for this proper synthesis to occur. Strong collaborations are very important here, and this means generating the proper dialogue and environment for a strong interdisciplinary team.

What do you see as the role of the IT desk in the learning commons?

To generalize, I think the idea of an "IT desk" is an old paradigm. The time of separation of IT from library functions has passed. IT desks need to be generalized into service desks and both librarians/cybrarians and technologists need to be working together in the service of patrons (faculty, students, and community members) at these desks. I also in general am not in favor of the whole idea of the technician/librarian behind the desk paradigm. So many learning commons projects in libraries involve strong collaborations between the people conventionally "behind the desk" and those in front that these definitions have been blurred. In the best projects with faculty, the technician is as much of an author or producer as the faculty or academic. Some of these role-based, more nineteenth-century paradigms need to be evolved. For the IT desk, too, even with basic "printer" functions, this really is an opportunity for the subject librarian to be helping with research, engaging the student, and providing a human face and help to these technologies. As I get older, I see a greater value for "human" mediation and remediation of the technology on a number of levels. We must be using the tools, not the tools using us. It is too easy to become robotic in our roles either as the subject librarian or specialists at the IT or 3D printer desks. This becomes especially dangerous at universities and institutions of learning. There is a lot of room for this whole metaphor and paradigm to be rethought in more interesting ways as the learning commons evolves.

What are the challenges of offering and managing technologies in the learning commons environment?

There are many challenges in offering and managing technologies in a learning commons environment. First and foremost, there are challenges of human resources. Many of these technologies and technological infrastructures are quite new. It is challenging to hire for these positions but also to determine who to train if one is training in house. These infrastructures are in libraries and in larger part have to do with the synthesis and organization of information into knowledge and artifacts on a larger level. My idea is to keep these with libraries and train people in house who have been acculturated to integrating library perspectives into these roles. This is a larger present challenge. In many institutions, these newer roles are being taken away from libraries with the tacit approval of the dean, say, for a makerspace to be managed by IT. These learning commons infrastructures need to be managed and brought into the larger library infrastructure so we are continuing and synthesizing the larger intellectual heritage of libraries as both producers and storehouses of knowledge. Another larger challenge is the very quick pace of technology and its movement forward. How to purchase say a viz wall when the technologies are changing so quickly. This is really a business problem. One cannot wait on the sidelines forever as one's library becomes obsolete. The problem of waiting for prices to come down is that one is not developing an in-house expertise or agile culture that is able to adapt to the pace of technological change. If this happens for long enough at a library, the learning commons infrastructure becomes divorced from the pace of technological change that is occurring. This should be avoided as much as possible and is a challenge. Decisions can be deferred, but one must be constantly deciding when to pull the trigger.

How do you plan for sustaining and upgrading learning commons technologies with the rapid changes in the industry that can make it difficult to identify future technological developments and needs?

My philosophy has been to always push to move forward. Technology is always changing. Universities and larger institutions, including libraries, are generally slow to move forward with change and technological endeavors. My philosophy has been to always take the opportunity, move forward with the next level of technological build, and keep track of current best practices on national and international levels. Even if one identifies a trend that fails to take hold, that trend usually evolves in the next build. Expertise is never lost. For example, the opportunities that are natural now with multimedia, one-button studios, and combining these with digital scholarship in the learning commons began long ago with a few pioneers building initial infrastructures which morphed and evolved over time. That expertise in a library or learning commons is always built upon. That is why valuing the expertise of your human resources by investing in people and creativity is extremely important.

Sustainability and upgrading is also driven by use. If both faculty and students are making such wide use of, say, a multimedia lab or data visualization space that its schedule is constantly full, that is an indication that an infrastructure should be sustained and upgraded. Relying on the advice of your frontline staff is crucial. If the staff feels they have to beg for new equipment and the faculty/students are constantly annoyed about the long waits to use a system or infrastructure, it's a signal that there is something wrong in the chain of command. Things need to be rectified at some level. Paradigm shifts are also constantly occurring. It is important for a leader to be cognizant of these large "shifts" and change the course of the larger ship if necessary.

In your experience, what do you see are the different sources for funding technologies in learning commons spaces?

There are many possibilities for funding technology in learning commons spaces. The IT budget for the university needs to be reconfigured to accommodate the learning commons and basic computing needs. Like it or not, the learning commons in the library is the university's main computing space. IT must understand this. If there is not a larger understanding here, education is needed. Secondarily, library budgets must be reconfigured. Currently, at least 80 percent of most library materials and acquisitions budgets is spent on electronic resources—that is, disciplinary and transdisciplinary databases. If this is not the case and there is still a large print budget (either serials or monographs), this needs to be reflected upon. Currently, the library I'm at is lucky enough to be part of university IT, but this is not the case at most academic libraries. In these cases, strong relationships at higher levels need to be engendered among administrative information technology (IT), associate vice presidents (AVPs), vice presidents for information technology (VPITs), chief information officers (CIOs), chief technology officers (CTOs), library deans (LDs), and vice presidents (VPs). If the library dean is lucky enough to serve close to the president's table, university higher administration needs to be educated and made aware of the new possibilities for libraries. If they aren't aware, junkets need to be planned with university higher administration, IT, and library staff to visit these best-in-class examples around the country to open eyes to possibilities. Technology is moving fast, but it never hurts to get a group together in this way, as community building on higher levels can pay off in spades for these types of large-dollar endeavors.

Finally, industry alliances need to be courted and quickly accepted. There should not be dillydallying or looking gift horses in the mouth. Alliances and gift in kind for equipment, infrastructures, and industry/learning commons projects need to be accepted. This is a win/win for both the university and the brand name involved. We live in a global capitalist environment. Libraries are not exempt from this model. At its best, a lifelong relationship is developed between the company and the learning commons environment.

Students and faculty are enabled, the company or industry is able to prototype and test new technologies, and synthetic collaborations are developed by the best and brightest on both sides of the divide. Academics, researchers, business entrepreneurs, companies, and students all have much to gain from these endeavors intellectually and in the pursuit of higher possibilities with the knowledge gained from these collaborations.

Are you surprised by the high student demand for technologies in the learning commons? What types of feedback or data might you possess that demonstrate student value and satisfaction with the technologies in the learning commons?

I'm not at all surprised by the high student demand for technologies in learning commons, and perhaps because I am on the technology side of the fence would expect it to be even higher. These generations have been fully raised with a laptop in the crib and are now entering a university; many of these students do not even turn on a broadcast television set, and YouTube is their preferred medium of choice. I'm more surprised that our older technologies actually have lasted so long and these encrusted infrastructures still remain. We should not be holding on to calcified infrastructures in libraries to their last dying days.

For the feedback and data on student value and satisfaction, we can see an endorsement of our efforts in how students are synthesizing the technology to produce new artifacts, tools, and ways of doing things. Similarly, for faculty we see an appropriation of library technology into the classroom that is always unexpected and not what we originally had thought. These types of bridges and conduits need to be strengthened, broadened, and explored further. Remnants of our classificatory, boxy nineteenth-century way of thinking still exist in our institutional infrastructures, and these need to be rethought in terms of what is organically happening in society. I'm in line with the whole idea of information ecologies and information anthropological fieldwork. Why not bring in new generations of anthropologists to study the habits of our millennials in our learning commons and use this as a feedback mechanism to build better infrastructures? These academics are trained in field notes and delineating societies, but the new dark continent is not some obscure tribe in Papua New Guinea but rather our new university community who are working in a different paradigm. We need these bridge figures to provide the contextualization. Also, I'm a big fan of Internet of Things methodologies for learning commons that are currently being enabled. Ideally, this type of sensor data tracking student movement with mobile devices, search strategies, and different learning centers needs to be married with these new anthropological information-ecology paradigms. Learning commons are fascinating, exotic technologically "constructed" environments, and really our explorations here have just begun.

Is there anything else you would like to add about technology in the academic library learning commons?

I am very excited about the possibilities for future learning commons and the evolution of the traditional academic library. We really are entering a renaissance or new Library of Alexandria phase for institutions of higher learning. The possibilities are mostly untapped. A wider scope of imagination is needed. Our library schools or computer science departments for the most part have not yet begun to teach these new methodologies. Best practices are currently being evolved by a few visionary examples that move with the flow of technological and imaginative possibilities. We will see an amazing evolution in the next ten to fifteen years in libraries. When I began as a student in academic libraries around thirty years ago, there were no learning commons or, for the most part, computers in libraries. The computers were relegated to small clusters of very rudimentary OPAC terminals or one or two CD-ROM PCs. Many students and faculty preferred the large wooden-cabinet card catalogs that still stood stalwart behind these new upstart terminals. As an undergraduate, I was a user and advocate of the terminal, but I did notice the faculty using the card catalog. I took time to learn both—everything at that time was still "not on-line." As I finished library school and began at an Association of Research Library (ARL) institution, the card catalog was relegated to a historical place in the library. To the larger group of terminals were added what was thought then to be a huge swathe of personal computers set up by IT on the main floor of the library. I remember, too, the back and forth between IT and the library. Who would manage all of these computers? We were also gutting the reference books from the first floor and making the main space "a computer lab." The orthodox librarians were not impressed. The university's School of Communication also made the enlightened decision that there was no future in multimedia and decided it could no longer afford the upgrades of the multimedia lab it had been given. Reluctantly, our quite visionary library director at the time accepted this equipment and lab. So began at that time the seeds of what was then known as an information commons.

Larger thinking is still required about the trajectory of these more visionary possibilities. As the years went by, I had a chance to build another early example of one of these infrastructures at the University of West Florida—the Skylab, which reconfigured a computer lab into an "information literacy" laboratory and combined this with a multimedia lab and digital archives studio—seeds of a more visionary learning commons with ideas of interdisciplinary, cross-campus collaboration, third space, and democratization of technology. Currently, I'm at an institution (Texas State University) where we have now just completed an offsite repository that will house a million books five miles down the road. The main library is to become a larger, multiphased seven-story learning commons with various themed centers and a richer application and synthesis of technological possibility.

Even though I started and still consider myself a technologist, I also consider myself a humanist and now need to remind everyone that this was never about the blind "application" of technology but rather a synthesis to introduce new learning and knowledge possibilities with enabling tools. These third spaces of the library allow different academics from various disciplines to meet informally and by serendipity and synchronicity collaborate and produce something which previously would not have been possible. These traditional new library spaces revive the library's role for the twenty-first century. Students and faculty will always need spaces to find inspiration, reflect, and actualize possibilities through both traditional books and technological infrastructures. These are core ideas of the "learning" commons, where learning is at the center of an ongoing synthesis of technology. The richness of the human mind is enabled with the breadth of our various communicative systems. Libraries and learning commons will always continue to serve a very important role for the production and organization of knowledge in our ongoing human quest.

ⓖ Popular Technologies Reported in the Learning Commons Survey

The Learning Commons Survey, introduced in chapter 3, "Partnerships and Strategies for Successful Programming," of this book, includes questions about the many technologies that are offered in learning commons spaces in order to identify the most common and popular technological offerings in academic library spaces. Overall, the technologies that were reported to be offered in the survey varied due to the respondents' differences in institutional missions, demographics, and financial and human resources and due to the many different sizes of libraries represented by those who participated in the survey. Even still, there were numerous common technologies reported to be widely offered within academic learning commons spaces. The answers to the Learning Commons Survey open-ended question "What are the most popular technologies offered in your learning commons?" are listed below. Those technologies at the top of the list were reported with the most frequency, and those technologies at the bottom of the list were reported less frequently. These technologies include

- desktop computing;
- laptop borrowing;
- printing (black and white, color, double-sided, wireless, 3D, large format or poster);
- scanning (flatbed and book);
- hardware checkout (headphones, equipment chargers, power adapters, data cables, calculators, audiovisual equipment, controllers, gaming devices, mice, keyboards, cameras and digital cameras, USB flash drives);
- whiteboards;
- group-collaboration media tables;
- tablet borrowing;
- charging stations;
- computer offerings in both PC and Mac;
- collaborative large-screen displays.

Other technologies reported by one or two respondents to be popular offerings include copy machines, thin client computers, portable and LCD projectors, GoPro cameras, and the Apple TV.

In addition to reporting on the most popular technologies offered in their learning commons spaces, respondents of the Learning Commons Survey were asked about the overall kinds of technologies that they offer. Again, these technologies were reported to be offered but not reported as the most popular. Differences in institutional missions and

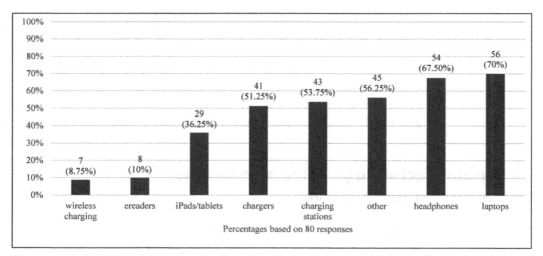

Figure 6.6. What kinds of technologies does your learning commons offer? Select all that apply. *Courtesy of the author*

available financial and human resources of the respondents' libraries are among some of the reasons for the varied availability and usage of these offerings. The answers to the Learning Commons Survey question "What kinds of technologies does your learning commons offer? Select all that apply" are listed in figure 6.6.

Some of the respondents who reported offering the technologies listed in figure 6.6 also listed additional technologies they offer. The forty-five (56.25 percent) people who responded to "other" when answering the question "What kinds of technologies does your learning commons offer?" reported the following technologies. This listing of offered technologies is in no particular order.

- Online booking software
- Virtual and augmented reality technologies
- Motion-controlled computers
- One-button studio (simplified video-recording technology)
- Arduino (open-source hardware and software)
- Bloomberg computers
- Podcasting rooms
- Video walls
- Microsoft Surface Hub (interactive whiteboard)
- Smartboards
- Makerspaces and technologies that are generally offered in these spaces, such as microphones, audio-recording studios, video cameras, camcorders, CD/DVD burners and players, TVs, digital voice recorders, multimedia editing software, robots, CNC routers, hand and power tools, laser cutters, sewing machines, die cutters, sun lamps, and power strips

Printing services were reported to be offered in all of the libraries that responded to the survey. Some variation to the different types of printing made available was reported. While black-and-white, color, double-sided, and wireless printing services were reported to be offered at a high rate, 3D printing and large-format/poster printing were reported to be offered less commonly (see figure 6.7).

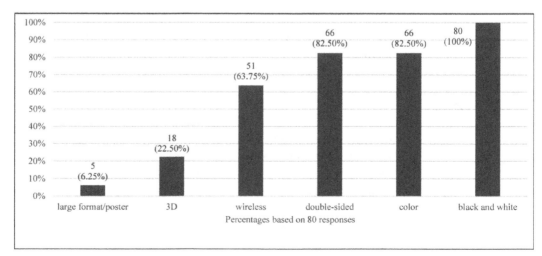

Figure 6.7. What types of printing do you offer in your learning commons? Select all that apply. *Courtesy of the author*

⑥ Key Points

While identifying, implementing, and offering a range of learning commons technologies that will fulfill your institutional mission and values and will also address the technological needs and expectations of your campus community, you and your team will want to consider the following recommendations:

- State-of-the-art academic library learning commons spaces offer integrated technologies via many diverse learning spaces and service points. Current-day learning commons spaces offer collaborative working areas that include individual and group study spaces that are flexible and offer a host of technologies.
- A technology needs assessment, carried out with a specialized technologist, can help to identify the technological offerings that may be lacking or that require more support within your learning commons.
- Surveys, interviews with users, and research can help your learning commons team gain relevant input that will aid in identifying needed and desired learning commons technologies.
- Knowledge of cutting-edge academic library learning commons institutional offerings can support a thoughtful and researched planning process.
- Technologies can be added iteratively. For example, once an initial 3D printer lab is established with a single printer, this lab can naturally expand over time to include more printers and other technologies as the resources become available.
- It will be necessary for campus IT to be involved in every step of planning, but the larger goal is to humanize the learning commons technologies and services for wider student and campus community use. "Nontechnical" subject librarians and other library staff need to be included and have leadership roles throughout the process. Strong collaborations among IT and nontechnical staff can generate the necessary dialogue and environment to create a strong interdisciplinary team to develop and offer technologies.

In the next chapter, the importance of promoting and marketing your new learning commons space will be addressed. Strategies for developing a marketing message that can be carried out through a variety of tools and communication formats will be identified. Best practices for promoting your learning commons resources and services on a regular basis are included.

⑥ References

Cooley, Christopher J., Thomas Malaby, and David Stack. 2011. "How Are Students Actually Using IT? An Ethnographic Study." *Research Bulletin*, November 29, 2011. https://library .educause.edu/~/media/files/library/2011/11/erb1117-pdf.pdf.

Foster, Nancy Fried, and Susan Gibbons. 2007. *Studying Students: The Undergraduate Research Project at the University of Rochester*. Chicago: Association of College and Research Libraries. www.ala.org/acrl/sites/ala.org.acrl/files/content/publications/booksanddigitalresources/ digital/Foster-Gibbons_cmpd.pdf.

McMullen, Susan. 2008. "US Academic Libraries: Today's Learning Commons Model." *PEB Exchange* paper 14. www.oecd.org/unitedstates/40051347.pdf.

Morgan, Kendra. 2017. "Technology Needs Assessment." WebJunction. www.webjunction.org/documents/webjunction/Technology_Needs_Assessment.html.

Pressley, Lauren. 2017. "Charting a Clear Course: A State of the Learning Commons." Paper presented at Association of College and Research Libraries (ACRL) Conference, Baltimore, MD, March 22–25, 2017.

CHAPTER 7

Marketing and Promotion

┌─────────────────── **IN THIS CHAPTER** ───────────────────┐

▷ Identifying chief objectives for your marketing and promotion

▷ Preparing the groundwork for designing effective communications

▷ Selecting strategies and vehicles for communicating your marketing message

▷ Launching your campaign through a variety of formats

▷ Identifying best practices for the future

COMMUNICATING AND PROMOTING a new library learning space will require the development of an effective marketing campaign. Extensive planning by stakeholders and access to a variety of resources will enable those vested in the project to reach their users with a targeted marketing message. This chapter will discuss the planning and collaboration involved in carrying out a successful library marketing campaign. Survey data from the Learning Commons Survey introduced in chapter 3, "Partnerships and Strategies for Successful Programming," of this book is also included. Specific marketing and promotional tools, strategies, and insights are offered. Recommendations for sustaining effective marketing and promotional efforts are included.

Identifying Chief Objectives for Your Marketing and Promotion

Planning for a groundbreaking renovation project such as a new learning commons and its myriad of offerings will require your library to develop a comprehensive campus communications and marketing campaign. This formal marketing campaign can assist library stakeholders in communicating the importance and details of the physical construction project to the campus community while simultaneously informing all campus and community members about the many new resources and services that will be available within your library's new learning commons. The objectives of the campaign will be to

1. inform students, staff, faculty, and the community about the construction project and what the new learning commons will provide and
2. build anticipation and excitement for the upcoming learning commons resources and services and grand opening event.

Your learning commons project stakeholders will want to consider using potential existing campus resources and to confer with campus marketing experts in order to develop a marketing plan that will meet users in as many formats and mediums as possible. Developing a communications campaign to encompass the aforementioned goals will require strategy and planning through the use of a variety of communication vehicles that will be carefully paced over the course of many months. Your overall marketing and promotional strategy may include phases due to the university's semester calendar and schedule.

Assessing the need for a carefully paced and multifaceted promotional campaign will require consideration of the many dynamics involved in disseminating information to many diverse communities that may not be aware of the renovation and future learning commons offerings. To help bridge communication and to involve students on campus within the planning process, library stakeholders can coordinate interactive in-person sessions, known as ideal space exercises, to acquire useful student feedback. During these sessions, students can be given the opportunity to "design" a library learning commons they would like to see and use on their campus. This will allow students to create diagrams of potential library learning commons physical spaces that include desired features such as more group study rooms and lounge areas. These student drawings can be assessed by the architects and project management team to help develop the design and layout of the learning commons. As an initial first step within the marketing communication process, these sessions will serve to inform students of the forthcoming construction project, enable assessment of student needs, and apprise library stakeholders of student desires and expectations. This experience also exposes students to the opportunity of what a learning commons can provide and how it may potentially impact their learning processes while at the library.

Assessing library user needs is another initial step to be carried out during this phase of the project in order to develop an effective learning commons marketing campaign. Many tools to assess the user needs of core library user groups—students, staff, faculty, and community members—include the use of

- surveys;
- comment cards;
- suggestion boxes;
- focus groups;
- mining census data;
- informal brainstorming with staff members;
- speaking directly with users (Alman 2007).

Once demographic and user information is gathered and assessed, it can be included within the development of the learning commons marketing plan. After the assessment of user groups has been carried out, the library administration can move forward to create an in-house marketing team assembled specifically for the campaign if your library does not have an existing marketing department or dedicated marketing staff member. This in-house marketing team will also need to work closely with campus marketing to coordinate any larger branding efforts.

⑥ Launching Your Promotional and Marketing Campaign

Launching a marketing campaign for a major renovation and the unveiling of a new space can be both intimidating and exhilarating all at the same time. A marketing project at such a large scale can present numerous challenges, including a compressed timeline due to the academic calendar, a finite budget, and most likely limited internal marketing experience. Informing students, staff, faculty, and the community about the construction from both a safety and user awareness standpoint and building awareness and excitement for the upcoming learning commons and opening event will be a major undertaking. In addition to these pressures, library leadership and staff may need to communicate with faculty and students about any anticipated print collection relocations and necessary weeding to make room for the new dynamic study spaces that your learning commons will occupy. As Paul Metz and Caryl Gray cautioned in their article, "Public Relations and Library Weeding" (2005), advance notice and strong and clear communication about physical changes to any collection help ward against poor public relations and negativity toward new library programming.

Those selected to serve on your learning commons marketing team can include librarians and staff members whose regular responsibilities and roles within the library warrant that their participation as essential for a communications campaign. Once established, the newly designated library marketing team can invite campus marketing faculty to assist in the development of a comprehensive campaign. If no campus marketing faculty member is available to participate in this manner, your campus administration might make other resources available to your team in an effort to develop a marketing campaign that can be implemented within a strategic timeline. The marketing plan should include goals and objectives as well as strategies for carrying out the plan (Alman 2007). Members of the marketing team can work with the library dean or financial officer to customize the plan to align with the library's allocated budget and resources for the campaign's implementation. Evaluation methods for the effectiveness of the campaign can also be considered at this stage in the process.

During the 2013 learning commons renovation of the Delmar T. Oviatt Library at California State University (CSU), Northridge, a marketing campaign was designed and carried out for the effective communication of the renovation and new offerings. A step-by-step "Marketing Action Plan," used by those at the Delmar T. Oviatt Library, can be found in appendix B. Elements of this specific marketing campaign include using a catchy tagline for the campaign—"Share the Commons Experience." Specific communication and marketing strategies were designed with this tagline to be carried out in two phases. "Share the Commons Experience" was included on all of the campaign's promotional materials and served to brand the project and message. Special consideration was given to the academic calendar since most students and faculty would be leaving in mid-May for summer and would return in early August for the fall semester. This required the campaign messages to be timed accordingly. Both phases of the campaign included tactics that focused on raising awareness of the library renovation and created anticipation and excitement about the new learning commons and its offerings. Both social media and traditional media platforms were targeted for distributing messages. During the spring of 2013, phase 1 of the campaign was aimed at creating a buzz about the construction project and about the many offerings the new learning commons would provide. Phase 1 of the communications task also included communicating service changes and collection relocation information to all library visitors. Once students returned to campus after summer break and in early fall, phase 2 continued to promote the upcoming learning commons offerings and build excitement for the grand opening event.

⊚ Selecting Strategies and Vehicles for Communicating Your Marketing Message

Selecting varied marketing and communication vehicles is an important step in message design within any promotional effort (Mathews 2009). Your multifaceted marketing campaign should be devised and structured to reach library users in the medium and format they most frequent. An online campaign can reach those users through Facebook, Twitter, Instagram, YouTube, and the library's website. Your library website banner should promote information about the upcoming learning commons construction project and future learning commons offerings. In addition, a library blog will be an effective tool in reporting about the project, and pages on your website dedicated to providing answers to questions about the construction project and future learning commons will be useful.

The use of videos can provide you and your library marketing team with an effective avenue to reach many of your user communities, in particular students. During the Delmar T. Oviatt Library's promotional campaign, several videos were developed throughout the eight-month project and were released during its different phases. An initial introductory video was created and released on the library's YouTube channel and sent out by email in late spring to reach faculty and students before the summer break. The video informed the campus community about the renovation project and provided details about what the new learning commons offerings promised. In spring, several time-lapse cameras were put into place within the learning commons construction areas in order to capture the renovation process. This footage was later used in a time-lapse video that showed library stakeholders firsthand the construction efforts that had taken place to develop the learning commons. The textbox provides links to these videos.

**VIDEOS THAT COMMUNICATE AND PROMOTE
DELMAR T. OVIATT LIBRARY, CSU NORTHRIDGE**

Initial introductory video, http://tinyurl.com/kpfmllo

Time-lapse renovation video, http://tinyurl.com/kfurdnc

Learning Commons video, http://tinyurl.com/mfdgoqo

The time-lapse video of the construction was edited by a cinema and television student, posted to the library's YouTube channel, and sent by email to many on campus. Midway through the promotional campaign, a librarian, two staff members, and the cinema and television student filmed and edited a *Learning Commons* video. Several minutes in length, the video describes the planning and construction processes as well as the promises of the learning commons. The video includes interviews with the campus president and other major stakeholders and was released on the library's website and YouTube channel and was sent by email mid–fall semester as another online vehicle to promote the new learning commons offerings.

Other promotional efforts can include online giveaways. Contacting database vendors for donations can be an effective way of garnering iPads or tablets and other items as giveaways. These online giveaways can involve the use of your library website and social media outlets as well. Delmar T. Oviatt librarians and staff developed a Facebook contest in which students who "shared" about the learning commons on Facebook would be entered in a drawing to win a tablet.

More traditional elements of any promotional campaign include the distribution and posting of banners, lawn signs, posters, A-frame posters, and flyers that can be developed by students within the graphic arts program or a library in-house graphic artist. These materials can be distributed throughout the dorms and campus grounds during the campaign. If library student assistants are available, they can help with the distribution of these materials. Promotional booths can provide library passersby with information about the learning commons and its offerings and a chance to win free movie passes or other inexpensive or donated items.

It also will be important to officially celebrate the opening of the new library learning commons space and its offerings with students, faculty, staff, and campus community members (see figure 7.1). Collaborating with campus colleagues in planning a successful

Figure 7.1. Learning commons ribbon cutting, Delmar T. Oviatt Library, California State University, Northridge. *Photo by Lee Choo. Courtesy of CSU Northridge*

grand opening event will yield the best results. Library marketing team members should consider contacting and collaborating with campus food services to arrange and provide food and rentals for the event. If collaboration with on-campus food services is not available, local restaurateurs or caterers who may be willing to offer their services at a discounted rate due to the significance of the event should be considered. Campus music faculty may be a great resource for arranging student musicians who can perform at the event. Finally, campus information technology and facilities departments should be contacted to coordinate the sound and ground management services. Working with a variety of colleagues on campus in this manner also will bring awareness to the celebration and ensure broader participation in the event. The community at large can be informed of the new learning commons offerings and event through press releases sent to the local press.

Important elements to consider including in your promotional campaign are

- grand opening event or celebration of the new space, services, and resources;
- online promotion through the use of social media, library website, blogs, videos, and email;
- posters in the library lobby communicating the learning commons;
- promotional booths;
- banners in the future learning commons area communicating the programming;
- promotional learning commons t-shirts worn by library staff;
- announcements made by librarians and campus faculty in classes;
- A-frames throughout campus communicating the learning commons;
- promotional buttons worn by library staff;
- campus newspaper ads;
- using sidewalk chalk to write ("chalk") messages on campus sidewalks;
- lawn signs throughout campus communicating the programming;
- table tents at campus eating locations;
- coffee sleeves on the campus coffee cups;
- articles in the campus newspaper communicating the learning commons;
- posters and flyers distributed throughout the dorms;
- banners on campus communicating the programming;
- press releases and contacting the local media.

⊚ Budgeting for Your Marketing Campaign

Historically, promotional and marketing budgets for libraries are nominal if existent. However, due to the significance of your learning commons renovation project and its anticipated impact on the campus community, it will be important to identify possible sources for funding. Perhaps your library dean's office will approve additional funding for a marketing campaign and grand opening event. However, other ways of acquiring and securing funding and donations for marketing purposes include

- collaborating with campus and/or community partners who provide services and resources for the programming;
- requesting donations from vendors, in particular database vendors;
- receiving financial donations from campus and community members;
- utilizing special library donated funds and/or grants.

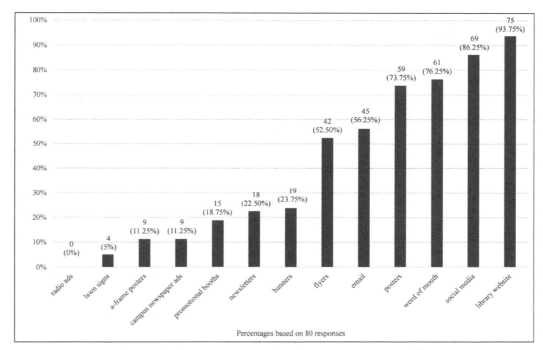 Marketing and the Learning Commons Survey

The Learning Commons Survey introduced in chapter 3, "Partnerships and Strategies for Successful Programming," of this book asked several questions about how academic libraries promote and market their learning commons spaces and offerings. Figure 7.2 illustrates the variety of communication vehicles employed by those who responded to the survey. The use of the library website, social media, and word of mouth were reported as the top three methods for promotion. Respondents of the survey were also asked "Who carries out the marketing and promotion for your learning commons?" Fifty-four (67.50 percent) respondents reported that a committee or team of employees handles the marketing and promotion for their learning commons spaces. The remaining twenty-six (32.50 percent) respondents reported having one individual person within the library assigned to those duties. Nearly a dozen people commented that neither an individual nor an official committee handles their marketing. Rather, there are many individuals and different departments within the library that handle marketing on an ad hoc basis.

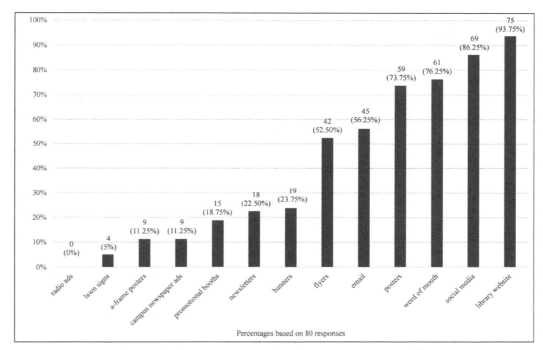

Figure 7.2. How do you market or promote your learning commons offerings and programming? Select all that apply. *Courtesy of the author*

Best Practices for Coordinating Library Marketing Campaigns

Marketing library resources and services may commonly involve large projects such as promoting a new learning commons, but just as often they will involve more specific communications programming such as the promotion of a single new service or resource. The following are suggestions and recommendations for coordinating and managing promotional efforts no matter the size of the marketing and communications campaign.

Get Organized

Create a marketing plan for your project. If you do not have a marketing staff member within your library for these purposes, look to see if your institution already has existing resources or a person within your organization who could serve as a marketing consultant. You may even want to consider hiring a consultant.

Utilize Research Skills

Supplement your promotional efforts with books that specifically discuss library marketing and programming. Many books are available that outline and describe the library marketing plan processes, including Bradford Lee Eden's *Marketing and Outreach for the Academic Library: New Approaches and Initiatives* (2016) and Robert J. Lackie and M. Sandra Wood's *Creative Library Marketing and Publicity: Best Practices* (2015). Using them to structure a marketing campaign to fit your library's specific size and marketing needs can make the development of a plan less daunting.

Customize the Plan

Overall, many library marketing plans will typically be varied in length and in their content according to your institution's size and goals. Marketing plans with smaller goals may only be several pages long, while more ambitious marketing campaigns may require a plan several times that length. Develop a library marketing plan that supports the specific needs of your library. When developing your marketing plan, keep in mind that most plans include the following: library demographic information, a SWOT analysis (strengths, weaknesses, opportunities, and threats to your plan), marketing project objectives and goals, a marketing strategy and tactics to be used to carry out the strategy, a list of team members who will carry out the plan, project costs and funding information, and methods for evaluating the promotional campaign (Alman 2007).

Other issues to consider when developing a marketing plan include the following:

- Creating a timeline and schedule for your marketing plan. Distribute the plan to all team members.
- Holding regular meetings to discuss programming and implementation needs.
- Ensuring someone is specifically assigned to each task; if no one is personally assigned, realize that no one will be accountable.
- Scanning your environment to see if there is talent or interest in the project by staff members even if they are not in your area. See if it is possible to invite them to participate.
- Collaborating with campus and/or community partners. These types of collaborations can produce additional assets such as funding, donated items, and the time and assistance of additional personnel. Such partners can also communicate the message of the campaign within their professional circles.
- Looking at other library award–winning marketing campaigns for ideas and inspiration. The John Cotton Dana Award winners' website, www.ebsco.com/about/scholarship-awards/john-cotton-dana, provides a listing of many successful marketing campaigns big and small.
- Planning accordingly but being open to changing the plan if necessary.

Today's libraries must rely heavily on marketing and promotion to remind users of the unique benefits that their services and collections offer. Whether a library is undertaking a new project; planning for a major renovation; or promoting new or existing products, programming, or services, it is imperative that marketing messages are well received by the target audiences the organization serves. Unfortunately, librarians do not traditionally receive formal training about marketing practices in graduate school programming. However, with proper planning and collaborative partners, in-house marketing strategies can succeed when creatively coupled with knowledge of your library clientele's demographics and needs. Key factors needed for success are (1) assembling a dedicated team to work on marketing needs and (2) diligently working to ensure that each promotional facet will be delivered within the planned timeline targets and budget.

Key Points

When planning to promote your library learning commons and its offerings, consider the following recommendations and guidelines in order to establish and maintain an effective marketing and promotional campaign:

- An effective marketing campaign will require a strategy that uses a variety of communication vehicles that will be carefully paced over the course of many months. This will require the identification of short-term and long-term communications and messaging goals.
- Library user needs will require assessment at the onset of the process in order to develop an effective learning commons promotional campaign.
- If there is no established committee or individual designated to carry out marketing activities, a learning commons marketing team will need to be developed from those within the library. Also, campus marketing faculty and/or campus administration may be able to assist in the development of a comprehensive campaign.
- The marketing plan to be developed and carried out by your marketing team will include overall goals and objectives as well as specific strategies.
- A multifaceted marketing campaign will include both print and online efforts and should be structured to reach library users in the mediums and formats they most frequent. The use of varied marketing and communication vehicles will support effective messaging.

In the next chapter, reference services and library instruction within the learning commons setting will be discussed. The importance of outreach programming and its role in developing a vibrant and robust learning commons space also will be explored.

A version of this chapter previously appeared as chapter 9, "If You Build It, Will They Come? Marketing a New Library Space," by Coleen Meyers-Martin and Lynn D. Lampert, in Creative Library Marketing and Publicity: Best Practices, *ed. Robert J. Lackie and M. Sandra Wood (Lanham, MD: Rowman & Littlefield, 2015), 119–36.*

ⓖ References

Alman, Susan Webreck. 2007. *Crash Course in Marketing for Libraries*. Westport, CT: Libraries Unlimited.

Eden, Bradford Lee. 2016. *Marketing and Outreach for the Academic Library: New Approaches and Initiatives*. Lanham, MD: Rowman & Littlefield.

Lackie, Robert J., and M. Sandra Wood. 2015. *Creative Library Marketing and Publicity: Best Practices*. Lanham, MD: Rowman & Littlefield.

Mathews, Brian. 2009. *Marketing Today's Academic Library: A Bold New Approach to Communicating with Students*. Chicago: American Library Association.

Metz, Paul, and Caryl Gray. 2005. "Public Relations and Library Weeding." *Journal of Academic Librarianship* 31, no. 3: 273–79. doi:10.1016/j.acalib.2005.01.005.

Meyers-Martin, Coleen, and Lynn D. Lampert. 2015. "If You Build It, Will They Come? Marketing a New Library Space." In *Creative Library Marketing and Publicity: Best Practices*, edited by Robert J. Lackie, and M. Sandra Wood, 119–36. Lanham, MD: Rowman & Littlefield.

CHAPTER 8

Teaching and Learning in a Learning Commons Space

Reference Services, Instruction, and Outreach

AMID CURRENT ACADEMIC LIBRARY trends in digitization, discovery systems, and the promotion of cutting-edge services such as makerspaces, it is easy to potentially overlook the centrality and value that reference, instruction, and outreach services can provide within learning commons environments. Such an oversight will likely prove detrimental to the development of a learning commons that aims to provide students with a central place to learn, socialize, access information, participate in outreach programming, and most importantly, improve their bourgeoning information literacy skills. The act of opening a learning commons will not, in and of itself, create opportunities for student learning. The best recipe for developing a learning commons space that optimizes student learning, both peer and individual, calls for combining the teaching and learning services provided by your library's reference and instruction librarians with campus entities and/or programming that support cocurricular learning to improve nascent research, writing, and studying skills.

A review of the recent literature studying the roles that reference librarians play during the development and later operation of a learning commons reveals that far too many institutions and/or administrators may not include frontline reference and instruction librarians and/or assess the need for consulting reference services within the critical planning and programming phases of learning commons design. This is unfortunate, as reference librarians can contribute to an institution's dialog about a learning commons [LC] by doing the following:

- preventing wholesale adoption of models that do not fit patron needs
- helping set appropriate goals and outcomes for the LC
- coordinating the library services with the curriculum needs" (Wolfe, Naylor, and Drueke 2010, 110)

In addition to helping shape and match the programmatic aspects of a learning commons to campus clientele (i.e., students and faculty), reference librarians are also "perfectly positioned to collaborate with other stakeholders in the development of a learning commons model" due to their strong footing in offering services in both virtual (text and email reference) and physical settings (Wolfe, Naylor, and Drueke 2010, 111). Moreover, within ideal learning commons layouts that provide for proximity to computer workstations, library instruction classrooms, reference collections, reference assistance at a reference desk, or within reference librarians' offices, students can become immersed in a learning space that offers multiple options for peer learning, tutoring, and research consultations.

In addition to the pivotal role that reference librarians can play in developing learning commons programming that supports information literacy and outreach efforts, it is also imperative to consider how the critical services that reference librarians and reference departments provide may be impacted by augmentations to academic library spaces. Reference services within academic libraries, such as the staffing of a reference desk and teaching and managing the reference collection, are signature services that librarians perform at most colleges and universities. Students and faculty steadfastly rely on being able to consult authoritative information sources and receive assistance from helpful campus librarians for all their information and research needs. A recent national survey that examined recent trends in reference services found that the overall quality of reference services remains very strong in the face of the recent trends in reference service staffing changes, service innovations, and the adoption of reference technology (Coleman, Mallon, and Lo 2015). The authors of this study also stated that the following trends were the most pressing within academic library reference services:

- A decline in reference questions
- An increase in online reference services
- A call for eliminating or de-emphasizing reference desks

Unfortunately, this study and the literature that they cited does not examine whether the reported decreases in "in-person" reference questions and the growth of a reliance in using online reference services had anything to do with students and other patrons avoiding coming into reference departments due to a library's potentially aging and uncomfortable physical reference room atmosphere. It is disappointing to see that many recent surveys, such as the *Learning Commons Benchmarks* study (Primary Research Group Staff 2015) did not choose to assess whether reference services existed within a physical learning commons. Future research on reference services trends within libraries that offer a learning commons should focus on examining whether reference transactions increased after the remodel/addition of the learning commons by comparing pre- and post-occupancy assessment data and by interviewing students. Significant studies on the impact that reference desks and reference librarian staffing make within highly programmed learning commons have not emerged since the publication of "Reference Librarians at the Reference Desk in a Learning Commons: A Mixed Methods Evaluation" (Fitzpatrick, Moore, and Lang 2008). More studies that employ qualitative data gathering, qualitative interviews, and focus groups that examine students' perceptions and use of reference services should be conducted in both the learning commons planning phase and post-occupancy.

Given the reported likelihood of dwindling library reference transaction statistics, it is also important for any library to examine precisely how their reference services might best be delivered within any new learning space. Will professional MLIS-degree-holding librarians staff the reference desk? Or will tiered reference services be deployed? Within a tiered reference system, "the initial reference contact point is with trained students or paraprofessionals at a general service desk. These non-librarians field all manner of questions, including directional, computing, and occasionally reference. They answer any 'basic' reference questions they can and refer advanced questions to an actual librarian" (Gardner 2006). In the long transition from information commons to learning commons models, the question of whether to staff a desk with professional librarians remains fiercely debated. One sound recommendation, which follows the sage advice of Laura MacWhinnie, implores us to remember that "the complexity of library resources provided in a Learning Commons creates a greater need for research assistance from librarians" (MacWhinnie 2003, 242).

In the Learning Commons Survey introduced in chapter 3, "Partnerships and Strategies for Successful Programming," of this book, fifty-eight (72.50 percent) of the eighty respondents reported that their learning commons offered reference services within their learning commons spaces (see figure 8.1).

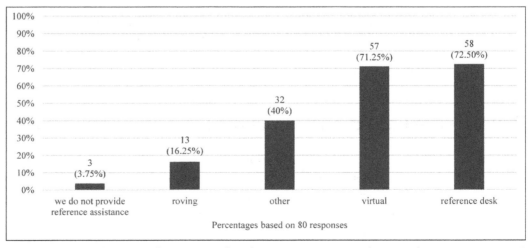

Figure 8.1. In what ways do you provide reference assistance within your learning commons? Select all that apply. *Courtesy of the author*

A considerable number of respondents indicated they provide "other" types of reference assistance. The thirty-two (40 percent) respondents who answered "other" reported providing reference services through different options such as telephone or by office appointment. Every institution will need to individually evaluate its reference services, both virtual and physical, and ultimately determine which services will need to be retained, highlighted, and marketed within a new learning commons. In addition to evaluating how and where reference interviews will be conducted within a learning commons, the implementation team will also likely need to gauge where their physical reference collection will be housed. Figure 8.2 illustrates research assistance at the knowledge commons assistance desk, Marriott Library, University of Utah. Further discussion of reference services within learning commons offerings can be found in chapter 10, "Successful Learning Commons Partnerships," of this book.

Figure 8.2. Knowledge Commons assistance desk at the Marriott Library, University of Utah. *Photo by Marriott Library, University of Utah*

Reference Collections within the Library Learning Commons

The print collection most often impacted by learning commons space implementations is the reference collection. This happens because many learning commons are situated on the first floor of academic libraries, where reference services and collections are commonly targeted for placement. With most reconceptualizations of library space aiming to make room for new peer-learning furnishings, group study rooms, coffee shops, and other learning commons features on the main floor of a library, many libraries find they must remove shelving and relocate or reduce print collections to make room for new learning commons elements. Learning commons projects often trigger the need to relocate or reduce an academic library's print reference collection. Depending on the location, size, and use of a reference collection, trying collection-management decisions may emerge when automated storage facilities or other locations are not viable alternatives for relocation. Citing the 2014 *Spec-Kit 342: Next-Gen Learning Spaces* (Brown et al. 2014), Cindy Pierard and Sever Bordeianu note that learning commons teams are regularly forced to make "decisions to weed, pair-down or relocate physical collections, to transition from print to electronic collections, and to develop collections to support new learning services, programs, and collaborations" (2016, 411).

⑥ Instructional Services and the Library Learning Commons

Four types of academic learning categories typified the twenty-two recent library renovation projects examined in Project Information Literacy's 2016 study, *Planning and Designing Academic Library Learning Spaces*. These four academic learning categories, in descending order, were (1) collaborative learning, (2) individual study, (3) point-of-need learning, and (4) "occasional" classes taught by campus instructors (Head 2016). While the availability of individual and peer-learning spaces within a learning commons is critical to its success, the proximity of instructional classrooms is also beneficial to creating a complete learning space. When a learning commons is planned within an academic library, it is characteristic to try to create and/or improve library instruction classrooms to better support existing library instructional programming. Most library instruction classrooms contain an instructor workstation, screen, projector, whiteboards, and student desk space and seating with either dedicated desktop computers or the availability to deploy laptops or wireless computing devices such as tablets from a precharged storage cart. Depending on the volume of library instruction that the library offers, more than one classroom may be needed to accommodate scheduled formal library instruction programming such as one-shot sessions, workshops, and/or credit-based information literacy courses offered by the library.

Instructor-led learning spaces designed for a library's learning commons may not all be reserved for library instructional sessions. Many types of learning spaces may be more flexible and suitable for faculty and other personnel to offer classes within the learning commons. As Arlee Turner, Bernadette Welch, and Sue Reynolds note, "The importance of spatial designs that encourage and support dynamic, engaged and inspired learning behaviors is a fundamental feature of the learning spaces trend. The impact of 'spaces' becomes more prominent as pedagogical practices in higher education start to move away from the traditional, teacher-centered approach to a more flexible, student-centered approach" (2013, 231). An example of such a "fluid space" can be found in the active learning classroom model that is appearing in some learning commons.

⑥ The Active Learning Classroom and Other Nonlibrary Instruction Classrooms

Since 2000, active learning classrooms (also known as *smart* or *flexible classrooms*) have begun appearing within and beyond information and learning commons settings at universities around the globe. These active learning classrooms are designed as cooperative learning environments that boost student collaboration and peer teaching by placing students and sometimes faculty in technology-rich, flexible spaces where work can be shared on large viewing screens. Victoria Karasic notes that within the last decade, active learning classrooms have "become popular features of libraries, both to provide new life for underused or outdated library spaces, and to reevaluate the ways in which collaborative teaching and learning occur, all in a flexible, high-tech library space conveniently and centrally located in the library" (2016, 55). Figure 8.3 depicts an active learning classroom at the Charles E. Odegaard Undergraduate Library at the University of Washington. Karasic also points out how recently libraries, including those at the University of Iowa (TILE classroom) and Virginia Tech University Libraries (SCALE-UP classroom), have successfully implemented active learning classrooms (Soderdahl 2011; Virginia Tech University Libraries 2013).

Figure 8.3. Active learning classrooms at the Charles E. Odegaard Undergraduate Library, University of Washington. *Photo by @LaraSwimmerPhotography, www.swimmerphoto.com*

According to Paul Soderdahl (2011), active learning classrooms are typically equipped with both collaborative furnishing (small group tables) and technology-rich features, including video screens, group shared laptops, wiring for video plug-ins, and outlets for BYOD (bring your own device) needs as well as data cables. It is now also commonplace to find portable or mounted projectors and screens facilitating more adaptable pop-up classroom scenarios within flexibly designed learning commons spaces. These kinds of adaptable pop-up lecture/teaching spaces can adroitly transform a learning commons seating area into a guest speaker landing zone within a learning commons, providing a flexible landing spot for campus, community, and library outreach programming needs. See chapter 3, "Partnerships and Strategies for Successful Programming," of this book for more information about active learning classrooms.

⊚ Opportunities for Outreach in Learning Commons Spaces

Unlike traditional academic library spaces of decades past that offered quiet reading areas and cubicle desks for independent reading and study, today's library learning commons offers multifunctional and flexible spaces for students to socialize, collaborate, explore, and to use many different types of state-of-the-art technologies. "The flexible design of the learning commons facilitates change by offering students a place that provokes their imagination. . . . The design of the space is effective because it provides a welcoming environment for students to congregate, collaborate, and create" says Jennifer Calvo (2009, 38). A typical afternoon for a student in a learning commons may allow the student to meet with classmates and take part in a study group project, eat a meal at the commons coffeehouse, use a scanner to scan parts of a book for a class, take a study break with friends, play a video or board game, and find help from a librarian in locating scholarly sources for a research paper (Calvo 2009). The learning commons setting is conducive to serving the many interests and needs of the busy millennial college student, and it offers a unique opportunity to develop and provide specialized library outreach programing. Addressing and serving the different needs of students makes the learning commons and its outreach offerings unique to academic institutions. "The learning commons affords a more robust conception of student success, one that incorporates cognitive development and scholarly pursuits, but also other aspects of student growth and development as well as embracing the philosophy of integrative learning" (Hinchliffe and Wong 2010, 213).

The work of Lisa Hinchliffe and Melissa Wong (2010) describes the research of Bill Hettler (1980), who brought the concept of wellness to student affairs with a framework of six dimensions. Hinchliffe and Wong assert that Hettler's framework is the basis for a "wellness wheel" model that describes the factors that influence wellness and impact one's overall health. This wellness wheel model of six dimensions can be used as a practical approach for working with students in higher education to develop programming that addresses a wide range of student learning needs. These six dimensions can be associated with various forms of outreach and programming efforts. Below are Hinchliffe and Wong's (2010), six wellness wheel dimensions with possible corresponding supportive outreach activities:

- Intellectual dimension—This outreach programming can take the form of learning commons displays and exhibits that showcase library collections and engage students through curricular interests outside of the classroom.
- Emotional dimension—Outreach efforts of this nature can include partnering with campus counseling and health centers to offer low-cost massages. Organized visits with therapy dogs can also be effective tools as well.
- Physical dimension—For this programming, learning commons staff can promote the areas in the library collections that support health and nutrition. They can also partner with the campus health center to offer wellness tips during stressful finals week periods.
- Social dimension—Learning commons spaces by their nature are geared to support students socially. This programming includes, but is not limited to, providing a variety of spaces where students can interact individually or as a group.
- Occupational dimension—Outreach efforts in this area can support students by promoting library collections that address careers, education, and financial aid.

- Spiritual dimension—This outreach programming can involve offering meditation sessions during midterms and finals weeks. Speakers on spirituality who are tied to course curriculum could be brought into the library as well.

These six dimensions (Hinchliffe and Wong 2010) and corresponding library learning commons outreach programming efforts represent how learning commons spaces can impact student development in nontraditional ways. Unlike traditional library floor plans and offerings, learning commons spaces are able to accommodate such varied programming that can address the diverse range of student learning needs identified through the six dimensions. Learning commons spaces offer the ideal setting and provide the unique opportunity for outreach programming due to their flexibility and multifunctional spaces.

⑥ Outreach Programming That Takes Place in Libraries and Learning Commons Spaces

Publications in the field of library science include a wide range of research results that focus on outreach practices that underscore the continued growth and interest in outreach programming within libraries. According to Melissa Dennis, trends in higher education suggest a greater emphasis on "student success and connecting student engagement to academic achievement" (2012, 368). Within this research, Dennis discusses how the Association of College and Research Libraries revised their *Standards for Libraries in Higher Education* in 2011 to include "expectations for library contributions to institutional effectiveness" (ACRL 2011, 5), signaling that student engagement should be a priority for academic library missions and their student goals. Given the growth of outreach programming, and the vast range of opportunities available to those who pursue these activities, many existing outreach practices can be drawn upon when considering the development of programming for academic library learning commons spaces.

According to library outreach programming literature and the results of the Learning Commons Survey, introduced in chapter 3, "Partnerships and Strategies for Successful Programming," of this book, the following is a list of outreach events and initiatives that have been carried out in academic libraries that are specifically well suited for learning commons spaces and their offerings. Many of these initiatives have been included in specialized programming such as finals week destressing activities or to celebrate specific cultural or academic events, but they can also be offered on their own, outside of specialized programs. These events and programs can be scaled up or down depending on your individual library's funding, staff support, and other resources. Outreach activities to consider for learning commons spaces include

- exhibits about civic engagement and other curricular-based displays;
- presentations, including those about new library resources;
- lectures and panel discussions, library or other-curricular based;
- banned books readouts;
- Black History Month and other multicultural awareness enrichment programming, including speakers and displays;
- therapy dog visits (see figure 8.4);
- film or athletic game screenings;

- National Library Week exhibits and displays;
- arts and crafts activities;
- gaming and game nights—board and online;
- musical performances and open mics;
- book talks, book signings, poetry and book readings;
- graffiti walls or boards (see figure 8.5);
- art exhibits, displays, and programming;
- photo booths;
- raffles related to celebrating library events and for using resources in the library;
- exercise breaks, yoga, meditation, mindfulness exercises, and chair massages;
- specialized contests associated with library resources and services;
- tabling for counseling and psychological services;
- exhibits of student work, traveling photo collections, and other special collections displays;
- wellness tips from campus health and wellness centers;
- quick reference, citation support, résumé writing, and other workshops;
- Associated Students group meetings;
- panel sessions on social initiatives and curricular interests;
- coffee coupon giveaways for the library coffeehouse;
- National Novel Writing Month and other writing events. (Dennis 2012; Imhoff and Maslin 2007; Meyer 2014; Meyers-Martin and Borchard 2015; Pease 2015; Ruffin, Brannen, and Venable 2015)

Figure 8.4. Therapy dog visit at the Delmar T. Oviatt Library Learning Commons, California State University, Northridge. *Courtesy of the Delmar T. Oviatt Library, CSU Northridge*

Figure 8.5. Graffiti board at the Delmar T. Oviatt Library Learning Commons, California State University, Northridge. *Courtesy of the Delmar T. Oviatt Library, CSU Northridge*

Fifty-five (68.75 percent) respondents who participated in the Learning Commons Survey reported they had coordinated and offered a variety of outreach activities in their learning commons spaces, including many of the activities listed previously. Less commonly reported outreach learning commons programming, per the Learning Commons Survey results, included offering Halloween trick-or-treating, science "salons" featuring

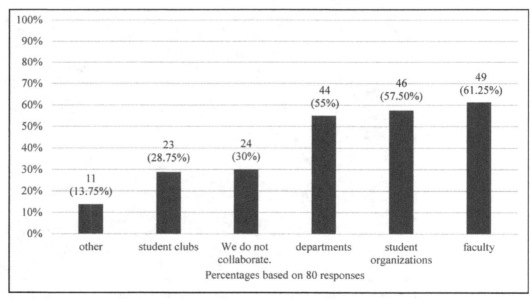

Figure 8.6. If employees in your learning commons collaborate with others on campus, . . . please tell us who they collaborate with for your learning commons programming. *Courtesy of the author*

doctoral student research, GIS (geographic information system) programming, suicide prevention and sexual assault and health awareness tabling, thesis presentations, tours, and student presidential debates and discussions. The respondents of the Learning Commons Survey also reported carrying out their outreach activities while working with a variety of campus colleagues. Figure 8.6 illustrates the many different groups and campus departments that collaborate with learning commons programming throughout the academic year. Respondents were asked to select all that applied.

Best Practices for Outreach Programming

With the abundance of outreach activities and efforts currently taking place in academic libraries, there lies a great opportunity for learning commons spaces to offer programming that fosters student engagement to address a wider range of student learning needs. Those who are assigned to the task of coordinating such outreach activities and events may want to consider the following programming tips and best practices for carrying out and offering outreach activities within learning commons spaces:

- Identify your outreach budget needs and the source for that budget. Common places to look for funding may be from a special library fund, donor support, or fundraising efforts.
- Identify the number of volunteers you will need to perform your outreach and secure them in advance. Let volunteers know ahead of time that if they need to cancel for any reason, they will need to replace themselves for the event or programming effort.
- Start your planning early. You may need to obtain approval or permission from library or campus units in advance for particular activities and events. Provide your colleagues with plenty of time to grant you the approval you need.
- Plan for your event to take place regardless of outside circumstances. For instance, if you are requesting approval for programming, submit your request and continue to plan your event. If you wait to plan your activity until after you gain approval, it may be too late to schedule the programming, particularly if the approval comes in at the last minute.
- Communicate the programming library wide. Even though the event may take place in the learning commons, let everyone in the library know about the outreach activity that is to take place. This welcomes all to participate, supports an inclusive working environment, and can help to create an initial "buzz" for the programming.
- Promote the programming through a variety of outlets, including social media, library website, campus newspaper, flyers, posters, banners, announcements in classes, and by word of mouth.
- Be flexible in coordinating the event in case last-minute changes need to be made.
- Partner with campus groups and communities when possible. Be mindful that programming is not only about specific outcomes for an event, but it can also be about building relationships with campus units and departments.
- Schedule programming during the best times for your students and/or faculty to attend. Partner with faculty members in selecting the day and timing for an event when appropriate and possible.

- Assess the programming to inform you and your team when planning for future events. This can take place through feedback from users attending the event, social media response, the number of attendees at the event, and through the distribution of questionnaires and surveys.
- Be able to illustrate and communicate the value-added aspects of the programming to ensure future interest and support (Meyers-Martin and Borchard 2015; Ruffin, Brannen, and Venable 2015).

Ⓖ Key Points

Reference services, user-centered information literacy instruction, and outreach programming efforts will continue to thrive due to the numerous and multifunctional collaborative areas and the resources and services that are available within today's academic library learning commons spaces. To best develop user-centered instruction, information literacy, and outreach programming within a learning commons, planning teams should remember the following:

- Reference librarians should be consulted during the design process of any learning commons.
- Pre– and post–learning commons occupancy assessments must be conducted to properly evaluate the functionality and impact of reference services and programming.
- The library's physical reference collection may need to be relocated or reduced to make way for peer and individual learning spaces and programming within the learning commons.
- Flexible active learning classroom options must be kept in mind when planning learning commons classroom spaces to optimize library information literacy programming environments.
- Each learning commons and library organizational structure is distinct, and there will be no single method for designing and implementing outreach programming.
- The learning commons setting is conducive to serving many interests of the busy college student and offers a unique opportunity to provide specialized library outreach programming.
- Partnering with campus colleagues, groups, and communities will support inclusive and well-rounded learning commons outreach programming.
- Communicating the value-added aspects of learning commons outreach programming with your administration and other stakeholders can help to ensure future interest and support.

In the next chapter, launching and assessing learning commons services will be discussed. Carrying out a successful assessment of your services and how that assessment will inform learning commons services specific to your institution will be addressed. A discussion about lessons learned while developing a new learning commons space will be included.

⊚ References

ACRL (Association of College and Research Libraries). 2011. *Standards for Libraries in Higher Education*. Chicago: Association of College and Research Libraries. www.ala.org/acrl/sites/ala.org.acrl/files/content/standards/slhe.pdf.

Brown, Sherri, Charlie Bennett, Bruce Henson, and Alison Valk. 2014. *Spec-Kit: 342 Next-Gen Learning Spaces*. Washington, DC: Association of Research Libraries.

Calvo, Jennifer. 2009. "Preserving the Vitality of Learning Commons Spaces through Dynamic Programming: The Learning Commons after Dark Series." *Against the Grain* 21, no. 4: 38–40. https://docs.lib.purdue.edu/cgi/viewcontent.cgi?article=2437&context=atg.

Coleman, Jason, Melissa N. Mallon, and Leo Lo. 2015. "Recent Changes to Reference Services in Academic Libraries and Their Relationship to Perceived Quality: Results of a National Survey." *Journal of Library Administration* 56, no. 6: 1–24. doi:10.1080/01930826.2015.1109879.

Dennis, Melissa. 2012. "Outreach Initiatives in Academic Libraries: 2009–2011." *Reference Services Review* 40, no 3: 368–83. doi:10.1108/00907321211254643.

Fitzpatrick, Elizabeth, Anne Moore, and Beth Lang. 2008. "Reference Librarians at the Reference Desk in a Learning Commons: A Mixed Methods Evaluation." *Journal of Academic Librarianship* 34, no. 3: 231–38. doi:10.1016/j.acalib.2008.03.006.

Gardner, Susan. 2006. "Tiered Reference: The New Landscape of the Front Lines." *Electronic Journal of Academic and Special Librarianship* 7, no. 3 (Winter). http://southernlibrarianship.icaap.org/content/v07n03/gardner_s01.htm.

Head, Alison J. 2016. *Planning and Designing Academic Library Learning Spaces: Expert Perspectives of Architects, Librarians, and Library Consultants*. Project Information Literacy Research Report. Practitioner Series. Seattle: University of Washington. www.projectinfolit.org/uploads/2/7/5/4/27541717/pil_libspace_report_12_6_16.pdf.

Hettler, Bill. 1980. "Wellness Promotion on a University Campus." *Family and Community Health* 3, no. 1: 77–95.

Hinchliffe, Lisa Janicke, and Melissa Autumn Wong. 2010. "From Services-Centered to Student-Centered: A 'Wellness Wheel' Approach to Developing the Library as an Integrative Learning Commons." *College & Undergraduate Libraries* 17, nos. 2–3: 213–24. doi:10.1080/10691316.2010.490772.

Imhoff, Kathleen, and Ruthie Maslin. 2007. *Library Contests: A How-to-Do-It Manual*. New York: Neal Schuman.

Karasic, Vickie Marre. 2016. "From Commons to Classroom: The Evolution of Learning Spaces in Academic Libraries." *Journal of Learning Spaces* 5, no. 2: 53–60. http://libjournal.uncg.edu/jls/article/view/825.

MacWhinnie, Laura. 2003. "The Information Commons: The Academic Library of the Future." *portal: Libraries and the Academy* 3, no. 2: 241–57. doi:10.1353/pla.2003.0040.

Meyer, Erin, E. 2014. "Low-Hanging Fruit: Leveraging Short-Term Partnerships to Advance Academic Library Outreach Goals." *Collaborative Librarianship* 6, no. 3: 112–20. https://digitalcommons.du.edu/cgi/viewcontent.cgi?article=1093&context=collaborativelibrarianship.

Meyers-Martin, Coleen, and Laurie Borchard. 2015. "The Finals Stretch: Exams Week Library Outreach Surveyed." *Reference Services Review* 43, no. 4: 510–26. doi:10.1108/RSR-03-2015-0019.

Pease, Lesley. 2015. "A New Learning Commons Connection with Art Students and Their Faculty." *College & Undergraduate Libraries* 22, no. 1: 107–16. doi:10.1080/10691316.2015.1001247.

Pierard, Cindy, and Sever Bordeianu. 2016. "Learning Commons Reference Collections in ARL Libraries." *Reference Services Review* 44, no. 3: 411–30. doi:10.1108/RSR-02-2016-0014.

Primary Research Group Staff. 2015. *Learning Commons Benchmarks*. New York: Primary Research Group.

Ruffin, Ingrid J., Michelle H. Brannen, and Megan Venable. 2015. "Library as Campus Main Street: Building Community via Engaging Programming and Spaces." In *Innovative Solutions for Building Community in Academic Libraries*, edited by Sheila Bonnard and Mary Anne Hansen, 269–91. Hershey, PA: Information Science Reference.

Soderdahl, Paul A. 2011. "Library Classroom Renovated as an Active Learning Classroom." *Library Hi Tech* 29, no. 1: 83–90. doi:10.1108/07378831111116921.

Turner, Arlee, Bernadette Welch, and Sue Reynolds. 2013. "Learning Spaces in Academic Libraries—a Review of the Evolving Trends." *Australian Academic & Research Libraries* 44, no. 4: 226–34. doi:10.1080/00048623.2013.857383.

Virginia Tech University Libraries. 2013. "SCALE-UP Classroom." Virginia Tech University website. www.lib.vt.edu/ instruct/classrooms/scaleupclass.html.

Wolfe, Judith A., Ted Naylor, and Jeanetta Drueke. 2010. "The Role of the Academic Reference Librarian in the Learning Commons." *Reference & User Services Quarterly* 50, no. 2: 108–13. https://digitalcommons.unl.edu/cgi/viewcontent.cgi?referer=https://www.google.com/&httpsredir=1&article=1232&context=libraryscience.

CHAPTER 9

Assessing Learning Commons Spaces and Reviewing Lessons Learned

---

IN THIS CHAPTER

▷ Examining how established academic library assessment methods, tools, and emerging practices can ideally inform post-occupancy learning commons assessment strategies

▷ Discussing approaches and considerations when assessing space and student learning within academic libraries: an interview with an assessment expert

▷ Exploring the lessons learned when developing an academic library's learning commons

▷ Identifying best practices for library learning space projects

---

ASSESSING THE USAGE OF SERVICES and collections remains standard practice within academic library settings. Librarians and library administrators still annually continue to measure and evaluate how their collections and services, such as reference and instruction, are used within their institutions by their primary clientele. However, output measures and collected data in the form of circulation, website, and instruction statistics are no longer the only sought-after indicators of how library clientele make use of a library's collection and programmatic services. As discussed in earlier chapters, within the past decade, factors such as decline of circulation and reference statistics, along with falling numbers of physical visitors, have caused many libraries to look for new ways to reengage students beyond access to collection materials and services by engaging in the repurposing and modernization of library spaces. The emergence of new learning spaces within libraries, through the development of learning commons spaces and other settings, has led to the need to move beyond traditional library assessment metrics. Indeed, libraries with learning commons and other newly configured student learning spaces and aligned services, are making concerted efforts to develop effective ways to assess how and why students are using their new learning spaces. Many within the field are working diligently to share evidence with their campus administrators and accreditation agencies that shows that the library contributes to student learning by maintaining spaces that support individual and social learning. As Mary Ellen Spencer and Sarah Barbara Watstein note,

> Because accrediting agencies also focus on the operation and maintenance of our physical facilities, they ask us to assess whether our campus libraries appropriately serve the needs of our institution's educational programs, support services, and other mission-related activities. Regional and specialized accreditation requirements and standards that pertain to learning resources and services invariably circle back to one thing—student learning. (2017, 390)

Keeping this in mind, it has become imperative when assessing informal learning spaces, like a learning commons, for libraries to develop plans to measure and hopefully demonstrate how, when, and why individual and social learning is occurring within the library. Many libraries currently employ various assessment methods to measure the usage of new and existing learning spaces (group study rooms, classrooms, and computer labs as well as individual- and group-seating configurations). A key task for any library developing a plan to effectively assess new or existing learning spaces is to decide how to measure space usage and the learning that is taking place within it.

Before embarking on developing any new assessment plan or strategy to measure the post-occupancy success of your new learning commons, there are some central things for your team to ask yourselves:

- Who among your staff will be involved in and/or responsible for carrying out the assessment of the library's learning spaces (learning commons spaces, services, and elements)?
- Who will be evaluating the results of your assessment? Campus administrators, donors, faculty, peer institutions, and so forth?
- How much effort and time will be needed to capture the data and information that you are thinking of collecting?
- Are there existing assessment resources available within your library or campus that can assist in your process? For example, an office of institutional research, software, an existing student ID/card swipe system.
- Will the library personnel charged with conducting the assessment need training or support to carry out their assigned duties?
- Does your library and/or institution participate in any system-wide or collective assessment efforts that may inform your strategies for measuring the effectiveness of student learning spaces?
- Which assessment techniques and methods can be applied, and how may they impact students (privacy, intrusion, burden, etc.)?
- Are you using an appropriate instrument or method to acquire the data or information that you need for the research question at hand?
- Will the accrediting agency expect to see certain measurements of student learning within these learning spaces or the library facility as a whole?

- Have you reviewed any collected pre–learning commons needs assessment data that you would like to follow up on (student satisfaction with library seating, technology, services, etc.)?

Reviewing the literature is another practical thing to do when tasked with developing effective ways for your team to assess different learning space offerings within a planned learning commons space. Table 9.1 illustrates the many wonderful studies that offer food for thought about how to approach the evaluation of everything from coffee shops and cafés to group study rooms and computer labs. Various examples of successful studies have evaluated emerging learning space elements and settings within academic library learning commons models. Some employ more passive observational ethnographic methods, while others rely more on surveys, focus groups, or other intake methodologies. While newer elements within academic learning commons spaces, such as makerspaces, still largely rely on quantitative measurement such as visitor or participant numbers, which fail to capture the impact of services on users, there are ample studies of learning commons spatial and programmatic elements that will help your assessment team discover ideas and proven methods to evaluate how space is being used for both traditional and social learning.

Table 9.1. Assessment Studies

TYPE OF LEARNING SPACE STUDIED/ASSESSED	PUBLISHED STUDY
Library cafés	Harrop and Turpin (2013)
Group study areas	Dallis (2016) Lange and Holder (2014) Kinsley et al. (2015) Montgomery (2014)
Social learning spaces/student social spaces	Bryant, Matthews, and Walton (2009) Carpenter (2011) Chan and Spodick (2014) May and Swabey (2015) Raish and Fennewald (2016)
Closed individual and quiet study spaces	Pierard and Lee (2011)
Computer stations/labs	Bailin (2011) Kinsley et al. (2015) May and Swabey (2015) Norton et al. (2013)

Before you consider modeling an assessment project after one of the published methods or developing a new plan from scratch to assess a new library learning space, it is a good idea for your learning commons assessment team to also consider how routine interactions with existing staff and services may assist you in data collection.

The research of Victoria Raish and Joseph Fennewald (2016) emphasizes that in addition to providing informal learning spaces that foster social learning, libraries also need to think about how the presence and positioning of personnel within these spaces may impact student engagement and learning. The authors specifically called out for future researchers to "devise a way that embedded managers can track student achievement in their space" (Raish and Fennewald 2016, 811). There are many ways to track the usage of space within libraries, such as tracking student usage through student ID swipe technology, taking head counts, and harnessing the power of software to analyze inputted data through tools like Suma and Tableau.

Examples of Assessment Software Tools

Suma (see figure 9.1) is software that was specifically designed to assist library personnel in capturing how learning spaces are being used within academic libraries. Developed at North Carolina State University (NCSU), "Suma is an open-source mobile web-based assessment toolkit for collecting and analyzing observational data about the usage of physical spaces and services" (NCSU [North Carolina State University] Libraries 2014). Suma

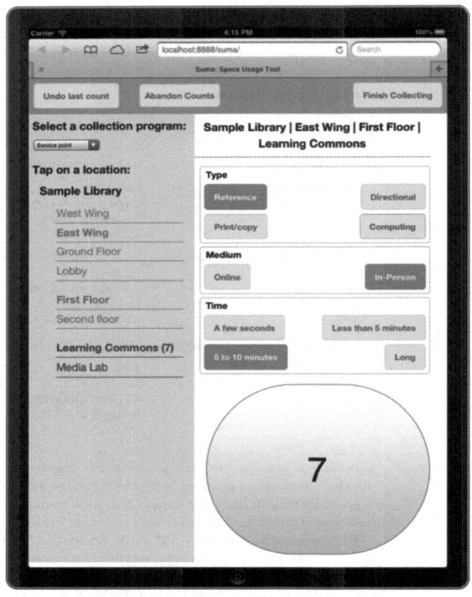

Figure 9.1. Screenshot of Suma data collection software in action on a tablet. *www .lib.ncsu.edu/projects/suma*

offers libraries the ability to capture data on space usage, including "building headcounts, service desk transactions, roaming reference services, laptop usage, group vs. individual study, media production activities and experimental space usage" (NCSU Libraries 2014).

Tableau is a more widely established library assessment tool that is growing in popularity within higher education. Many academic libraries are using Tableau to produce visualizations and dashboards of library data. "Tableau is a data visualization and analysis software that improves decision-making by giving libraries the ability to query, blend, explore, discover, and then analyze and present data in new and compelling ways ... and allows stakeholders and librarians to 'see and understand their data' using an intuitive drag and drop interface and a powerful data engine" (Murphy 2015, 482). Maggie Faber, the data visualization and analysis librarian at the University of Washington Libraries, notes in her online Tableau tutorial that Tableau allows librarians to construct a visual map of the learning space they are observing and then connect it to data (head count, card swipes, etc.). This allows libraries to study patterns and develop ways to more effectively gauge space and service desk usage (Faber 2016). Examples of how academic libraries and others are using Tableau to visually disseminate assessment data on their learning spaces can be found by searching Tableau Public (https://public.tableau.com/en-us/s/). Many academic libraries often report their gathered post-occupancy learning commons metrics within their annual reports. A simple Google search of "library learning commons annual reports" will retrieve a plethora of reports and information concerning learning commons offerings, with some assessment information if/when this data has been gathered. The *University of Iowa Libraries Learning Commons Reports* (www.lib.uiowa.edu/commons/home/monthly-reports) provides an example of how one academic library reports and assesses its learning commons offerings and space.

There are also many professional development opportunities available for library staff charged with learning space assessment projects. Some recurrent opportunities to learn more about the assessment of libraries and higher education learning spaces include the following conferences and workshops:

- The Association of Research Libraries Library Assessment Conference, http://libraryassessment.org/
- Next Generation Learning Spaces Conference, https://higheredlearningspaces.iqpc.com/

Regardless of how your team approaches the assessment of any library learning space, it is critical that those assigned these tasks receive the training and support needed to carry out their assignments. If your library does not have a resident assessment expert, it is also a good idea to reach out to assessment leaders within the field.

Interview with April Cunningham

April Cunningham (figure 9.2) provides a professional's view on assessing space and student learning within academic libraries and higher education. April is the instruction and information literacy librarian at Palomar College in San Marcos, California, where she also teaches in the library tech program. She earned her EdD in educational leadership from California State University, Fullerton, in 2012. She is the project lead for the Threshold Achievement Test for Information Literacy.

Please describe your recent work in assessment and the study of assessment of student learning and/or quality of services within academic libraries.

I assess student learning in our library instruction sessions and in the library tech courses I teach. I have used direct and indirect measures of students' learning, measures of their satisfaction and their professors' satisfaction with the instruction provided, librarians' reflections on observed learning, and item analysis of quizzes that we use at the end of some in-person and online instruction.

Figure 9.2.   April Cunningham

I have also served as a facilitator for other librarians' assessment planning through Assessment in Action, which I describe in more detail below, and by working with campus teams at the Western Association of Schools and Colleges Core Competencies Assessment Retreats in 2013 and 2014.

I also have experience creating information literacy tests. I was a consultant to the IL [Information Literacy] Framework Cooperative Project for At-Risk Student Success in Smaller Colleges in which an IMLS [Institute of Museum and Library Services]-grant-funded team of librarians in Maryland and Pennsylvania collaboratively developed curriculum and testing materials. And I am the project lead for the Threshold Achievement Test for Information Literacy.

Please tell us more about your role in ACRL's [Association of College and Research Libraries] Assessment in Action program and how you see programming like this helping libraries and librarians learn to effectively find ways to collect data that provides evidence of student learning and retention being influenced by library resources both physical (group study rooms, computing, learning spaces) as well as collections and services.

I was a curriculum designer and facilitator for ACRL's Assessment in Action (AiA) from 2012 to 2016. AiA was a fourteen-month program of training and support for librarians who were leading assessment teams, and we had three rounds of projects. The core concepts and lessons of AiA continue being offered now in a one-day workshop format. I am not involved directly with this new program, but I enthusiastically support it because I know how useful the content is for librarians who are ready to take on a new assessment project.

The strength of AiA is that it helps librarians to design assessments with the culture, needs, and values of their own institutions at the center from the beginning. There are so many decisions to make when designing an assessment project. Whether assessing something traditional like one-shots or something newer like a library's social media presence, it's always best to start by defining the audience for your results and what action you want that audience to support or to take. AiA emphasizes making decisions in the early stages about what type of data and what format of reporting will best help you make your case to the people you want to influence, even if it's just the librarian you share an office with. Because assessment should lead to some kind of action, you want to be strategic in your approach so that you increase the likelihood that your results will inspire action. A campus culture where numbers and charts are considered rigorous and authoritative calls for a different assessment approach than does a campus culture that values detailed stories illustrating the impact an intervention has had. And the same assessment design cannot investigate how the library might affect student persistence as well as how library spaces should be changed in order to attract student populations who are underrepresented among library users.

The assessment projects completed by AiA team leaders are available in a searchable database (https://apply.ala.org/aia/public). Less than 3 percent of the completed projects assessed physical spaces, and what I learned from those studies is that measuring any effects of library space on student outcomes, like completion or retention, presents a particularly difficult assessment challenge that often has disappointing results showing that the library space has no effect. I believe that is because success and retention are influenced by so many different factors beyond the library. On the other hand, doing a descriptive study of how students perceive and use the space can result in useful results for making decisions that benefit learners.

Given the established practice of academic libraries working to assess and then report on how their collections and services impact student learning, what are your thoughts on the recent trend of academic libraries working to assess how their physical spaces impact student learning (moving beyond LibQual qualitative assessments, etc.)?

The most important thing when evaluating the current space and/or gathering data to inform the design of new spaces is to keep the intrusion on students' time and attention to a minimum when they are actively using the library space. If libraries collect student ID numbers when they are using the spaces, then it could be interesting to use existing data regarding students' success (i.e., retention, persistence, and completion) to look for relationships between library use and student outcomes. But as I noted above, claims based on that type of data usually are not very strong because of all of the other confounding factors. We can also learn a lot about how students are using our spaces by keeping track of their questions at service points where they are asking, for example, about where to find a quiet place with access to an electrical outlet or whether it is okay to use a group study room to conduct a Skype interview or where they should sit with their kids to cause the least disruption while they do their research. But many students who are having trouble using our space will never ask about it.

That is why I think that the best approach for investigating the value of space is an ethnographic study or, at least, what Donna Lanclos and Andrew Asher (2016) call an "ethnographish" study that uses ethnographic methods even if the full power of open-ended ethnographic research is not achieved. Observational methods, whether as part of an ethnographic study or a user experience (UX) project, are best suited to evaluate library spaces so that students' experiences are foregrounded but their time in the library is as undisturbed as possible during the evaluation. For example, North Carolina State University librarians have been hailed for making quick decisions to change their information commons design after they saw students bringing their own furniture into a room the librarians had filled with bean bags. The librarians realized their original plan was not what students needed, and they pivoted to achieve the goal that we all have: to create a space free from barriers that impinge upon students' ability to pursue their own goals (Mathews 2011). Overall, as my colleague said, we want to avoid bothering students to ask them their opinion of furniture that is twenty years old so that we can pick the furniture we'll have after they graduate.

What do you think are some of the largest barriers that often cause libraries and librarians to fail to assess services, programming, and facilities?

I learned a lot about barriers to assessment by working with team leaders in AiA. Several team leaders struggled despite being highly motivated to define an assessment question and identify relevant assessment methods. I observed that this struggle often surfaced when the librarian was trying to assess something that she or he did not originally create because it was an existing space or service. When trying to assess the effects of something that already exists, the assessment design process gets more complicated. Normally, we would use backward design to (a) begin from a desired outcome; (b) create a service, space, or other intervention we think would achieve that outcome; and then (c) select assessment methods that make it possible to collect evidence of those outcomes so we can make decisions. But when we assess an existing space or service, we have to infer the goals and desired outcomes the original designers had when they established the service or space. It turns out that when we assess existing services or spaces, we often run into a misalignment between our assessment methods, which we selected because of their feasibility, the multiple ways users are interacting with the space, which have evolved and shaped the space over time, and the assessment goals that are driving the project. This misalignment is sometimes the cause of negative or inconclusive results that can be disappointing. The good news is that if you have designed your assessment with local culture, needs, and values at the center, then even disappointing results are likely to lead to interesting conversations and to new questions to inform future action as well as assessments.

Do you see value in linking library learning outcome goals to physical spaces (such as metrics for assessing how new spaces facilitate student learning and users' productivity at accomplishing research tasks)? If so, what evaluation metrics or strategies could possibly be considered when working to link learning outcomes to the planned goals of a library space renovation project?

To me, linking learning outcomes to planning for physical spaces seems like a stretch. We should always be thinking about library space in terms of how it will facilitate or impede users' goals, but I do not think that learning outcomes are a useful tool for planning or evaluating space. Even in instruction, where librarians often use student learning outcomes, the outcomes we care about most are not measurable because we do not get to observe our students applying their skills beyond our one-shot. Most of us cannot make any claims about learning transfer or about students' information literacy based on the instruction we do. Dominique Turnbow and Annie Zeidman-Karpinski (2016) have written a great article explaining the limitations of student learning outcomes assessment for instruction librarians, and their explanation shows why an even more significant misalignment exists between learning outcomes assessment and learning spaces. Turnbow and Zeidman-Karpinski recommend using the right tool for the job in order to get relevant feedback about learner satisfaction and knowledge gains on which to take action to improve future instruction rather than trying to extrapolate from weak evidence to support unsupportable claims about behavior changes or our impact on students' success. Learning outcomes define instructors' goals for students, but the best library spaces should make it possible for students to pursue their own goals. In our efforts to ensure that spaces are not creating barriers for students, we can get relevant and actionable insight by observing students, taking their frustrations seriously, and taking action when the library space is making it harder for them to achieve their goals.

ⓖ Lessons Learned and Best Practices

Each library learning commons project and its post-occupancy assessment will be unique to the institution implementing the renovations and the offerings of the new space. As such, each institution involved in the development of a new learning commons will need to consider the best way to carry out their individual plans, giving consideration to the size of their undertaking, institutional values, teaching pedagogies, financial support, and other available resources. During the often-lengthy process, stakeholders will need to continually ask themselves, "What will work best, for all involved, in moving this project forward given the specific circumstances at hand and our organizational goals?" The answer to this question will likely be very different each day and dependent on the distinct issues that arise during the many stages of the project. Reviewing the lessons learned by other institutions that have already completed and begun to assess their learning commons may be very beneficial to your planning process.

Project Information Literacy (PIL; Head 2016) research presents qualitative data that identifies the best approaches and practices in addition to the challenges associated with developing new learning commons spaces in academic libraries. This research is the result of forty-nine interviews conducted with academic librarians, architects, and library consultants, and the report offers a plethora of information concerning all aspects of the planning and development processes for learning commons spaces. Findings from the interviews, which were conducted between 2011 and 2016, include the determination that the

> success of library projects is dependent upon a shared knowledge and understanding of the sweeping learning, pedagogical, and research changes facing the academy. Librarians and architects need to work together to apply that knowledge and understanding to the unique environment and learning and teaching needs of their specific institution. (Head 2016, 3)

The PIL study (Head 2016) reports major findings associated with the myriad of issues involved during the development of a new learning commons space. See the PIL study for additional results from this report.

ⓖ Learning Commons Renovations: Lessons Learned

More often than not, library learning commons renovations present themselves on a grand scale, possessing many unforeseen pitfalls and numerous challenges. Due to the uniqueness of each learning commons project, a one-size learning commons renovation plan will not fit all. Each institution carrying out a learning commons project will need to consider the scope of their undertaking and how best to institute their plans considering their institutional mission, teaching pedagogies, and resources at hand. Regardless of the differences that exist among learning commons development projects, some broad recommendations may be useful for consideration.

The Learning Commons Survey, introduced in chapter 3, "Partnerships and Strategies for Successful Programming," of this book, asked survey participants for feedback about carrying out the development of a new learning commons space. Responses to the Learning Commons Survey about the lessons learned while undertaking a library learning commons renovation or building a learning commons space from the ground up were pragmatic and insightful. The question "What lessons has your organization learned in developing your learning commons and what advice would you give to those planning to create a commons within their library?" asked survey participates to provide input about their firsthand experiences. The following represents summarized feedback received from the eighty survey participants about their experiences during the development of their learning commons spaces. Comments that were similar or duplicated were combined, and the survey feedback has been categorized within areas that were most commonly described. Comments have been expanded for clarification where necessary.

Planning and Preparing

- Plan, read, and carry out research about how others have developed learning commons spaces. Visit other learning commons in order to gain ideas about what will work or not work for your particular library and institution.
- Develop campus and library buy-in at the beginning of the project. Reach out to campus colleagues and administration for collaboration, input, and support. The renovation or construction of a learning commons most often needs to be a campus-wide effort in order to ensure all of the financial support necessary.
- Develop a master plan for your library building first. The basis of this plan will confirm the need for the development of a learning commons and can outline future projects to be phased in at a later date.
- If your institution will be hiring a new library director in the near future, hire the new library director before or during the initial planning phases, not after the learning commons' mission, goals, and space have been developed and are in place.
- Make sure library representatives/librarians are a part of a continuous campus learning commons conversation in order to develop and preserve library space for library use. After your learning commons becomes popular, everyone will want a part of your new space.
- Plan the resources and services that will be offered in your learning commons and include a means for supporting, sustaining, and promoting these offerings. Learning commons resources, services, and programming must be grounded in a clear sense of ownership and ongoing support. Recognize that your learning commons space and services will need to constantly evolve in order to meet students' changing needs.

Assessment

- Carry out a needs assessment before the beginning of the project and carry out postassessments concerning your resources and services offered in your learning commons each year after its initiation. Modify your offerings if and as necessary.
- Collect and analyze learning commons user data at department levels in order to obtain department-based input and evidence rather than letting administrators dictate non-evidence-based decisions.
- Ask, pilot, assess, ask, pilot, assess. Then make decisions. Making the effort to find out the types of technologies and spaces your students want, before investing your time and financial resources, can save you from making mistakes in the long run.
- Obtain user data in order to evaluate user needs and carry out student focus groups for direct feedback. Find out what students want in a learning commons concerning furnishings, technologies, spaces, and services. Don't rely solely on the suggestions put forth in the design brochures.

- Carry out ethnographic assessments. Students will show you what they need. Forget what you think you know about academic libraries and observe the students. They can't always tell you what they want because they don't know the range of possibilities, but students will show you if you watch them often and carefully.
- Develop a post-occupancy assessment plan for your new learning space. Make certain to consider the frequency that assessments will be conducted and to review your data-gathering options annually.

Collaboration

- Collaborate, collaborate, and collaborate. Develop collaborative learning commons partnerships with campus colleagues and units. Don't be afraid to bring others into the library space.
- Move beyond colocation to collaboration and, where it makes senses, integration. Develop shared learning outcomes with all learning commons partners to inform pedagogies (curricular support, curriculum embedded, and curricular).
- Make sure all learning commons partners involved understand the institutional vision and goals for your learning commons. Communicate expectations about the roles each partner will play so that your learning commons doesn't end up with tenants rather than active collaborators.
- Develop a team approach to provide services across different service areas when possible. Other times, job duties will need to be defined and separated.
- Keep an open mind about the services that will be offered in your learning commons when partnering with campus collaborators.
- Meld the traditional librarian knowledge base and expertise with an information technology knowledge base and expertise to meet the full range of user needs.
- Be patient. Collaboration can be a slow process if the organizational units are managed separately.
- Be prepared to respond to an increased demand for services by adding additional staff as necessary.
- Establish a position for someone to be in charge of the learning commons. Provide the support necessary to maintain a learning commons staff.

Flexible Spaces and Furnishings

- Start out simple with offerings and spaces. Allow for plenty of room to grow.
- Include flexibility in space design and in staffing structure and procedures.
- Offer a variety of spaces that include different furnishings, computing, and technology options. Spaces with noise levels that range from collaborative to very quiet should be available in addition to offering different privacy levels to support both independent and collaborative study.
- Create a space that is conducive to different learning styles and that offers visual cues to support hands-on learning and consultations.
- Plan for more restrooms and additional unisex restrooms.
- Offer students plenty of seating, computing, and whiteboards.
- Be prepared to maintain heavily used furniture and equipment. Furniture should be professionally cleaned and maintained each semester.
- Buy good furniture with warranties.

- Flexibility in space design is important, but offering a variety of ready-made spaces can help students define how they want to use the space as well.
- Ensure there is proper ventilation and that your learning commons areas offer a variety of lighting options.
- Be aware that your new learning commons will be nosier than anyone ever expected.
- Remember that the learning commons is a student space, and be willing to allow students to use the space as they see best. What made sense during the planning stage may not work later as had been anticipated. Be willing to go with the flow.

Communication

- Take the lead among your learning commons partners in establishing communication and setting a tone that will help to facilitate cross-training and to ensure that questions are referred appropriately. It is also important to communicate to building partners that being a library is the library's main function and that the work that students carry out in the library is important.
- Develop relationships with colleagues who will be colocated within your learning commons before the move. Make sure everyone involved knows what a learning commons is and how a learning commons model may change the way work is carried out.
- Maintain ongoing communications about the learning commons project with vested partners and community members at large during the entire process.
- Explain the vision of the learning commons to library staff as the learning commons will involve changes to space as well as to job responsibilities. Everyone needs to feel included and good about the vision. Keep communication open and transparent (no meetings behind closed doors), and include staff in visits to other libraries with learning commons. Remember, developing a learning commons is not all about technology. It's about relationships: relationships with students and relationships with staff. Build spaces and services that nurture these relationships and your learning commons will be successful.
- Make sure students know what a learning commons is, what a learning commons offers, and what they can accomplish in the new space.
- Place ample signage in your learning commons to support students in the successful use of the space.
- Promote your learning commons resources and services actively.

Student Involvement

- Involve students in the planning of your learning commons and in making decisions. Don't just ask them what they want. Include students at the table, making decisions.
- Get students involved in the beginning of your learning commons project so that when it is finally up and running, they will think of it as their own space.
- Consider using a campus student marketing class to carry out a needs assessment for the library and an architecture class to develop initial designs. Many of these ideas could be used in your actual space. This will not only save you work, but it will also generate student ownership of the space. By the time the learning commons opens, everyone will be very excited to see the finished design and space.

- Keep talking to students about what they want to see offered in their learning commons once the space is in use.
- Remember to involve students in the assessment of your learning commons during the post-occupancy phase. Consider focus groups, surveys, and establishing a student advisory board to generate feedback channels.

Technology

- Make a well-trained staff available to assist with a variety of technological questions and needs.
- Collaborate with others on campus to gain support for new technological initiatives and/or to obtain new technologies for your learning commons.
- Offer more electrical outlets than you believe your learning commons space will need.
- Plan a technology infrastructure you can't imagine yet. Assume everything will be different in five years.

ⓖ Best Practices

The lessons-learned responses from the Learning Commons Survey offer many approaches and information in support of developing best practices for carrying out the development of new academic library learning commons spaces. The PIL study (Head 2016) also offers best practices for academic library learning space projects. Table 9.2 illustrates the best practices stated by those interviewed within the PIL study.

Table 9.2. Best Practices for Academic Library Learning Space Projects

	AS STATED BY STAKEHOLDERS PIL INTERVIEWED:		
	LIBRARIANS	ARCHITECTS	CONSULTANTS
1. Talk to librarians, staff, student, and faculty so the design process is inclusive and there is a large amount of user input.	✔	✔	✔
2. Ask lots of questions during design discussions to make sure the opportunity for giving input is not missed.	✔	✔	✔
3. Hire experts to advise where there is a lack of expertise on a project (e.g., project managers, IT specialists, library consultants, civil engineers, and landscape architects).	✔	✔	
4. Be sure to document the planning and design process, so that decisions and outcomes can be revisited and verified.	✔	✔	
5. Develop and document the scope for a project early on; one that has goals that are realistic, affordable, and achievable.		✔	✔

(continued)

Table 9.2. *(continued)*

	AS STATED BY STAKEHOLDERS PIL INTERVIEWED:		
	LIBRARIANS	ARCHITECTS	CONSULTANTS
6. Ensure there is a shared vision for a design across all library units before renovation or building of a new structure begins.	✔		✔
7. Hold frequent check-in meetings with individual library units (e.g., circulation or reference) and also bring everyone together in library-wide meetings.	✔		
8. Tour other campus libraries (and new learning spaces) to find out what design worked well, and what did not.	✔		
9. Find champions within the faculty to communicate the value of the project, since faculty often needs to be convinced how new spaces will impact their research and teaching.	✔		✔
10. Have continuous communication with campus constituents about the project's progress. Use different channels (e.g., web, social media, in person presentations given at request of departments).	✔		
11. Trust the architectural design process, it's intentionally slow so there is a greater sense of ownership for a project as it develops.		✔	
12. Conduct continual user assessments of what needs are (and are not) being met. Modify design goals to resolve problems.	✔		
13. Create and sign a Memo of Understanding (MOU) between the library and learning partners, especially when partners are contributing funds for space in the library.	✔		
14. Make sure the architectural firm and the construction company have an integrated process for the construction phase of library spaces.	✔		
15. Provide a translation session between librarians and architects to define architectural vocabulary to help manage expectations.	✔		
16. Good lighting and the proper acoustic treatment are necessary to the success of library projects.		✔	
17. Anticipate change 10 years from now, so that spaces can expand and contract as needed. Plan for flexible designs.		✔	✔

Source: Head, Alison J. 2016. *Planning and Designing Library Learning Spaces: Expert Perspectives of Architects, Librarians, and Library Consultants*. Project Information Literacy Research Report, Practitioner Series. Seattle: University of Washington. www .projectinfolit.org/uploads/2/7/5/4/27541717/pil_libspace_report_12_6_16.pdf.

Note: Ordered from most to least mentioned best practices in interviewees' discussions about their projects. N=49 stakeholders, N=22 academic library learning space projects. Some of the best practices listed may be additional to the themes discussed in the "Detailed Findings" section of the PIL report.

⑥ Key Points

Preassessment and postevaluation of your learning commons offerings and space will be essential to the success of your new space and necessary to support students in your learning commons moving forward. Being mindful of the many hidden pitfalls that exist with such an undertaking, and considering the many lessons learned of colleagues who have previously carried out such an endeavor, you and your team will want to keep in mind the following recommendations:

- New and more established academic library assessment methods, software tools (Tableau and Suma), and emerging practices will help shape your post-occupancy learning commons assessment strategies.
- A campus and/or peer institution assessment expert who has experience in academic space usage assessment can be consulted during the planning phase of the project.
- It will be important for all stakeholders and personnel to be involved in your assessment strategies for an inclusive process.
- Student involvement in the beginning of your learning commons project will be essential so that when it is finally up and running, students will think of it as their own space.
- The learning commons team will need to plan the resources and services that will be offered in your learning commons but also include a means for supporting, sustaining, and promoting these offerings. Learning commons resources, services, and programming must be grounded in a clear sense of ownership and ongoing support.
- Learning commons user data must be collected and analyzed at the department levels in order to obtain department-based input and evidence.
- After your learning commons becomes popular, everyone will want to be a part of your new space. It will be essential to include librarians in the continuous campus learning commons conversation in order to develop and preserve library space for library use.
- Offering a variety of spaces that include different furnishings, computing, and technology options will support learning. Spaces with noise levels that range from collaborative to very quiet should be available in addition to offering different privacy levels to support both independent and collaborative study.
- When possible, it will be helpful to develop relationships with colleagues who will be colocated within your learning commons before they move in. During the course of communications, everyone involved in the process must know what a learning commons is and how a learning commons model may change the way work is carried out.
- An effective technology infrastructure plan will project five years into the future and yet still be flexible, as everything will be different in five years.

In the next chapter, the importance of developing successful learning commons partnerships will be addressed. Strategies for collaborating with a variety of campus colleagues and units will be identified, and services and collaborative partnerships reported in the Learning Commons Survey will be discussed.

⦿ References

Bailin, Kylie. 2011. "Changes in Academic Library Space: A Case Study at the University of New South Wales." *Australian Academic & Research Libraries* 42, no. 4: 342–59. doi:10.1080/0004 8623.2011.10722245.

Bryant, Joanna, Graham Matthews, and Graham Walton. 2009. "Academic Libraries and Social and Learning Space: A Case Study of Loughborough University Library, UK." *Journal of Librarianship and Information Science* 41, no. 1: 7–18. doi:10.1177/0961000608099895.

Carpenter, Cathy. 2011. "Transforming the Georgia Tech Architecture Library into a Social Space." *Art Documentation: Journal of the Art Libraries Society of North America* 30, no. 1: 79–83. www.jstor.org.libproxy.csun.edu/stable/27949571.

Chan, Diana, and Edward Spodick. 2014. "Space Development." *New Library World* 115, nos. 5/6: 250–62. *Art Documentation: Journal of the Art Libraries Society of North America* 30, no. 1: 79–83. doi:10.1108/ NLW-04-2014-0042.

Dallis, Diane. 2016. "Scholars and Learners: A Case Study of New Library Spaces at Indiana University." *New Library World* 117, nos. 1/2: 35–48. doi:10.1108/NLW-04-2015-0023.

Faber, Maggie. 2016. "Library Space Assessment in Tableau: A Step by Step Guide to Custom Polygon Maps and Dashboard Actions," *visualibrarian* (blog), October 7, 2016. https:// visualibrarian.wordpress.com/2016/10/07/library-space-assessment-in-tableau-a-step-by -step-guide-to-custom-polygon-maps-and-dashboard-actions/.

Harrop, Deborah, and Bea Turpin. 2013. "A Study Exploring Learners' Informal Learning Space Behaviors, Attitudes, and Preferences." *New Review of Academic Librarianship* 19, no. 1: 58–77. doi:10.1080/13614533.2013.740961.

Head, Alison J. 2016. *Planning and Designing Academic Library Learning Spaces: Expert Perspectives of Architects, Librarians, and Library Consultants.* Project Information Literacy Research Report. Practitioner Series. Seattle: University of Washington. www.projectinfolit.org/uploads/ 2/7/5/4/27541717/pil_libspace_report_12_6_16.pdf.

Kinsley, Kirsten, Rachel Besara, Abby Scheel, Gloria Colvin, Jessica Evans Brady, and Melissa Burel. 2015. "Graduate Conversations: Assessing the Space Needs of Graduate Students." *College & Research Libraries* 76, no. 6: 756–70. doi:10.5860/crl.76.6.756.

Lanclos, Donna, and Andrew D. Asher. 2016. "'Ethnographish': The State of the Ethnography in Libraries." *Weave: Journal of Library User Experience* 1, no. 5. https://quod.lib.umich.edu/w/ weave/12535642.0001.503?view=text;rgn=main.

Lange, Jessica, and Sara Holder. 2014. "Looking and Listening: A Mixed-Methods Study of Space Use and User Satisfaction." *Evidence Based Library and Information Practice* 9, no. 3: 4–27. doi:10.18438/B8303T.

Mathews, Brian. 2011. "Building a Competitive Advantage." *American Libraries*, October 28, 2011. https://americanlibrariesmagazine.org/2011/10/28/building-a-competitive-advantage.

May, Francine, and Alice Swabey. 2015. "Using and Experiencing the Academic Library: A Multisite Observational Study of Space and Place." *College & Research Libraries* 76, no. 6: 771–95. DOI 10.5860/crl.76.6.771.

Montgomery, Susan E. 2014. "Library Space Assessment: User Learning Behaviors in the Library." *Journal of Academic Librarianship* 40, no. 1: 70–75. https://scholarship.rollins.edu/cgi/ viewcontent.cgi?article=1216&context=as_facpub.

Murphy, Sarah. 2015. "How Data Visualization Supports Academic Library Assessment: Three Examples from the Ohio State University Libraries Using Tableau." *College & Research Libraries News* 76, no. 9: 482. https://crln.acrl.org/index.php/crlnews/article/view/9379/10546.

NCSU (North Carolina State University) Libraries. 2014. "Suma: A Tablet-Based Toolkit for Collecting, Managing and Analyzing Data about the Usage of Physical Spaces." NCSU Libraries website. www.lib.ncsu.edu/projects/suma.

Norton, Hannah F., Linda C. Butson, Michele R. Tennant, and Cecilia E. Botero. 2013. "Space Planning: A Renovation Saga Involving Library Users." *Medical Reference Services Quarterly* 32, no. 2 (April–June): 133–50. doi:10.1080/02763869.2013.776879.

Pierard, Cindy, and Norice Lee. 2011. "Studying Space: Improving Space Planning with User Studies." *Journal of Access Services* 8, no. 4: 190–207. doi:10.1080/15367967.2011.602258.

Raish, Victoria, and Joseph Fennewald. 2016. "Embedded Managers in Informal Learning Spaces." *portal: Libraries and the Academy* 16, no. 4: 793–815. https://muse-jhu-edu.libproxy.csun.edu/article/632346.

Spencer, Mary Ellen, and Sarah Barbara Watstein. 2017. "Academic Library Spaces: Advancing Student Success and Helping Students Thrive." *portal: Libraries and the Academy* 17, no. 2: 389–402. https://muse-jhu-edu.libproxy.csun.edu/article/653212.

Turnbow, Dominique, and Annie Zeidman-Karpinski. 2016. "Don't Use a Hammer When You Need a Screwdriver: How to Use the Right Tools to Create Assessment That Matters." *Communications in Information Literacy* 10, no. 2: 143–62. www.comminfolit.org/index.php?journal=cil&page=article&op=view&path%5B%5D=v10i2p143&path%5B%5D=238.

Successful Learning Commons Partnerships

IT IS NOT UNUSUAL TO FIND an office and/or the personnel of one or multiple student support services units embedded within a library's learning commons floor plan. Indeed, many learning commons housed within academic libraries offer students access to either full service or satellite posts for face-to-face assistance with such campus services as information technology (IT) support, tutoring, career counseling, or student advisement. Initially, most information and learning commons designs incorporated assistance with campus technology assistance units through the addition of IT help desks or increased computer lab presence within a library's commons setting. However, as time has passed, many library design teams opted to incorporate more extensive and collaborative campus programming within their learning commons. The motivation behind these decisions resides in the belief that the placement of these services within the library learning commons will increase a student's proximity to and use of critical support services delivered through student services and/or student affairs divisions or other campus-wide programs and initiatives. Identified learning commons services are typically selected because both library and university administrators firmly believe that their cohabitation with a centralized library building will enhance a student's success and overall engagement with the university's programming and initiatives.

Examining the Evolution of Library-Campus Partnerships within Learning Commons Settings

For over a decade, many academic libraries have built extensive partnerships with various campus programs and student services. Initially, these partnerships emerged to support students' access to computing and information technology and to improve the campus community's recognition and support of the library's information literacy instruction initiatives. As information resources began to go digital in the 1990s, more and more universities began to realize the need to meld library and IT support services. When it became clear that students and faculty needed access to enhanced networked environments, the information commons learning space model gained popularity. The growing need for additional services to holistically support the multitude of student learning needs that require continual attention outside of the traditional classroom setting helped launch today's typical learning commons design, as previously discussed in chapter 1, "Learning Commons Library Spaces."

As Emily Love and Margaret Edwards noted in their article "Forging Inroads Between Libraries and Academic, Multicultural and Student Services," "Since 2005 . . . many academic library partnerships include units such as career centers, writing centers, cultural centers and non-traditional groups such as fraternities, sororities and registered student organizations" (2009, 21). A careful review of current learning commons literature or an online search for existing learning commons partnership programming will reveal the following frequently found campus partners within academic libraries:

- Writing centers
- Tutoring centers
- Information technology help desks
- Advisement centers
- Career services
- Study-abroad centers
- Campus testing centers
- Assistive technology centers/disabled student services

In addition to these more commonly found embedded student support services and offerings, a search of the literature also reveals the growing establishment of embedded campus-wide initiatives being marketed and serviced from within academic library learning commons environments. Examples of campus-wide initiatives services, offices, and/or programs being located or run from within an academic library's learning commons include the following:

- Campus sustainability and recycling programming:
  Oregon State University's Compost Collection Program (Hussong-Christian 2016)
- Wellness and mindfulness:
  Kansas State University and Humboldt State University (Wachter 2018)
- Fitness and health initiatives:
  FitDesk bicycles at Clemson University Library (Chant 2013)
- Veterans support services:
  Veterans Reading Room at the University of Massachusetts Dartmouth Claire T. Carney University Library (Claire T. Carney University Library 2017)

- Community engagement:
  All Pikes Peak Reads (APPR) at Pikes Peak Community College,
  https://libguides.ppcc.edu/events

As Rebecca Sullivan notes often, "In order to enact an institutional mission, a learning commons must reach across campus to form partnerships with other initiatives" (2010, 133). It is important to remember that partnerships, whether forged with units or initiatives, do not have to result in structural mergers with the library to succeed. Citing the sage advice offered in Barbara Fister's 2004 "Common Ground: Libraries and Learning," Sullivan reminds library learning commons planners that partnering units housed within a learning commons do not need to be "administratively merged to work together" (Sullivan 2010, 134). Typically, the intersection of missions and goals matter more than reporting lines when it comes to the factors that ultimately result in successful learning commons partnerships. In addition to forging partnerships to support student learning, many learning commons partnerships also are forged to support faculty teaching and professional development. It is not uncommon to find faculty development centers housed within or nearby a library's learning commons. Other common faculty services housed within learning commons environments also include faculty technology-assistance centers.

⑥ Discussing How Library and Student Services Partnerships Can Strengthen a Learning Commons

For the past fifteen or more years, many academic libraries within the United States have actively participated in a great number of the programs and initiatives that have developed from the emergence of highly successful collaborative programming between student and academic affairs divisions. Examples of such programming include first-year and transfer experience programs, service-learning initiatives, and student-success initiatives. The fact that so many academic libraries now have permanent first-year experience (FYE) librarian positions on staff speaks to the fact that the library's participation in these collaborative programming endeavors has not been halfhearted. Indeed, the active and successful participation of librarians in FYE programming activities such as orientation, common reads, and cohorted curricular learning communities in many ways has paved the way for the newer and noncurricular partnerships that are now emerging within learning commons nationwide. As librarians taught FYE information literacy sessions, helped support common read programming and marketing, and assisted with orientation outreach services, campus administrators took note of the collaborative strengths that a teaching library and its personnel offer the entire campus. The relationships forged among librarians, student affairs staff, and faculty affairs officers in the past decade have truly made the collaborative promise of a learning commons seem bankable to university administrators searching for ways to centrally align and house services. As Nancy Schmidt and Janet Kaufman note, the learning commons model epitomizes the highest complete synthesis of a "one-stop-shop model of academic support services where students can (1) get help with research; (2) obtain assistance with reading, note taking and writing papers; (3) attend a study group; (4) meet with friends to discuss a group project; and (5) access computers to complete their learning tasks" (2007, 243). Alongside each of these services, students typically interact with librarians, faculty, staff, student-service professionals, peer tutors, and information technologists.

Love and Edwards (2009) explain that much of the successes that these typical library student services collaborations achieve are the result of shared goals and missions directed at supporting student success and the similarly aligned academic statuses that librarians and student services professionals hold within the university setting. If academic libraries are willing to expand their vision of what services can be found within their walls while not losing sight of their primary mission and/or surrendering space to potential partners who do not intend to fully collaborate in the long term, then partnerships can succeed and benefit all involved. Anne Moore and Kimberly Wells note that "students embrace the learning commons environment with its integrated social and academic lifestyle. The convenience of academic support services such as reference, technology, writing, advising, and supplemental instruction adds another dimension to higher education success" (2009, 84).

However, housing personnel and services from different units and divisions together under a learning commons umbrella does not automatically result in harmonious communication or clear and consistent customer service. As Bridget Farrell notes, "Ironically, the learning commons' 'one-stop-shop' service model is supposed to simplify service to users, but in learning commons where partners do not communicate clearly or are unfamiliar with other service units, the service model can prove frustrating for users" (2015, 232). There are several key things that need to occur for learning commons partners and partnerships to continue to flourish beyond the ribbon-cutting photo and grand opening. These include

- ensuring, through training, orientations, or annual open-house events, that all staff within the building are familiarized with the services offered in learning commons offices and service desks;
- creating recurring meetings (annually or as needed) to make certain that learning commons partners stay abreast of each other's individual and collaborative initiatives, goals, and needs;
- marketing all learning commons services equally within the library learning commons;
- offering clear physical signage and visible representation on the learning commons website;
- listing all learning commons services on library directories to make students aware that the services are housed within the library;
- working to align operational hours of all learning commons partners to the library's operational hours to thwart the tendency to have closed offices and service points on nights and weekends;
- sharing opportunities, across all services housed within the library, to design assessments that elicit shared feedback from students about their experience in using each and every learning commons service.

🌀 Developing Successful Learning Commons Collaborations

Successful library learning commons partnerships and collaborations with campus units and programs have the ability to streamline student services and at the same time support many university and departmental goals. Such collaborations also establish campus-based networking opportunities, educate others involved in the programming about services of other campus units, raise the visibility of the library on campus, and finally, promote student success (Ferer 2012; Seal 2016; Swartz, Carlisle, and Uyecki 2007). Establishing successful partnerships within a library learning commons space will be a unique undertaking for each institution. Existing resources and available space within a commons can often dictate the types of collaborations that may be beneficial and developed. Available university resources will also play a factor. Considerations for developing a learning commons partnership will reflect the needs and opportunities of each space; however, according to Robert Seal (2016), the following general questions must be asked before attempting to develop any library learning commons partnership:

- What perceived needs are not being met currently?
- What are the ultimate goals of the collaboration?
- How will this collaboration enhance services to current users, students, and faculty?
- What resources will be required for the partnership?
- Where will this new service be offered, and is there space available in the library or somewhere else on campus?
- When will the new service begin to be offered?
- Are there existing library staff members available to undertake the project?
- Have other institutions attempted to carry out the collaboration under consideration?
- If so, what challenges arose during their process? (129)

Once the answers to these questions have been identified, it will be necessary to consider potential campus partners and to determine the resources available and the responsibilities to be undertaken by each partner in order to support the establishment of a successful collaboration. Identifying partners will require an awareness of campus programs and special projects that could potentially share common goals. It will be vital for members on the library learning commons team to be or to become well connected to and knowledgeable about the campus and its many institutional programs and units. Being aware of current academic programming and what is taking place within different departments on campus will assist in identifying partners who will benefit mutually. This may require learning commons project team members and their respective partners to visit each other's spaces and to become knowledgeable about each other's fields. It will also be necessary to become familiar with each other's practices, procedures, services, and resources. Attending presentations or workshops held by the other partner in order to gain firsthand experience of their offerings will be essential (Elmborg 2006; Ferer 2012).

Following the identification of potential partners, the next step in the process will require each party in the collaboration to determine programming goals, the nature of the proposed service, and the responsibilities and desired outcomes for each party (Seal 2016). Library team members and campus partners may want to consider keeping the initial collaborations small but include the opportunity for more growth over time, once initial successes have been achieved. Regular meetings should take place in an effort to provide an opportunity for communication to occur on a regular basis. During these meetings, each partner will have the ability to address issues of concern and/or offer suggestions that support the continued growth of the programming. Early on in the process, it will also be necessary to obtain the support of the library's administration. This will likely include a programming proposal that outlines and communicates the benefits and challenges as well as the perceived needs of the partnership.

Carrying out these steps successfully will serve as the foundation of a collaboration that will have the ability to evolve over time. However, Michele Giglio and Constance

Strickland (2005) emphasize the importance of good communication and listening skills for all parties involved during the ongoing process. They also recommend extending sensitivity to and acceptance of different working styles for everyone within the project. While there are many recommendations to consider for developing a fruitful collaboration, Seal's (2016) elements of success for a meaningful and effective partnership provide an outline of factors to follow:

- Identification of the right partners for collaborating
- Mutual respect and understanding
- Sufficient resources, including space, personnel, and funding
- Administrative support
- Shared goals and values
- A jointly developed memorandum of understanding (MoU)
- Sufficient planning and preparation
- Regular meetings and close communication
- Assessment and adjustments to programming as needed (130)

Developing successful learning commons partnerships with campus units and colleagues provides an opportunity to improve student services and to meet library and campus departmental goals. Existing resources within the library and university will impact the types of collaborations that can be established. However, taking the time to identify campus partners who share mutual goals and to develop programming that addresses your particular library and campus needs has the potential to support a collaboration that will not only serve students well but will also create meaningful and rewarding partnerships among campus colleagues.

Services and Collaborative Partnerships Reported in the Learning Commons Survey

The Learning Commons Survey introduced in chapter 3, "Partnerships and Strategies for Successful Programming," of this book asked participants about the many services offered in their learning commons spaces and about the collaborations that take place in association with those services. Survey respondents reported a variety of services and collaborative arrangements that offer the opportunity to enhance services with campus partners who share mutual programming goals. These services and partnerships provide students with access to state-of-the art technologies, tutoring and writing consultations, and many forms of research assistance through individual service desks and/or blended service desks. Other learning commons services and campus partnerships reported in the survey results include art exhibits, student advisement, and campus-related event programming.

Service Centers

Respondents of the Learning Commons Survey reported offering learning commons service points that varied due to many factors, including type and size of each institution in addition to the available resources of individual campuses and library learning commons spaces. However, the learning commons service centers most cited in the survey results are as follows: fifty-nine (73.75 percent) respondents reported offering reference desks, and nearly as many survey participants, fifty-seven (71.25 percent), reported offering circulation desks. Fifty-one (63.75 percent) respondents reported offering both information technology desks and tutoring or writing centers, while forty-two (52.50 percent) survey participants offer technology-lending centers. Additional services centers are included in figure 10.1, which illustrates the types and number of services reported in the survey. Twenty (25 percent) respondents reported "other" to describe their service centers. The most commonly reported "other" service was single-service-point desks that offered blended services. The types of help reported to take place at these single-service-point desks varied; some desks provided only research and writing support, others offered circulation services and loaning of equipment in one location, and still others provided help in all areas of service and equipment loaning within their learning commons. Finally, multimedia-production service desks or multimedia-production labs were mentioned as individual service centers several times within the survey results comments. See chapter 3, "Partnerships and Strategies for Successful Programming," of this book for previous discussion of learning commons services and service centers.

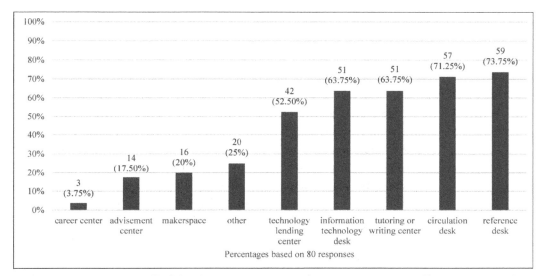

Figure 10.1. What are all of the service centers your learning commons offers to your student users? Select all that apply. *Courtesy of the author*

Support for Technology and Reference Questions

The majority of Learning Commons Survey respondents reported offering staff equipped to answer technology-related questions in their learning commons. When asked, "Do you have a dedicated staff to answer technology-related questions within your commons?" fifty-nine (73.75 percent) respondents answered yes. Twenty-one (26.25 percent) survey participants answered no to this question. When asked, "If you have dedicated staff to answer technology-related questions, is your staff comprised of professionals, students or a combination?" forty-one (51.25 percent) respondents answered a combination of professionals and students provide this service, while eighteen (22.50 percent) survey participants reported they do not offer a dedicated staff for technology-related questions, and seventeen (21.25 percent) respondents reported students provide this service. Finally, four (5 percent) respondents reported professionals as to those who provide this service in their commons. Per the survey results, figure 10.2 illustrates the breakdown of those who answer technology-related questions in learning commons spaces.

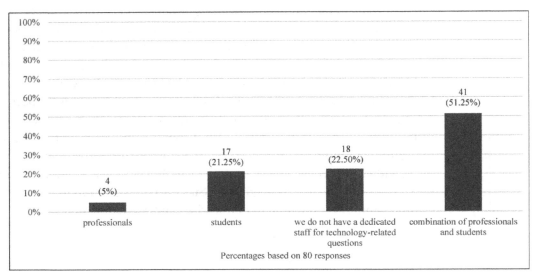

Figure 10.2. If you have dedicated staff to answer technology-related questions, is your staff composed of professionals, students, or a combination? *Courtesy of the author*

Reference assistance was reported to be offered in a variety of formats in most learning commons of those who participated in the Learning Commons Survey. Fifty-eight (72.50 percent) respondents reported offering a reference desk, fifty-seven (71.25 percent) survey participants offer virtual reference, while thirteen (16.25 percent) reported offering roving reference, and three (3.75 percent) reported offering no reference services in their learning commons. Thirty-two (40 percent) people who participated in the survey chose "other" to describe the manner in which they offer reference services in their commons. The most common "other" responses were reference services offered through consultation or appointment, followed by telephone reference and some form of service desk that offered librarian services on call. Several respondents mentioned that reference services were available through a writing and research center, and several other respondents reported librarian assistance available at single-service-point desks such as those that include technology lending and information help. Two respondents reported to house librarian offices in their learning commons. Figure 10.3 illustrates the variety of formats in which reference assistance is provided in the learning commons spaces of survey participants. Those that provide reference assistance in learning commons spaces per the survey results can be seen in figure 10.4. A combination of librarians and/or students and staff provides the majority of reference assistance with forty-six (57.50 percent) of those reporting such a service, while twenty-three (28.75 percent) respondents reported librarians as those who provide reference assistance. An additional discussion of reference services within learning commons offerings can be found in chapter 8, "Teaching and Learning in a Learning Commons Space: Reference Services, Instruction, and Outreach," of this book.

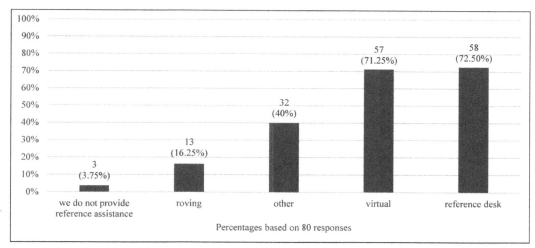

Figure 10.3. In what ways do you provide reference assistance within your learning commons? Select all that apply. *Courtesy of the author*

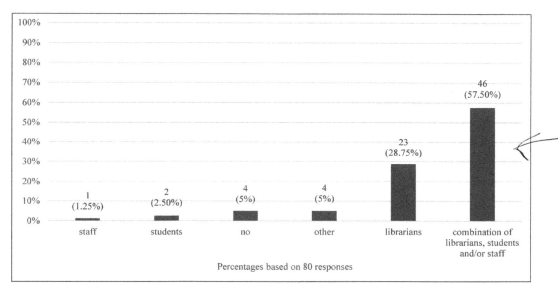

Figure 10.4. Do you have dedicated librarians or staff to answer reference questions within your commons? *Courtesy of the author*

Tutoring and Writing Centers

Tutoring or writing centers were commonly reported services offered in learning commons spaces according to the Learning Commons Survey results. The majority of survey respondents, forty-five (56.25 percent), reported offering a writing or tutoring center in their commons. Nineteen (23.75 percent) of those participating in the survey reported no writing or tutoring center services in their learning commons, while sixteen (20 percent) respondents reported a tutoring center in their library building but not in the learning commons area. Those that provide tutoring and/or writing services in learning commons spaces varied. The majority of respondents, thirty-one (38.75 percent), who offer these services in their commons reported a combination of peer mentors and/or faculty and/ or professional writing instructors/staff as those who provide the tutoring. Twenty-seven (33.75 percent) survey respondents reported peer mentors as those who provide these services. Figure 10.5 illustrates the answers to the question "If your learning commons provides a writing or tutoring center, who provides the tutoring? Select all that apply."

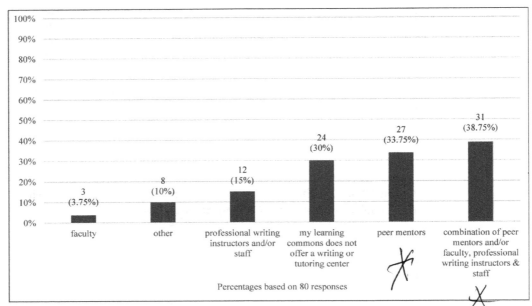

Figure 10.5. If your learning commons provides a writing or tutoring center, who provides the tutoring? Select all that apply. *Courtesy of the author*

Advisement

Although reference assistance and technological and tutoring services have been common offerings in library learning commons spaces for some time, providing formal academic advisement has not been a significant offering within many academic library learning commons spaces in the past. However, a variety of formal and informal advisement has been reported to occur according to the Learning Commons Survey results. Approximately fifteen (18.75 percent) respondents reported to provide advisement services in their learning commons. Eight (10 percent) respondents reported advisement was available in their library building but not within their learning commons, and fifty-seven (71.25 percent) respondents reported offering no advisement in their learning commons spaces or libraries.

Fifteen (18.75 percent) respondents reported campus counselors as those who advise students, while ten (12.50 percent) survey participants reported peer mentors, and finally, two (2.50 percent) faculty members were reported to provide advisement in learning commons spaces. Figure 10.6 illustrates the reported individual groups that provide advisement within learning commons spaces of those who participated in the survey. In addition to the numbers included in figure 10.6, several survey participants commented on other types of informal advisement that take place in the learning commons. It was noted that some first-year advisors use the learning commons space and offer pop-up advisement for students, and other students and faculty meet there as some faculty members hold office hours in the learning commons.

According to the Learning Commons Survey respondents, it is less common for career centers to be housed in learning commons spaces. The majority of respondents

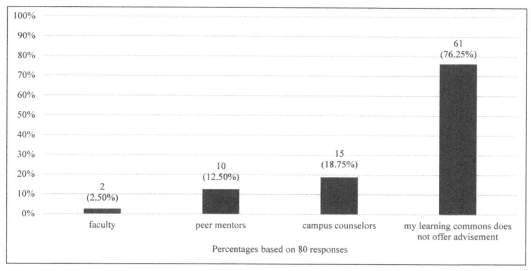

Figure 10.6. If your learning commons offers advisement, who serves as the advisors? Select all that apply. *Courtesy of the author*

of the Learning Commons Survey, seventy (87.50 percent), responded no to offering a career center in their learning commons. Six (7.50 percent) survey participants reported to offer a career center in the library building but not in their learning commons, and four (5 percent) survey respondents reported to house a career center in their commons space.

Art Exhibits and Gallery Spaces

The respondents of the Learning Commons Survey who reported to offer gallery space and/or who display art in their learning commons described a variety of partnerships and methods for showcasing art. The answers to the questions "Does your learning commons offer gallery space? If so, what types of shows/art are displayed and what makes your gallery space unique?" are illustrated in figure 10.7. Thirty-five (43.75 percent) respondents reported offering a gallery space in their learning commons, while approximately twenty-three (28.75 percent) survey participants responded no to offering a gallery space, and an equal number of respondents, twenty-three (28.75 percent), reported a gallery space in the library building but not in the learning commons.

Many of the respondents provided additional feedback about their partnerships in displaying art in their learning commons through comments. Those who display art in their commons reported their most common method for obtaining and displaying art was to collaborate with campus partners. Those specifically mentioned as campus collaborators include photography instructors and photography clubs, art and photography departments, art and photography classes, as well as obtaining art from the university community as a whole. In addition to partnering with art and photography classes, other classes were mentioned—for example, a botany class collaborated with the campus photography club, whose members took photographs of greenhouses. These photographs were showcased in the learning commons. The comments also indicate that the majority of art displayed in learning commons spaces was student art, followed by art exhibits made up of library special collections materials. Less commonly mentioned art collaborators or art displays

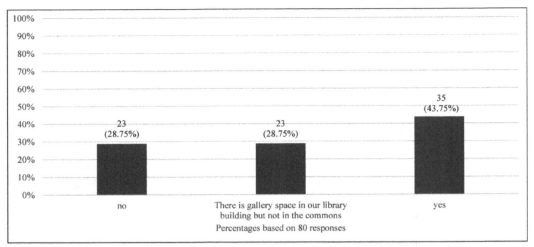

Figure 10.7. Does your learning commons offer gallery space? If so, what types of shows/art are displayed and what makes your gallery space unique? *Courtesy of the author*

include local or visiting artists, permanently installed art and/or electronic or video wall displays. Overall, some respondents reported designated spaces for displaying art in their commons, while others reported using any available space on their learning commons walls in order to showcase works.

Event Programming

Participants of the Learning Commons Survey were asked if they collaborate with campus colleagues and units in order to offer events and programming in their learning commons spaces. The majority of those who responded to the survey, fifty-five (68.75 percent) respondents, answered yes to the question "Do employees in your learning commons collaborate with faculty, departments, or students to develop outreach event programming that takes place in your commons?" Twenty-five (31.25 percent) respondents answered no to collaborating with events that take place in their commons. Chapter 8, "Teaching and Learning in a Learning Commons Space: Reference Services, Instruction, and Outreach," provides further details about the different organizations, departments, and colleagues that collaborate and the variety of events and programming that take place in learning commons spaces.

> The *Learning Commons Benchmarks* study by the Primary Research Group (Primary Research Group Staff 2015) presents further data and information from forty-four college and university learning commons.

🌀 Key Points

Successful learning commons partnerships and collaborations offer networking opportunities with campus colleagues and educate others on campus about library resources and services. Such collaborative programming also raises the visibility of the library on campus and, most importantly, promotes student success. When establishing learning commons partnerships, keep in mind the following recommendations:

- Identified partners should be willing participants interested in long-term collaborations that share student services connections and impact student learning and success.
- Communications between the personnel of all partners need to be clear and consistent.
- Recent assessment data that shows student perceptions of potential partnering services such as campus writing centers, career services, tutoring centers, and so forth will be a useful planning tool.
- Reporting lines may or may not stay the same depending on whether partners are relocating to the learning commons location permanently or as a satellite post.
- Vision, goals, and scope for your learning commons partnerships should be established at the beginning of the collaboration.
- Campus colleagues, units, or departments that share mutual programming goals are good candidates for partnering.
- Administrative support for your collaborations that includes resources, staff, and funding needs to be secured in the early stages of the process.
- Programming partnerships must be assessed and changes made as necessary.

Finally, chapter 11, "The Future of Library Learning Commons Spaces," will consider how dynamic learning commons offerings continue to shape the future of libraries. Trends in learning commons spaces and considerations for developing state-of-the-art makerspaces will also be addressed.

References

Chant, Ian. 2013. "Fit for the Library: Clemson Students Study on Bikes: Clemson Psych Professor to Analyze Results in Study of Exercise and Learning." *Library Journal* 138, no. 19 (2013): 12–14. http://libproxy.csun.edu/login?url=https://search-proquescom.libproxy.csun.edu/docview/1449807208?accountid=7285.

Claire T. Carney University Library. 2017. "Veterans Reading Room at UMass Dartmouth Claire T. Carney University Library." North Dartmouth: University of Massachusetts Dartmouth. www.lib.umassd.edu/about/veterans-reading-room-claire-t-carney-library.

Elmborg, James K. 2006. "Locating the Center: Libraries, Writing Centers, and Information Literacy." *Writing Lab Newsletter* 30, no. 6: 7–11. https://ir.uiowa.edu/cgi/viewcontent.cgi?article=1004&context=slis_pubs.

Farrell, Bridget. 2015. "Using Interviews to Improve Relationships with Library Partners: A Case Study." *Reference Services Review* 43, no. 2: 251–61. doi:10.1108/RSR-01-2015-0001.

Ferer, Elise. 2012. "Working Together: Library and Writing Center Collaboration." *Reference Services Review* 40, no. 4: 543–57. doi:10.1108/00907321211277350.

Fister, Barbara. 2004. "Common Ground: Libraries and Learning." *Library Issues* 25, no. 1. http://homepages.gac.edu/~fister/LIcommonground.html.

Giglio, Michele R., and Constance F. Strickland. 2005. "The Wesley College Library and Writing Center: A Case Study in Collaboration." In *Centers for Learning: Writing Centers and Libraries in Collaboration*, edited by James K. Elmborg and S. Hook, 138–47. Chicago: Association of College and Research Libraries.

Hussong-Christian, Uta. 2016. "If You Build It, Will They Sort It? Compost Collection in the Academic Library Learning Commons." *Library Management* 37, nos. 6/7: 340–51. doi:10.1108/LM-04-2016-0026.

Love, Emily, and Margaret B. Edwards. 2009. "Forging Inroads between Libraries and Academic, Multicultural and Student Services." *Reference Services Review* 37, no. 1: 20–29. doi:10.1108/00907320910934968.

Moore, Anne Cooper, and Kimberly A. Wells. 2009. "Connecting 24/5 to Millennials: Providing Academic Support Services from a Learning Commons." *Journal of Academic Librarianship* 35, no. 1: 75–85. doi:10.1016/j.acalib.2008.10.016.

Primary Research Group Staff. 2015. *Learning Commons Benchmarks*. New York: Primary Research Group.

Schmidt, Nancy, and Janet Kaufman. 2007. "Learning Commons: Bridging the Academic and Student Affairs Divide to Enhance Learning across Campus." *Research Strategies* 20: 242–56. doi:10.1016/j.resstr.2006.12.002.

Seal, Robert A. 2016. "Resource Sharing Begins at Home: Opportunities for Library Partnerships on a University Campus." *Interlending & Document Supply* 44, no. 3: 127–34. doi:10.1108/ILDS-01-2016-0003.

Sullivan, Rebecca M. 2010. "Common Knowledge: Learning Spaces in Academic Libraries." *College & Undergraduate Libraries* 17: 130–48. doi:10.1016/j.resstr.2006.12.002.

Swartz, Pauline S., Brian A. Carlisle, and E. Chisato Uyeki. 2007. "Libraries and Student Affairs: Partners for Student Success." *Reference Services Review* 35, no. 1: 109–22. doi:10.1108/00907320710729409.

Wachter, Ronnie. 2018. "A Space Apart: College Libraries Contemplate Meditation Rooms." *American Libraries* 49, nos. 1–2: 14. https://americanlibrariesmagazine.org/2018/01/02/library-meditation-rooms-space-apart/.

CHAPTER 11

The Future of Library Learning Commons Spaces

IN THIS CHAPTER

▷ Exploring popular trends in recent learning commons design

▷ Reviewing the literature on predicted future features of library learning spaces

▷ Defining library learning commons makerspaces

▷ Considering future expansion opportunities for learning commons spaces

---

UCH HAS BEEN WRITTEN about the future of libraries and library space design. In the last two decades, the immense growth of information available via the Internet and the overall impact of the digital age have changed the parameters of discussions about the future of libraries in terms of their mission, acquisitions foci, and physical layouts in general. In fact, the growth of online resources available to libraries in the 1990s led many people to question if libraries even had a future. Many wrongly predicted that people would stop coming into libraries altogether. As Kathleen Crowe notes in the preface to *The Future of Library Space*, "They couldn't have been more wrong! Libraries have transformed their foci from being repositories for materials into thriving centers for their communities where people gather to learn, collaborate and create" (2017b, xiii).

Many libraries, such as those surveyed for this book, have already begun to physically transform their floor layouts and related programming to accommodate their users' needs while simultaneously working toward establishing new spaces and programming that foster both future growth and the library's sustained grounding as a pivotal hub of learning on their college campus. In doing so, some libraries have launched learning commons within their new, reinvigorated library spaces that feature creative spaces that allow for both socialization and learning for students to work within. Others have added new learning spaces and more cutting-edge and technology-driven services without establishing a formal learning commons within their library building. Determining how a library learning space will be programmed, whether the new area is ultimately called a *learning commons* or not, is no easy task. Politics, funding, and the competing needs of any library's potential collaborative partners or donors, who may be needed to fund a space redesign project, can pose real hurdles that take time to work through.

In the end, if a learning commons design team weighs what services and features students and other stakeholders want against identified library user satisfaction data obtained through assessment efforts, it may be possible to achieve a balanced and successful approach to any new space redesign. The key is to make certain to explore fully and vet all potential space programming options and to resist the external pressure to make decisions based on short timelines or other extenuating circumstances. To fully examine the range of potential space functions, your team will need to become very familiar with all the current trends and possibilities that are currently being employed or theorized for learning commons programming. The space planning team also needs to learn something about how to best approach planning for a library's future space needs. It is critical to never lose sight of the fact that your library's space is likely finite, and programming and building mistakes are costly and can linger in a building for years to come. Your planning team will need to choose wisely and not give in to foolhardy space concepts that do not take student needs or the central library mission into account.

> Knowing the user community and having a thorough understanding of the mission and strategic direction of the library and/or the organizations of which it is a part is extremely helpful in another way; saying a firm "no" to some new idea. There are more opportunities and ideas for creative spaces than there will ever be time or money or personnel to implement. It is crucial to be able to draw lines around the services and technologies on offer and say, "We do this, yes, but we don't do that." (Johnson 2017, 27)

Inevitably, during any leaning commons design or even a learning commons expansion plan phase, a learning commons team will be approached by a campus administrator or another stakeholder, external to the library, who passionately believes that the library can afford to give up space for a new or relocating concept, program, or service. It is imperative that your team weigh how each proposed space concept will impact students, staffing, services, and the physical atmosphere within the building now and in the future. Many current and popular library learning commons space programming trends may not remain viable in the next five to ten years. Many campus leaders positioned outside the library are likely reading futurist articles that focus on higher education trends, and they may not be aware of the realities of your library and its operations. This is especially true when one considers the fast pace with which technologies are emerging and changing within libraries and college campuses. Therefore, it is imperative for your team to scrutinize what futurists are calling for and then compare those options with what your local assessment leads you to believe may work best for your library learning space and users.

⑥ Exploring the Current Trends in Library Future Planning and Learning Commons Design

In a July 2014 article that appeared in *portal*, Brian Mathews extended some sage advice to librarians. Mathews wrote,

> Librarians could discuss ad infinitum the predictions, proclamations, worries, fears, hopes, and dreams about what libraries are becoming. In fact, as a profession, librarians are ob-

sessed with talking about our future. Books, articles, blog posts, conference sessions, and webinars offer a steady stream of speculation. But honestly, all of this speculation does not matter. *We should not concern ourselves with the future of libraries.* Instead, we should focus on the factors driving change within the communities we serve and partner with. (2014, 460)

Mathews goes on to state that is it imperative for library leaders to be both cautious and strategic when thinking about the future. He implores us that it is most important to examine how librarians are thinking about the future rather than merely reviewing the latest trends and projections that futurists and technologists are prognosticating for today's and tomorrow's libraries. Indeed, an online search of the literature on library scenario planning and/or libraries of the future yields a large volume of results. Some recent helpful publications and blog posts that may be insightful to read when pondering the future of library space and academic libraries in general include *The Future of Library Space* (Hines and Crowe 2017); "Back to the Future: From Book Warehouses to Library Learning Commons" (Uzwyshyn 2017); "Space: The Final Frontier" (Little 2014); and "Thirty Trends Shaping the Future of Academic Libraries" (Attis and Koproske 2013).

In addition to those articles that focus on emerging future trends, Barbara Blummer and Jeffrey Kenton (2017) have written an exhaustive literature review focused on identifying learning commons themes in academic libraries. Their research found 103 articles published since 2001 that describe learning commons development themes and highlight the increasing importance that learning commons spaces are playing within academic libraries. Beyond the Primary Research Group's 2015 *Learning Commons Benchmarks* (Primary Research Group Staff 2015) and Project Information Literacy's 2016 *Planning and Designing Academic Library Learning Spaces* publications (Head 2016), there are no other truly significant studies that examine the current programmatic trends occurring within learning commons layouts. The research conducted for this book suggests that the following elements are becoming the most visible programmatic spaces gaining popularity within academic library learning commons designs:

- Writing centers
- Student-advising centers
- Tutoring centers
- Presentation rehearsal rooms
- Exhibition spaces
- Technology centers
- Digitization centers
- Data-visualization centers
- 3D printing labs
- Makerspaces

The key commonality that almost all the above-listed possible learning commons services or areas share is that they all represent an element of creation taking place within libraries. Unlike past library service points, where students would come to access previously stored created information, almost all of these possible learning commons elements allow for students to create or get assistance in creating/authoring something. They share a commonality that supports a maker mind-set or what Emily Thompson describes as a "maker mentality" (Thompson 2013). Thompson posits that the maker mentality is already present within academic libraries when librarians consider that students produce and create when they write, discuss, and share. Some students and majors may be more inclined to discover a way to express their ideas beyond writing by venturing into the realm of turning an idea or concept into a physical reality. In short, when library programming focuses more on creating and learning with new media rather than just acquiring and marketing shiny new tools—such as 3D printers—that students may use to create something, libraries are fully embracing the maker culture and maker mind-set.

David Lang, the author of *Zero to Maker* (2017), contends in his chapter titled "Maker Mentality" that a maker mind-set values sharing what you know and going beyond learning a tool or technology to embracing the mind-set that you ultimately create with your mind, not just with your hands or implements. While the sentiments of Thompson (2013) and Lang (2017) are valid, many library leaders are looking to create dedicated spaces within their learning commons areas that offer students the ability to learn new technologies and explore cutting-edge software and experimentation. These spaces are typically called *makerspaces*, and they have generated the most recent futuristic buzz when many discuss the future of library learning spaces.

ⓖ What Are Library Makerspaces?

Library learning commons spaces have continued to develop and evolve during the last two decades, providing collaborative-learning opportunities that engage students in new and innovative ways. Approximately ten years ago, library makerspaces were first introduced in the United States as a unique space in order to create, experiment, and learn. They are often found within learning commons spaces and can be described by many terms. Erin Fisher defines makerspaces as places where students come together to build and design projects. These spaces "typically provide access to materials, tools, and technologies to allow for hands-on exploration and participatory learning" (Fisher 2012). Many library learning commons spaces are now either incorporating makerspaces or have plans to create makerspaces within their offerings to support the collaborative programming in their commons. These makerspaces provide students with a distinct opportunity to explore in innovative ways. "Makerspaces, sometimes also referred to as hackerspaces or Fab-Labs, are creative, DIY (do-it-yourself) spaces where people can gather to create, invent, and learn. In libraries they often have 3D printers, software, electronics, craft and hardware supplies, and tools, and more" (Willingham and De Boer 2015, 1). According to Heather Moorefield-Lang (2015), no two makerspaces are alike. Some makerspaces focus on technology, with 3D printers, music studios, laser cutters, and computer programming, while others emphasize crafting, painting, or more artistic pursuits. Yet still other makerspaces combine a mix of the arts and technologies.

Alex Baddock (2016) asserts that despite the wide range of makerspace foci, these spaces can be distinguished in different ways depending on the basis of their offerings. It is important for developers of makerspaces to know their users' and curricular needs as there are a variety of tools and materials to be offered in these spaces; however, there are essentially two different types of equipment found in library makerspaces. "Dirty" equipment includes tools that leave a lot of dust and debris with use, while "clean" equipment does not leave any remains with use, and so the "clean" equipment does not have the potential to impact other equipment in a negative manner. Both types of resources provide distinct opportunities for creation and learning. "Dirty" equipment includes table saws, drill presses, computer numerical control (CNC) lathes, routers, mills, and other manual tools. "Clean" equipment includes 3D printers, 3D scanners, vinyl and laser cutters, injection molders, vacuum formers, and computers. If a makerspace includes both "dirty" and "clean" equipment, there should always be designated "dirty" and "clean" spaces, as the two spaces need to be clearly separated, even if the separation is a collapsible wall. Without a separation, there will be the risk of dust and debris infiltrating costly "clean" equipment (Baddock 2016). Regardless of the specific types of tools offered, overall a makerspace can be "define[d] by what it enables: making" (Maker Media 2013, 1). Due to the variety of participatory learning opportunities that makerspaces provide, they will continue to develop and grow in libraries and in library learning commons spaces.

Considerations for Developing a Makerspace

Developing a makerspace in a library learning commons will require teamwork on the part of those within the library and campus community as well as university stakeholders. Many reputable guides and resources exist that provide step-by-step information about how to develop a library learning commons makerspace. The following contains general recommendations, with references to other detailed resources, for undertaking such a project. However, to begin the process of developing a learning commons makerspace, a needs assessment must be carried out in order to determine the type of makerspace—"clean," "dirty," or both—that will support curricular, student-body, and campus-community needs. Stakeholders within and outside the library will need to be identified and committees or teams developed in order to begin building a foundation for the project. These project development teams will help to coordinate the production and communication of the project. Architects and designers will also play a role in determining the scope, design, and overall plans for the new makerspace. The development of a makerspace will require its own budget, distinct from a learning commons budget, and as such it will be necessary for library and/or campus administration to locate sources of funding and to develop a budget for the programming that includes both development and maintenance monies. While there will be those on the project development teams who will help to communicate and market the programming, it will also be the responsibility of the library administration to communicate the project throughout the library as well as campus-wide at meetings, presentations, and town halls. Building support for the project within and outside of the library will help to create an inclusive environment in which those within the library and on campus, not just those on the project development teams, feel a connection to and/or ownership of the new space. Finally, assessment strategies and tools must be carried out annually in order to determine the effectiveness of the offerings and programming. Changes must be made accordingly using the assessment feedback. There are many considerations to keep in mind when undertaking the development of a new library learning commons makerspace. However, the following are twelve questions to ask when planning a learning commons makerspace, loosely based on architect Tiffany Nash's (2017) recommendations:

1. Who will use the space?
2. What are the curricular goals of the makerspace, if any?
3. How will the space be used, and what will be the focus of the space (dirty, clean, or both)?

4. How will the makerspace be funded, and will the funding include maintenance costs?
5. What campus colleagues, faculty, units, and/or library staff will serve on the teams to develop the makerspace?
6. What architects and/or designers are available to serve on the project?
7. Where is the best location for the makerspace?
8. Who will staff the makerspace, and what space will be needed for staffing?
9. What will be the storage needs for the makerspace?
10. What will be the lighting, electrical, and mechanical needs of the space?
11. What will be needed for technology, display, and audiovisual needs and support for these technologies?
12. What will be needed for soundproofing, enclosures, furniture, and flooring?

Identifying the answers to these questions will be the beginning of the process in developing a new library learning commons makerspace. For further reading and information for creating a library makerspace, see *Makerspaces in Libraries* (Willingham and De Boer 2015); *Makerspaces: A Practical Guide for Librarians* (Burke and Kroski 2018); and *Library Makerspaces: The Complete Guide* (Willingham 2018).

Learning Commons Survey Results

The Learning Commons Survey, introduced in chapter 3, "Partnerships and Strategies for Successful Programming," of this book, asked participants about the existence of makerspaces in their learning commons offerings. When asked, "Does your learning commons provide a makerspace or another form of media lab that provides resources for students to work on digital design projects? If so, what is this space called and what is its focus?" more than thirty (37.50 percent) respondents reported offering a makerspace or media lab, while approximately fifty (62.50 percent) respondents answered no to this question. Figure 11.1. illustrates the Learning Commons Survey results for the number of learning commons that offer makerspaces or media labs.

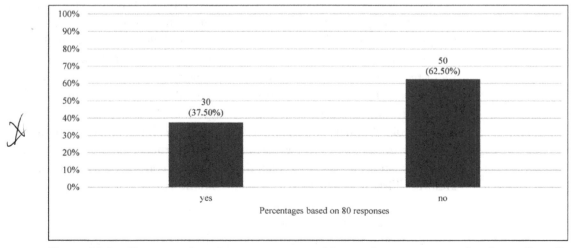

Figure 11.1. Does your learning commons provide a makerspace or another form of media lab that provides resources for students to work on digital design projects? If so, what is this space called and what is its focus? *Courtesy of the author*

Those who provided additional feedback about their makerspaces reported using a variety of names to call these spaces. The word *media* was the most commonly reported word to be used to describe the makerspaces of those who completed the survey. Many respondents reported calling their makerspace some form of *media lab*, *media center*, or *media services*, followed by calling their spaces different forms of *digital studios* or *technology centers*. Others combined several of these terms to describe their spaces as some form of *digital media center*, *lab*, or *digital commons*. Finally, a handful of respondents reported using the word *maker*, such as *makerspace*, *maker commons*, or *maker lab*, when referring to their makerspace offerings. These comments from the Learning Commons Survey about what makerspaces are being called within learning commons spaces suggest that those who have developed makerspaces within their programming name these spaces to reflect their unique curricular offerings and their campus and library cultures.

Respondents to the survey also reported a range of foci for their makerspaces. The most commonly reported focus and offering was 3D printing, followed by a multimedia or digital media focus associated with audiovisual projects. A technology focus for makerspaces was mentioned several times. Other noteworthy comments within the survey results included the fact that the makerspaces of those participating in the survey were not always located within their library learning commons. Sometimes their makerspaces were located in another location within the library or in another location on campus.

◎ Themes for Future Expansion Found in the Learning Commons Survey

The Learning Commons Survey also asked survey participants if they would like to further develop any of their learning commons offerings. When asked, "Are there areas in your learning commons you would like to expand upon or develop, and if so, what would they be?" more than sixty-three (78.75 percent) respondents answered yes, while approximately eighteen (22.50 percent) respondents answered no. Figure 11.2 illustrates the Learning Commons Survey results for the number of survey participants who would like to expand their learning commons offerings.

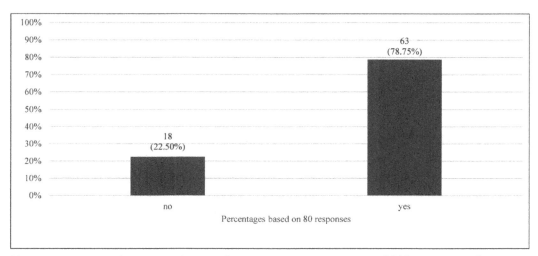

Figure 11.2. Are there areas in your learning commons you would like to expand upon or develop, and if so, what would they be? *Courtesy of the author*

While the majority of respondents reported the desire to expand upon their learning commons offerings, the areas in which they would like to develop varied. However, there were some common themes identified in the responses. The following illustrates the ways in which survey respondents would like to develop or expand their learning commons spaces as found in the comments section of the answer to the question. Comments that are included in the themes below were mentioned at least two or more times by the survey participants.

- **Overall space**—Many of the survey respondents expressed the desire to expand their overall learning commons space into additional areas of their libraries. They would like to add more collaborative open areas and study spaces. Several respondents who have learning commons spaces without cafés noted the desire to add a café. Finally, there were those who participated in the survey who reported the wish to expand the physical space of their learning commons but that no physical space exists for this to occur.
- **Collaboration**—Many of the survey comments noted a desire to develop more partnerships with campus units in their learning commons spaces, and others reported the desire to develop better and more meaningful collaborations with the existing service units in their commons. Adding a writing center was also reported as a means of expansion for many respondents, as was developing more overall programming to take place within their learning commons.
- **Technology**—Respondents of the survey expressed a strong interest in developing makerspaces and/or media labs associated with multimedia production within their learning commons spaces. Instruction and practice presentation rooms for students were also a highly mentioned offering many survey respondents reported to wish to develop. Adding more technology lending and additional information technology support were commonly expressed upgrades to learning commons spaces within the feedback of the survey results. Finally, adding 3D printing and upgrading computers and computer labs were also included within the desires of learning commons expansions.
- **Teaching and learning**—Survey respondents also mentioned the desire to develop research space specifically for faculty members in the form of some sort of faculty development center. Providing specific services for graduate students was also included in the feedback results. Many survey participants commented on the need to develop more group study rooms, and others mentioned adding more overall service support. Expanding book display and/or popular literature sections within learning commons spaces were also mentioned as additional desired offerings.

⑥ Current and Future Learning Commons Spaces

According to Eric D. M. Johnson in "The Right Place at the Right Time: Creative Spaces in Libraries" (2017), much of the focus in libraries has been on making information resources and services available in support of the consumption of content rather than the creation of content. But during the last several decades, there has been a shift in the development of library spaces that provides users with much more ability to create content. Now, due to "falling prices, increased ease of use, supportive communities of users, and expanded familiarity with the products and processes of creative endeavors, library creative spaces are now both socially and fiscally responsible" (Johnson 2017, 3). Johnson asserts that these influences have come together in the early twenty-first century and will continue to influence libraries and their spaces for some time to come. The confluence of four principal threads that have come together to make developing creative library spaces possible are

> a recognition at a societal level of the value and necessity of creativity and related skills and attributes; the philosophies, values, and missions of libraries; the rise of participatory culture benefiting from inexpensive technologies and improved communications; and library experience and historical practice in matters related to creativity. (2017, 24)

Those who are looking to the future of library and learning commons spaces will want to consider the paths that scholarship, education, and technologies are taking and how these paths can merge and intersect. According to Kathryn M. Crowe in *The Future of Library Space* (2017), current and future trends in libraries include the development of digital media centers, gaming labs, makerspaces, and flexible classrooms. She also foresees the likelihood of an increase in offerings related to data visualization, GIS (geographic information systems), and digital humanities. The focus will be on creating and maintaining nimble organizational structures that can respond to user-defined needs, not librarian-defined needs (Crowe 2017). Finally, keep an eye on what the cutting-edge libraries are creating in their spaces and offering with their technologies and services. Looking toward other forward-thinking institutions may provide you and your organization with inspiration concerning how your future spaces may be redefined to meet your own user expectations and needs.

Key Points

Libraries across the country and beyond have been undergoing major changes in their efforts to develop spaces and programming that engage and support innovative student learning during the last two decades. Feedback from the Learning Commons Survey provides insight into future library learning commons programming and where it is headed. As such, it appears that library learning commons spaces will continue to grow and offer new and exciting learning opportunities for students. Technologies, collaborative partnerships, and the continued development of participatory work and study areas, such as learning commons makerspaces, will continue to offer students innovative ways to learn. Aspiring organizations with library learning commons will want to consider the following recommendations for their spaces:

- Examine current popular trends in recent learning commons design.
- Study the current futurist predictions for learning commons space development within higher education.
- Determine if a proposed space and its usage is a good and unique fit for your user population's current and future needs.
- Identify curricular goals and whether your makerspace or media lab will include both "dirty" and "clean" equipment early on in the development of your space.
- Assess all learning commons and makerspace programming and offerings annually, and make changes as necessary.

- Consider the paths that scholarship, education, and technologies are taking and how these paths can merge and intersect.
- Keep an eye on what the cutting-edge libraries are creating in their spaces and offering with their technologies and services.

◎ References

Attis, David, and Colin Koproske. 2013. "Thirty Trends Shaping the Future of Academic Libraries." *Learned Publishing* 26, no. 1: 18–23. doi:10.1087/20130104.

Baddock, Alex. 2016. "6 Essential Tips for Designing Your Makerspace's Layout." *Make:*, September 23, 2016. https://makezine.com/2016/09/23/6-tips-makerspace-layout-design.

Blummer, Barbara, and Jeffrey Kenton. 2017. "Learning Commons in Academic Libraries: Discussing Themes in the Literature from 2001 to the Present." *New Review of Academic Librarianship* 23, no. 4: 329–52. doi:10.1080/13614533.2017.1366925.

Burke, John J. 2018. *Makerspaces: A Practical Guide for Librarians.* 2nd ed. Revised by Ellyssa Kroski. Lanham, MD: Rowman & Littlefield.

Crowe, Kathryn M. 2017a. "The Future of Library Space." SirsiDynix webinar, February 22, 2017. http://go.sirsidynix.com/The-Future-of-Library-Space-SD-Webinar.html.

———. 2017b. "Preface: The Future of Library Space." In *The Future of Library Space*, edited by Samantha Schmehl Hines and Kathryn Moore Crowe, xiii–xvi. *Advances in Library Administration and Organization* 36. Bingely, UK: Emerald Group.

Fisher, Erin. 2012. "Makerspaces Move into Academic Libraries." *ACRL TechConnect* (blog), November 28, 2012. http://acrl.ala.org/techconnect/post/makerspaces-move-into-academic-libraries.

Head, Alison J. 2016. *Planning and Designing Academic Library Learning Spaces: Expert Perspectives of Architects, Librarians, and Library Consultants.* Project Information Literacy Research Report. Practitioner Series. Seattle: University of Washington. www.projectinfolit.org/uploads/2/7/5/4/27541717/pil_libspace_report_12_6_16.pdf.

Hines, Samantha Schmehl, and Kathryn Moore Crowe, eds. 2017. *The Future of Library Space. Advances in Library Administration and Organization* 36. Bingely, UK: Emerald Group.

Johnson, Eric D. M. 2017. "The Right Place at the Right Time: Creative Spaces in Libraries." In *The Future of Library Space*, edited by Samantha Schmehl Hines and Kathryn Moore Crowe, 1–35. *Advances in Library Administration and Organization* 36. Bingely, UK: Emerald Group.

Lang, David. 2017. *Zero to Maker: A Beginner's Guide to the Skills, Tools, and Ideas of the Maker Movement.* San Francisco, CA: Maker Media.

Little, Geoffrey. 2014. "Space: The Final Frontier." *Journal of Academic Librarianship* 40, no. 6: 632–33. doi:10.1016/j.acalib.2014.10.006.

Maker Media. 2013. *Makerspace Playbook.* Sebastopol, CA: Maker Media. https://makered.org/wp-content/uploads/2014/09/Makerspace-Playbook-Feb-2013.pdf.

Mathews, Brian. 2014. "Librarian as Futurist: Changing the Way Libraries Think about the Future." *portal: Libraries and the Academy* 14, no. 3: 453–62. doi:10.1353/pla.2014.0019.

Moorefield-Lang, Heather. 2015. "Change in the Making: Makerspaces and the Ever-Changing Landscape of Libraries." *TechTrends* 59 no. 3: 107–12. https://link.springer.com/content/pdf/10.1007%2Fs11528-015-0860-z.pdf.

Nash, Tiffany. 2017. "10 Questions to Ask before You Plan Your Library Makerspace." *Demco Interiors* (blog), July 5, 2017. http://demcointeriors.com/blog/10-questions-help-plan-library-makerspace.

Primary Research Group Staff. 2015. *Learning Commons Benchmarks.* New York: Primary Research Group.

Thompson, Emily. 2013. "Maker Mentality in the Learning Commons." Morning keynote presented at the Indiana Online Users Group Fall Meeting, Indianapolis, IN, November 1, 2013. https://prezi.com/tqdiwlsmergd/maker-mentality-in-the-learning-commons-iolug -keynote-nov-1-2013/.

Uzwyshyn, Ray. 2017. "Back to the Future: From Book Warehouses to Library Learning Commons." RayUzwyshyn.net. http://rayuzwyshyn.net/TXU2016/BacktotheFutureUzwyshyn.pdf.

Willingham, Theresa. 2018. *Library Makerspaces: The Complete Guide*. Lanham, MD: Rowman & Littlefield.

Willingham, Theresa, and Jeroen De Boer. 2015. *Makerspaces in Libraries*. Lanham, MD: Rowman & Littlefield.

Appendix A: Learning Commons Survey

THANK YOU FOR TAKING THE TIME to share your thoughts about academic library learning commons spaces. This survey is intended for those who work in academic libraries that offer learning commons spaces. We are collecting data for a book to be published with Rowman & Littlefield entitled *Creating a Learning Commons: A Practical Guide for Librarians.*

We estimate that the survey will take 10–20 minutes to complete. *You will have the ability to add to or alter your responses up until the survey closure date of December 19, 2016.*

Thank you,
Lynn Lampert and Coleen Martin
California State University, Northridge
Oviatt Library
lynn.lampert@csun.edu
coleen.martin@csun.edu

1. Do you work in an academic library that offers a learning commons?
   ___ Yes
   ___ No

2. What type of institution are you affiliated with?
   ___ 4-year public
   ___ 4-year private
   ___ 2-year public
   ___ 2-year private
   ___ vocational
   ___ other (please specify)

3. Are you a librarian, staff member, or an administrator at your library?
   ___ librarian
   ___ staff member
   ___ administrator
   ___ other (please specify)

4. Your role and title in the library? (optional)

5. When was your learning commons established or when will it open?

6. Do you have any needs assessment instruments your organization utilized to evaluate the need to establish a learning commons within your library? If so, would you be willing to share these instruments with us?
   ___ Yes
   ___ No
   If you are willing to share your needs assessment instruments with us, please provide the best way to contact you.

7. Do you have planning documents or planning checklists your organization utilized while developing your learning commons? If so, would you be willing to share those documents and/or checklists with us?
   ___ Yes
   ___ No
   If you are willing to share your planning documents with us, please provide the best way to contact you.

8. Would you be willing to share pictures of your learning commons for possible inclusion in our book?
   ___ Yes
   ___ No
   If you are willing to share pictures of your learning commons with us, please provide the best way to contact you.

9. Would you be willing to highlight any specialized area in your commons by writing a short vignette?
   ___ Yes
   ___ No

10. What areas does your learning commons promote or offer in terms of student life and learning? Select all that apply.
    ___ collaborative spaces
    ___ research assistance
    ___ quiet reading spaces/reading support
    ___ writing center
    ___ studying rooms
    ___ tutoring
    ___ advisement
    ___ library instructional classrooms
    ___ computer labs
    ___ makerspaces
    ___ technology support
    ___ equipment checkout
    ___ printing
    ___ community activity space
    ___ café or coffee shop
    ___ campus faculty development center
    ___ other (please specify)

11. Please describe specific types of activities that your users engage in within your learning commons.

12. When developing your learning commons, did your organization carry out a needs assessment specific to technology? If so, would you be willing to share your technology needs assessment instruments with us?
   ___ Yes
   ___ No
   If you are willing to share needs assessment instruments, please provide the best way to contact you.

13. Does your learning commons or library have a technology plan? If yes, would you be willing to share your technology plan with us?
   ___ Yes
   ___ No
   ___ Don't know
   If you are willing to share your technology plan, please provide the best way to contact you.

14. What kinds of technologies does your learning commons offer? Select all that apply.
   ___ laptops
   ___ iPads/tablets
   ___ ereaders
   ___ headphones
   ___ charging stations (groups of electrical outlets for charging)
   ___ wireless charging stations (groups of charging pads or units)
   ___ chargers
   ___ other (please specify)

15. What software programs does your learning commons provide? This can include any software offered in a makerspace.

16. If your learning commons provides charging stations, how many charging stations are available within your commons?
   ___ one designated area with up to 50 outlets
   ___ several designated areas with 50 outlets or more (up to 150 outlets total)
   ___ more than three areas with 50 outlets or more (more than 150 outlets)
   ___ my learning commons does not provide charging stations
   ___ other (please specify)

17. What are the most popular technologies within your learning commons?

18. What types of printing do you offer in your learning commons? Select all that apply.
   ___ black and white
   ___ color
   ___ 3D
   ___ wireless
   ___ double-sided
   ___ other (please specify)

19. Do you have dedicated staff to answer technology-related questions within your commons?
    ___ Yes
    ___ No

20. If you have dedicated staff to answer technology-related questions, is your staff comprised of professionals, students, or a combination?
    ___ professionals
    ___ students
    ___combination of professionals and students
    ___We do not have a dedicated staff for technology-related questions.

21. Does your learning commons offer a café or a way to access food?
    ___ Yes
    ___ No

22. Do you have dedicated librarians or staff to answer reference questions within your commons?
    ___ librarians
    ___ staff
    ___ students
    ___ combination of librarians and/or students and/or staff
    ___ No
    ___ other (please specify)

23. In what ways do you provide reference assistance within your learning commons? Select all that apply.
    ___ reference desk
    ___ roving
    ___ virtual
    ___ We do not provide reference assistance.
    ___ other (please specify)

24. Does your learning commons allow for louder noise?
    ___ Yes
    ___ No

25. Is noise an issue for your students? If so, please explain.
    ___ Yes
    ___ No
    If noise in your learning commons is an issue for your students, please describe here.

26. Do you take steps to assess your learning commons, and if so, what methods do you employ? Select all that apply.
    ___ in-person surveys
    ___ gate count
    ___ headcount or attendance at events
    ___ focus groups
    ___ interviews
    ___ ethnographic tools
    ___ feedback from social media

___ email or library website questionnaires
___ other (please specify)

27. Do you have a successful assessment plan you utilize to gauge the success of your learning commons programming? If so, would you be willing to share this information with us?
___ Yes
___ No
If yes, please list the best way to contact you.

28. Does your learning commons have a career center?
___ Yes
___ No
___ There is a career center in our library building but not in the immediate commons area.

29. Does your learning commons provide student presentation rooms or active learning classrooms that offer specialized technologies (not traditional group study rooms)? If so, what are the technologies offered in these rooms/spaces?
___ Yes
___ No
If technologies are offered, please describe these rooms/classrooms and list the technologies offered.

30. Does your learning commons offer gallery space? If so, what types of shows/art are displayed and what makes your gallery space unique?
___ Yes
___ No
___ There is gallery space in our library building but not in the immediate commons area.
If shows/art are displayed, please describe what makes your gallery space unique.

31. Does your learning commons provide a makerspace or another form of media lab that provides resources for students to work on digital design projects? If so, what is this space called and what is its focus?
___ Yes
___ No
If you provide a makerspace, please describe its name and focus here.

32. Does your learning commons offer advisement?
___ Yes
___ No
___ Advisement is available in our library building but not in the immediate commons area.

33. If your learning commons offers advisement, who serves as the advisors? Select all that apply.
___ campus counselors
___ peer mentors
___ faculty
___ My learning commons does not offer advisement.
___ other (please specify)

34. Does your learning commons offer a writing or tutoring center?
    ___ Yes
    ___ No
    ___ There is a tutoring center in our library building but not in the immediate commons area.

35. If your learning commons provides a writing or tutoring center, who provides the tutoring? Select all that apply.
    ___ peer mentors
    ___ professional writing instructors/staff
    ___ faculty
    ___ combination of peer mentors and/or faculty and/or professional writing instructors/staff
    ___ My learning commons does not offer a writing or tutoring center.
    ___ other (please specify)

36. Do employees in your learning commons collaborate with faculty, departments, or students to develop outreach event programming that takes place in your commons? Examples may include hosting poetry readings, viewing or speaking events, musical performances, and more collaborations specific to your campus.
    ___ Yes
    ___ No

37. If employees in your learning commons collaborate with others on campus to develop outreach event programming that takes place in your commons, please tell us who they collaborate with and the types of events that take place. Examples may include hosting poetry readings, viewing or speaking events, musical performances, and more collaborations specific to your campus. Select all that apply.
    ___ faculty
    ___ departments
    ___ student organizations
    ___ student clubs
    ___ other
    ___ We do not collaborate with campus colleagues or students for outreach event programming.
    If you collaborate, please provide details about the types of events that take place.

38. If you have writing and/or advisement centers within your commons, how well do the library and centers collaborate to integrate services? Select the statement that most closely reflects your situation.
    ___ We are highly collaborative and work together to develop programming.
    ___ We work together but we would like to see more collaboration take place.
    ___ We work in the same area/building but do not collaborate in a measurable fashion.
    ___ other (please specify)

39. What are all of the service centers your learning commons offers to your student users? Select all that apply.
    ___ reference desk
    ___ circulation desk

___ tutoring or writing center

___ advisement center

___ career center

___ makerspace

___ information technology desk

___ technology lending center (for borrowing tablets and laptops etc.)

___ other

Please describe how your service centers may be unique in serving your students.

40. If you have developed successful learning commons programming partnerships, would you be willing to be contacted to provide more specifics about your programming?

___ Yes

___ No

If yes, please provide the best way to contact you.

41. How do you market or promote your learning commons offerings and programming? Select all that apply.

___ library website announcements

___ posters in the library and/or campus

___ banners in library and/or campus

___ flyers in the library and/or campus

___ social media

___ email

___ word of mouth

___ A-frame posters on campus

___ lawn signs on campus

___ campus newspaper ads

___ promotional booths

___ radio ads

___ newsletters

___ other (please specify)

42. Who carries out the marketing and promotion for your learning commons?

___ One individual within the library handles marketing and promotion.

___ A committee or team within the library handles marketing and promotion.

___ other (please specify)

43. Has your learning commons attracted funding from donor support? If so, please describe.

___ Yes

___ No

If your learning commons has attracted donor funding, please describe here.

44. Has your learning commons been recognized for awards based on design or functionality? If so, may we contact you?

___ Yes

___ No

If yes, please provide the best way to contact you here.

45. Are there areas in your learning commons you would like to expand upon or develop, and if so, what would they be?

___ Yes

___ No

If yes, please describe how you would like to further develop your commons.

46. What lessons has your organization learned in developing your learning commons and what advice would you give to those planning to create a commons within their library?

47. May we follow up with a phone call or email to get more detailed information about your learning commons?

___ Yes

___ No

If yes, please specify email or phone.

48. If you would like to share the name of your library with us, please enter it in the box below. (optional)

49. What is the name of your library learning commons (if applicable)? Would you like to share it with us? (optional)

___ My learning commons does not have a specific name.

If your learning commons has a name and you would like to share it with us, please enter it here or skip.

50. Please enter the name of your institution below if you would like to share it with us. (optional)

51. Please list your library's state.

52. Please enter your name if we may contact you. (optional)

53. Please list your email address if we may contact you. (optional)

54. Please enter the best phone number to reach you if we may contact you. (optional)

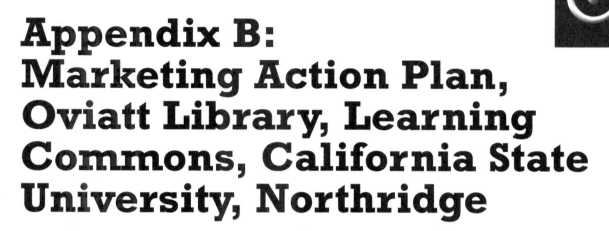

Appendix B: Marketing Action Plan, Oviatt Library, Learning Commons, California State University, Northridge

Share the Commons Experience!—Fall 2013

⊚ Raising Awareness: February to May 2013

- Stakeholder presentations to select groups of students, faculty, and staff (carried out by library dean, associate dean, and department chairs)
- Classroom presentations (carried out by librarians)
- Department presentations (carried out by library administration and librarians)
- Public relations—campus newspaper, meeting with editor, construction tour, constant updates, media alerts 8/13, grand opening press release (carried out by associate dean and library communications staff member)

⊚ Implementation

Phase 1: Building Anticipation: "The Learning Commons Is Coming"

4/16/13—**Launch the Learning Commons Marketing Campaign:** The goal of phase 1 is to create buzz that the learning commons is coming. The date or details will not be revealed at this stage.

4/16/13—Online Marketing: Begin posting "Share the Commons Experience" on Facebook and #campaigntagline on Twitter. Run ads on the library website banner. Create library webpage and blog describing the learning commons construction process and upcoming offerings of the new commons. All online marketing tactics will have a link to the library website. (Carried out by two librarians, webmaster, and webmaster assistant)

4/16/13—Chalking: Using sidewalk chalk, write ("chalk") "Share the Commons Experience" and library.csun.edu/evolution by Sierra Tower and by Freudian Sip, University Student Union. (Carried out by student assistants overseen by librarian or staff member)

4/16/13—Lobby Signage: Hang one large banner in the lobby that reads "Share the Commons Experience" and includes the blog URL in addition to two column banners that advertise the commons. Two learning commons "safety" posters (due to construction) will be placed within the entrance of the lobby (entrance and exit of escalators). These posters will describe the construction timeline. Five adhesive window messages that say "Pardon our dust during construction" will be placed on entrance doors. (Carried out by in-house graphic designer, librarian, and staff member)

4/16/13—Email Message: Send an email blast message to library-subscribed members and all campus communicators with the phrase "Share the Commons Experience" and a link to the learning commons blog. Ten lucky winners who reply "I'm in!" will receive a learning commons giveaway. Instructions about how to reply will be prominent on the oviatt.csun.edu homepage. (Carried out by library communications staff member and librarian)

4/16/13—*Sundial* Ads: Run print and online/mobile ads beginning 4/16. These ads will inform readers of the upcoming learning commons. Several of the ads will include contests such as completing a crossword puzzle, Sudoku, and matching games in order to win a "Share the Commons Experience" T-shirt. (Carried out by in-house graphic designer and librarian)

4/16/13—"Share the Commons Experience" Printed Materials: 155 posters; 5,000 fliers; 20 lawn signs; 20 A-frames; and 3 banners (1 Eucalyptus Hall and 2 University Student Union [USU]). All printed materials will include a QR code and the URL for blog. The QR code will link to a video after May 6. (Carried out by in-house graphic designer and librarian)

4/16/13—"Share the Commons Experience" Buttons: Provide all library staff and student assistants with promotional buttons. Everyone in the library will wear buttons to entice questions regarding the grand opening date. When asked about the button, participants will give the patron a "Share the Commons Experience" flier. (Carried out by in-house graphic designer, librarian, staff member, and student assistants)

5/1/13—400 "Learning Commons" Internal T-Shirts: Staff and student assistants will be given a "Share the Learning Commons Experience" T-shirt to wear to promote the commons. (Carried out by student assistants, managed by staff member and librarian)

5/1/13—Freudian Sip Coffee Sleeves: "Share the Commons Experience" coffee sleeves will be distributed to all Freudian Sip locations on campus. There will be twelve cases of coffee sleeves, which equates to 14,400 sleeves made with recycled newspaper. The main goal is to raise awareness about the learning commons. (Carried out by in-house graphic designer and librarian)

5/6/13—Introduce the *Learning Commons* video on the library's websites, YouTube, Pinterest, Facebook, and Twitter. (Carried out by an in-house video production team, which includes two staff members, a librarian, and a student assistant. A library communications staff member will help to distribute the video once it is completed.)

5/6 to 7/31/13—Continuation of Phase 1: Lawn signs, posters, banners, and fliers will still be displayed within the library and on campus grounds. Online marketing also will continue with the use of social media.

Phase 2: Grand Opening Ramp-Up

8/1/13—Introduce the Second Phase of the Learning Evolution Campaign: This phase will focus on the promotion of the grand opening. The grand opening date will be introduced. Marketing materials must include the date or a countdown timer.

8/1 to 8/24/13—New Student Orientation: Set up promotional booths at each day of orientation to provide giveaways and promote the grand opening. Present information via video and in-person presentations. Five thousand grand opening fliers will be distributed at new student orientation booths as well as at the library, dorms, Redwood Hall, Sierra Hall, USU, Student Recreation Center (SRC), Satellite Student Union (SSU), and targeted classrooms throughout campus. (Volunteers will serve at the booths [approximately ten] and materials will be coordinated by a librarian. The volunteers can be librarians or staff members.)

8/1/13 to October Opening—Online Marketing: Post "Share the Commons Experience at the Grand Opening on October 3" on Facebook and #LearnCommons on Twitter. Introduce countdown timer on the front page of the Oviatt website. Send an email blast message to your listserv. Run ads on the Oviatt website banner. (Carried out by two librarians, a library communications staff member, and the webmaster)

8/1/13—"Share the Commons Experience" Printed Materials: 155 posters; 2,500 fliers; 20 lawn signs; 20 A-frames; and 3 banners (1 Eucalyptus Hall, 1 on library, and 1 at USU). All printed materials will include a QR code and the Oviatt/Evolution website. (Carried out by in-house graphic designer, librarian, staff member, and a team of student assistants)

8/1/13—*Sundial* Ads: Run print and online/mobile ads beginning 8/1. These ads will promote the grand opening and include a contest to win a free "Share the Commons Experience" T-shirt. (Carried out by in-house graphic designer, librarian, and staff member)

8/1/13—Chalking: Chalk "The Commons Experience Is Here!" along with grand opening details, the event date, and the website on sidewalks by Sierra Tower and by Freudian Sip, USU. (Carried out by student assistants overseen by a staff member or librarian)

Late August—Table Tents: Table tents promoting the commons and the grand opening will be placed on tables in the Plaza del Sol and at all The University

Corporation (TUC) food courts (library, Arbor Grill, Freudian Sip, Sierra Center, Geronimo's, Pub Sports Grill, and Book Store Food Court; carried out by in-house graphic designer, a librarian, and several student assistants)

8/24/13—Dorm Displays: Print approximately seventy 22" x 34" posters with grand opening graphics to place on each floor of campus dorm displays. (Carried out by in-house graphic designer and a team of student assistants managed by a librarian)

8/24/13—Start of the Facebook Contest: Have the library's website banner promote "Share the Commons Experience" and link students to a set of instructions. For example, "Share the Commons Experience on Facebook." Enter those students who share about the learning commons grand opening in a raffle to win a Samsung mini tablet. Place posters and fliers on each floor of the library to promote the Facebook contest. The winner will be announced soon after the grand opening and featured on the library's blog. (Carried out by two staff members and a librarian)

9/13—On three separate occasions, set up marketing tables with fliers and giveaways to promote awareness about the learning commons. Give away popcorn, candy, and T-shirts and offer students an opportunity to enter in a raffle for two movie passes. (Carried out by volunteers of several librarians and staff members coordinated by librarian)

Mid-September—Introduce the time-lapse *Learning Commons* video on the library's website, YouTube, Pinterest, Facebook, and Twitter. (Carried out by an in-house video production team, which includes two staff members, a librarian, and a student assistant. A library communications staff member will help to distribute the video once it is completed.)

Day of Event and Mid-October

10/3/13—Online Marketing: The goal is to create a buzz about the grand opening. Start posting comments like "The Commons Experience is HERE!" on Facebook and #learningevolved on Twitter. Send an email blast message to the library listserv and run ads on the website. Add an event to the campus calendar of events and submit a request to the California State University, Northridge (CSUN), webmaster to have the event on the CSUN homepage. All online marketing tactics will have a link to the Oviatt blog. (Carried out by two librarians, webmaster, and library communications staff member)

10/3/13—Ten Grand Opening 2' x 3' A-Frame Posters: A-frames will be strategically placed by Sierra Quad, Sierra Food Court, Redwood Hall, Chaparral Walkway, Fitness Centre, Arbor Grill, Matador Bookstore, and in front of the Oviatt Library. Work with Associated Students (A.S.), USU, Matador Involvement Center (MIC)— borrow additional A-frames. (Carried out by staff member or librarian and a team of student assistants)

10/3/13—Twenty Grand Opening Lawn Signs: Grand opening lawn signs will be strategically placed on the east and west sides of the Oviatt Library. (Carried out by staff member or librarian and a team of student assistants)

10/3/13—Grand Opening Banner: Hang one large grand opening banner in front of the library. (Carried out by staff member and librarian)

10/3/13—*Sundial* Ads: Run half-page *Sundial* ads for three consecutive days beginning the day of the event announcing the opening and offerings. (Carried out by in-house graphic artist and librarian)

10/3/13—Grand Opening Giveaway: Distribute 275 special learning commons–branded microfiber cloth giveaways at the event. (Carried out by in-house graphic artist, librarian, and team of student assistants)

Mid-October—Introduce the *Making of the Learning Commons* video on the library's website, YouTube, Pinterest, Facebook, and Twitter. (Carried out by an in-house video production team, which includes two staff members, a librarian, and a student assistant. A library communications staff member will help to distribute the video once it is completed.)

Implementation action plan based on marketing plan by Kevin Lizarraga.

Index

Page references for figures are italicized.

focus groups, 24–25
furniture, 125; ergonomics, 31, 51
furniture fairs, *18*

group study spaces, 25–26, 30–31, 76, 78, 117, 154

information commons, xv–xvi, 85, 103, 134; emergence
    of within academic libraries, 2–5
instructional services, 30, 105–6

Jones, Amber, 51–53

leadership, 17, 21–22, 81
Leadership in Energy and Environmental Design
    (LEED certification), 47
learning commons: best practices, 123–28; *Best
    Practices for Academic Library Learning Space Projects*,
    127–28; budgeting, 59–61; cafes and coffee shops
    within, 17, 30, 76, 104, 117; definition of, 2; design,
    47–49; event programming within, 10, 144; floor
    plans, 20, 29–30, 40, 47, 57; future of, 153–55;
    gallery spaces within, 143–44; growth of physical
    learning commons spaces, 5–6; history of, 1–5; noise
    mitigation within, 57–58; planning methods, 15–27,
    46–47; programming, 20, 29–44, 110, 147–50;
    renovation lessons learned, 123–27; services, 40–42;
    socialization aspects, 29–30, 34, 147; space design,
    24–26, 30–33, 45–47; ties to campus-wide initiatives,
    4, 134–35; trends, 31, 47
learning commons project management teams, 22–23
Learning Commons Benchmarks (Primary Research
    Group), 5, 103, 144, 149
Learning Commons Survey: advisement, 142–43; art
    exhibits and gallery spaces, *144*; campus IT, 81–82;
    design and distribution of, 37–39; event programming,
    144; marketing, *97*; partnerships reported, 138–44;
    popular technologies reported, 85–87; printing,
    87; reference services reported, 103–4; renovations
    lessons learned, 123–27; services centers, *42*, 138–39;
    technology and reference, 139–41; tutoring and
    writing centers, 141–42
Learning Space Rating System, 40, 46
library spaces, 4–5, 7, 26, 51–52, 154–55; future of, 11,
    72, 147–50; trends within United States, 31, 49
LibQual+, 30–31, 121

makerspaces, 11, 78, 80, 117, 150–53
marketing, 91–99; learning commons to students, 18

McKee, Nate, 69–72
Miller, Brent, 49–51

NCSU Learning Space Toolkit. *See* North Carolina
    State University Learning Space Toolkit
noise, 57–58
North Carolina State University Learning Space Toolkit,
    32–33, 46, 72; Learning Space Taxonomy, *33*; *Role of
    the Technologist*, 68

outreach services: best practices, 111–12; events, 108–12;
    opportunities, 107–8; programming, 108–12

partnerships, 40–43, 133–44; advisement, 142–43; art
    exhibits and gallery spaces, 143–44; campus IT,
    81–82; developing campus partnerships, 135–39;
    event programming, 144; first year experience, 135;
    identifying collaborative partners, 133–38; service
    centers and desks, 40–43, 138–39; technology and
    reference, 139–41; tutoring and writing centers,
    141–42
printing, 42, 53, *86–87*; 3D printing, 69, 81–82,
    86–87, 153
programming, 29, 40–43, 147–50; outreach, 108–12;
    partnerships, 133–44; reference and instruction,
    101–5
Project Information Literacy (PIL): 2016 study *Planning
    and Designing Academic Library Learning Spaces*,
    18–19, 105, 123; best practices, 127–28
project manager: interview with a project manager,
    54–57
promotion, 91–99

reference: Learning Commons Survey results, 42–43,
    139; reference collection, 104–5; reference services,
    102–5, 140–41

SCALE-UP Classrooms at North Carolina State
    University, 35–36
services, 40–42; Learning Commons Survey results,
    42–43, *139*; partnerships, 133–44; reference and
    instruction, 101–5; technology loaning centers, 41, 76
space design usage software: FLEXspace, 39–40; Suma
    data collection software, 118–19, 129
strategic planning: organizational plans, 65–66;
    technology, 63–67
student advisement services, *142*; Learning Commons
    Survey results, *143*

student services partnerships, 10–11

student support services, 41–42

students: assessing satisfaction with current or future library facilities and services, 17; focus groups, 18, 23–25; input on desired learning commons features and services, 126; needs assessments, 23–26

Tableau software, 119, 129

TEAL classroom at MIT, 36

technologists: interview with a technologist, 68–72; role in learning commons planning, 67–72

technology, 63, 68–72, 75–78; design planning, 72–73; interview with a technology expert interview, 80–85; loan services for laptops and tablets, 41, 79; needs assessments, 78–79; popular trends within learning commons spaces, 85–88

technology plans, *64*, 65–67, 72–73

TILE classroom at the University of Iowa Library, 36–37

tutoring services, 141; Learning Commons Survey results, *142*

University of Southern California (USC): Leavey Library Information Commons, 2–3

USC Leavey Library. *See* University of Southern California

Uzwyshyn, Ray, 80–85

writing centers, 141–42

About the Authors

Lynn D. Lampert is the coordinator of information literacy and instruction at California State University (CSU), Northridge. Lynn served as a key member of the Oviatt Library's Learning Commons Planning Team, which managed the $2.5 million learning commons renovation project. Lynn also helped develop and design the learning commons' new makerspace area, which opened to students in the fall of 2014. She has also served as a consultant for other recent learning commons projects.

Lynn's publications have focused on how library public services can transform students' learning. She has specialized in the area of information literacy instruction and campus collaborations for student success since she began her professional career as an academic librarian in 1998. Lynn has authored two books, *Combating Student Plagiarism: A Librarian's Guide* and *Proven Strategies for Building an Information Literacy Program*, as well as many peer-reviewed publications in the field of information literacy and academic librarianship, both within and outside the field of library and information science, appearing in such publications as the *Reference Librarian*, the American Historical Association's publication *Perspectives*, and the Association of College and Research Libraries' *C&RL News*.

Since joining the library faculty at CSU Northridge in 2001, Lynn has served as the chair of research, instruction, and outreach services (2005–2014); coordinator of information literacy and instruction (since 2001); and interim associate dean (2014–2015). Prior to 2001, Lynn worked as an information specialist at California Lutheran University. Lynn received both her MLIS in library and information science and her MA in history from the University of California, Los Angeles, in 1998. She earned a BA in history from the University of California, Santa Barbara, in 1994.

Coleen Meyers-Martin is coordinator of outreach services at California State University (CSU), Northridge's Oviatt Library. In 2013, she coordinated a multifaceted marketing campaign, which promoted the library's $2.5 million learning commons renovation to students, faculty, staff, and community members.

Many of Coleen's publications address marketing and promoting library programming, resources, and services as well as issues in the area of information literacy. Coleen has authored many articles and other publications, including "The Finals Stretch: Exam Week Library Outreach Surveyed" and "One-Minute Video: Marketing Your Library to

Faculty," appearing in such publications as *Reference Services Review*, *Education Libraries*, and the Association of College and Research Libraries' *C&RL News*.

As coordinator of outreach services at CSU Northridge since 2008, Coleen has overseen many of the library's outreach and promotional efforts. Prior to 2008, Coleen worked as a children's librarian in the Altadena Library District. She received her MLIS from San Jose State University in 2006 and her BA in political science from Cal Poly Pomona in 1993.